THE FLOURISHING OF JEWISH SECTS
IN THE MACCABEAN ERA:
AN INTERPRETATION

SUPPLEMENTS

TO THE

JOURNAL FOR THE STUDY OF JUDAISM

Formerly Studia Post-Biblica

Editor

JOHN J. COLLINS

The Divinity School, University of Chicago

Associate Editor

FLORENTINO GARCÍA MARTÍNEZ

Qumran Institute, University of Groningen

Advisory Board

J. DUHAIME – A. HILHORST – M.A. KNIBB
M. MACH – J.T.A.G.M. VAN RUITEN – J. SIEVERS
G. STEMBERGER – J. TROMP – A.S. VAN DER WOUDE

VOLUME 55

THE FLOURISHING OF JEWISH SECTS
IN THE MACCABEAN ERA:

AN INTERPRETATION

BY

ALBERT I. BAUMGARTEN

BRILL

LEIDEN · NEW YORK · KÖLN

1997

This book is printed on acid-free paper.

Library of Congress Cataloging-in-Publication Data

Baumgarten, Albert I.
The flourishing of Jewish sects in the Maccabean era : an
interpretation / by Albert I. Baumgarten.
    p.   cm. — (Supplements to the journal for the study of
Judaism, ISSN 1384-1261 ; v. 55)
    Includes bibliographical references and index.
    ISBN 9004107517 (cloth : alk. paper)
    1. Jewish sects.   2. Judaism—History—Post-exilic period, 586
B.C.- 210 A.D.   I. Title.   II. Series.
BM175.A1B38   1997
296.8'1—dc21   97-5232
                                                                   CIP
                                                                   r97

Die Deutsche Bibliothek – CIP-Einheitsaufnahme

Baumgarten, Albert I.:
The flourishing of Jewish sects in the Maccabean era : an
interpretation / by Albert I. Baumgarten. – Leiden ; New York ; Köln
: Brill, 1997
    (Supplements to the journal for the study of judaism ; Vol. 55)
    ISBN 90-04-10751 7   Gewebe
[Journal for the study of judaism / Supplements]
Supplements to the journal for the study of judaism. Supplements. –
Leiden ; New York ; Köln : Brill
    Früher Schriftenreihe
    Bis Vol. 48 (1995) u.d.T.: Studia post-biblica
Vol. 55. Baumgarten, Albert I.: The flourishing of Jewish sects in the
Maccabean era. – 1997

ISSN   1384-1261
ISBN   90 04 10751 7

PRINTED IN THE NETHERLANDS

FOR RITA

CONTENTS

Indices

PREFACE

In June 1987 the Institute of Jewish Studies at the Hebrew University convened a colloquium of Israeli scholars in honor of the fortieth anniversary of the discovery of the Dead Sea Scrolls. Invited to speak at that event on "Qumran and Jewish Sectarianism," I utilized the opportunity to reflect on some traits of Second Temple sectarian groups, as well as ponder the reasons for their pre-eminence at that time.

In the published version of my presentation ("Qumran and Jewish Sectarianism," in M. Broshi, S. Japhet, D. Schwartz and S. Talmon (Eds.), *The Scrolls of the Judaean Desert: Forty Years of Research* (Jerusalem, 1992), 139–151 [in Hebrew]), I offered some preliminary reflections on these questions. In particular, I ventured the suggestion that the flowering of sectarian groups might have had something to do with an atmosphere of imminent eschatological hope. An interest in applying insights from other instances of sectarianism, as well as from the social sciences, was already apparent in that paper. In making these proposals, I tried to buttress them with an appeal to what could be learned from 4QMMT, word of whose contents was already circulating: at the June 1987 colloquium, in fact, Y. Sussmann delivered the paper later published in full as "Research on the History of the Halacha and the Scrolls of the Judean Desert," *Tarbiz* 59 (5760), 11–76 [in Hebrew].

Since that colloquium, and since 1990 in particular, I have returned often to search for the connections between context and consequence, which will help illuminate the flourishing of ancient Jewish sects in the Maccabean era. The intellectual approaches broached in my initial paper are now more fully developed in this book, in as full-scale a set of answers as I believe possible.

In a project spread over so many years the support of a wide range of institutions, friends and family is a great blessing. I must therefore thank the administration and my colleagues at Bar Ilan University, who invited me to make my home in Israel. Sabbatical appointments at San Diego State University and at the Jewish Theological Seminary, as well as a year as a Fellow at the Institute for Advanced Studies, Jerusalem, facilitated research, reflection and writing.

Friends whose academic interests are diverse, such as Magen Broshi, Michael Heyd, Richard Landes, Doron Mendels, and Ed Sanders, read and commented on drafts of the work while in progress. Nor were relatives exempt from this chore: Elisheva Baumgarten, Rita Baumgarten and Murray Baumgarten made many helpful suggestions. John Collins, in his capacity as editor of the series, read the penultimate version, offering much good advice. Without his encouragement, this book might never have left its comfortable niche in the memory of my computer.

All the members of my immediate family – my wife Rita, and daughters Elisheva, Shoshana, Margalit and Naama – have helped me labor at the questions addressed here. Each of them in turn listened to my latest notions, but also prompted me to press on and finish, thus aiding me to reach the point where I feel that I have written below as much as I can say.

Opportunities to lecture at other universities, including Ben Gurion University of the Negev, the Hebrew University, McMaster University, University of Oregon, Princeton University, Rice University, University of California at San Diego, Yale University and York University all offered chances to present my ideas to audiences, and benefit from comments and criticism. At the very least, these occasions forced me to abandon the overly simplistic notions with which I began this project.

In the Spring of 1996 I recorded a series of lectures based on the argument of this book for Israel Army Radio, as part of their "Broadcast University" Series. This provided one more chance to refine the exposition of the ideas elaborated below.

Comment on drafts, discussion with colleagues and public presentations of different sorts, in short, evoked much revision. For that reason, the usual reminder that "I alone am responsible for the contents" applies with special force. As the reader will notice, I have modified my view on any number of issues taken up in this book, referring to my own earlier treatments of questions with which I no longer fully agree. Hence, someone who heard or read an earlier version of some aspect of a matter presented here – even if it was one of those rare occasions at which one scholar agreed that another's argument was sound, absolutely convincing and wished that the point were his or her own – cannot be held responsible for the case as it now appears.

Believing as I do that there is an intimate connection, best explicitly acknowledged, between the work produced by a scholar and the world in which he or she lives, I conclude by noting the Israeli context of the discussion to follow. I doubt if the questions asked below would have occurred to me with such force, or the answers proposed seemed so convincing, if I were still living full-time in North America. Offering up the fruits of my labors to other inquirers, I declare that they are proof that I have settled physically and intellectually in the land promised to our ancestors, in which we are to live (Dt. 26:3).

Jerusalem
December 6, 1996
First Day of Channukah 5757

INTRODUCTION

One of the dominant characteristics of Jewish life in Palestine in the period preceding the destruction of the Temple by the Romans was the prominence of Jewish groups, such as Pharisees, Sadducees, Essenes and those who lived at Qumran,[1] alongside a much larger population

---

[1] As should be clear from the formulation, I believe one should distinguish as carefully as possible between the Essenes and Qumran. For a full statement of my position see A.I. Baumgarten, "The Rule of the Martian as Applied to Qumran," *Israel Oriental Studies* 14 (1994), 179–200; "The Temple Scroll, Toilet Practices, and the Essenes", *Jewish History* 10 (1996), 9–20. On this view, classical sources on the Essenes have no privileged place in explaining the Dead Sea Scrolls, and vice versa. I am not concerned to reconcile differences between the two bodies of evidence, and am content to let contradictions stand. For a slightly different perspective on these issues, but reaching a conclusion I share wholeheartedly, see now M. Goodman, "A Note on the Qumran Sectarians, the Essenes and Josephus," *Journal of Jewish Studies* 46 (1995), 161–166. See also S. Talmon, "Qumran Studies: Past, Present and Future," *Jewish Quarterly Review* 85 (1994), 11–14; 17–18.

Prominent in recent treatments of Qumran texts have been the inter-related questions of (1) the unity of the cave finds and (2) the connection between the scrolls found in caves and the settlement uncovered by the archaeologists. On the first issue, do the texts, as we are now coming to know them in their full variety, represent the works of a single group, or are compositions of different origins to be found in the caves? On the second, what was the connection between the settlement and texts found in caves up to several kilometers from that site? For a summary of my view on these issues, arguing that there was a connection between the settlement and the scrolls, but that not all works found in the caves were truly sectarian, see A.I. Baumgarten, "Crisis in the Scrollery: A Dying Consensus," *Judaism* 44 (1995), 401–402. See also D. Dimant, "The Qumran Manuscripts: Contents and Significance," in D. Dimant and L. Schiffman (Eds.), *Time to Prepare the Way in the Wilderness* (Leiden, 1995), 23–58. For a judicious assessment of the question see also J. Collins, *The Scepter and the Star: The Messiahs of the Dead Sea Scrolls and Other Ancient Literature* (New York, 1994), 4–11; cf. P.R. Davies, "Was There Really a Qumran Community?" *Currents in Research* 4 (1995), 9–35. For a fuller account see L. Schiffman, *Reclaiming the Dead Sea Scrolls* (New York, 1994), 31–61. Note also the comments of M. Smith, "The Dead Sea Sect in Relation to Ancient Judaism," *New Testament Studies* 7 (1960), 347: "Even if we suppose that all books came from the official library, we cannot be sure that everything in the library reflected faithfully and directly the beliefs of its owners – that sort of absurd supposition should be left to the secret police."

It was characteristic of Smith to raise issues which would later pre-occupy scholars, well before others broached them. For a vigorous defense of Smith's originality and the significance of his contributions in response to recent criticism see S.J.D. Cohen, "Are There Tannaitic Parallels to the Gospels?" *Journal of the American Oriental Society* 116 (1996), 85–89.

To the extent possible, my conclusions concerning the Qumran community will be based on the strictly sectarian works, such as the Manual of Discipline (1QS), the

who were not members of any of these groups. Indicative of the
place of these movements in Second Temple Judaism was Josephus's
sense that his reader would not understand events of that era ade-
quately if he did not include an extensive excursus discussing Pharisees, Sadducees and Essenes in Book 2 of his *War*;[2] in a similar section
in *Ant.* 18 he added an explicit account of the so-called Fourth Philosophy.[3] Indeed, as the story of Second Temple Judaism unfolds in
Josephus's works, these groups play a major role, from the place of
Pharisees and Sadducees in the courts of John Hyrcanus, Alexander
Jannaeus and Salome Alexandra, to the accounts of Pharisees and
Essenes during the reign of Herod, culminating in the part played
by the Fourth Philosophy in preparing the groundwork for the Great
Revolt and the activity of all four groups and their leaders at the
time of the Great Revolt.

If scholars of our century fault Josephus, it is not for placing too
much emphasis on the divisions within Judaism,[4] but rather for not
being detailed enough. Thus, while Josephus included descriptions of
three groups in the excursus in *War* 2 and of four in *Ant.* 18, it is
clear from his own narrative that there were others, such as the
Christians,[5] the followers of John the Baptist (who aroused crowds
by his sermons, and whose adherents were still present in the diaspora,
a generation after John's death, according to Acts 18:24–19:7), or
the disciples of the hermit Bannus, with whom Josephus himself spent

---

Messianic Rule (1QSa), the Scroll of Blessings (1QSb), the Thanksgiving Hymns
(1QH), the *pesharim*, the War Scroll (1QM), and the Halachic Letter (4QMMT). On
the place of the Damascus Document (CD) see below Introduction, n. 62.

  The analysis, in the pages below, is not dependent on any particular theory of
Qumran origins. It requires the minimalist conclusion that the site was occupied by
a community of Jews devoted to a particular way of life, reflected in the strictly
sectarian works, who lived there from sometime in the second century BCE until
the era of the Great Revolt.

  [2] *War* 2.117–166.

  [3] *Ant.* 18.9–25.

  [4] Josephus himself could ignore these divisions when it suited his purposes. See
Ag. Ap. 2.65–67, 179–181. For a general assessment of Josephus's reliability as evidence
for ancient Jewish sectarianism see below, Chapter One, n. 2.

  [5] I agree with the many scholars who consider the reference to James the brother
of Jesus in *Ant.* 20.199–201 to be genuine, and who believe that Josephus did write
something about Jesus at *Ant.* 18.63ff. (where the *Testimonium Flavianum* now can be
found), whether or not the latter Josephan original can be reconstructed or restored.
For a brief treatment of the *Testimonium Flavianum* and its difficulties see the comments
of L. Feldman *ad loc.* in the *LCL* translation of Josephus; J. Meier, "Jesus in Josephus:
A Modest Proposal," *Catholic Biblical Quarterly* 52 (1990), 76–103.

three years.[6] If only Josephus had provided more than the scattered information on the latter groups, and included a comprehensive account of them in at least one of his excursuses! Another focus of criticism concerns Josephus's depiction of Pharisees, Sadducees and the Fourth Philosophy: he stressed their beliefs and ideology, while many contemporary scholars wish that he had written a more specific account of their legal practice (the exotic Essenes fared somewhat better – their way of life was so unusual that it merited extensive description).

For the groups he described in these excursuses, Josephus indicated the wider social and intellectual context in which he wished to place them, calling them philosophies (*War* 2.119; *Ant.* 13.289; 18.9, 11, 23), *haireseis* (*War* 2.137; *Ant.* 13.171, 293) a word whose basic meaning is "choice" or a *proairesis* (*Ant.* 13.293; 15.373). Specifying further the overlap between Jewish and Greek philosophies, Josephus explained to his reader that the Pharisees were similar to the Stoics (*Life* 12), and that the Essenes followed the way of life taught by Pythagoras (*Ant.* 15.371).

Philo of Alexandria, who devoted several pages to a summary of the ways of the Essenes, employed terms which overlap at least in part with those of Josephus: he called the Essenes a *proairesis*, in which membership was based on choice, not birth (*Hyp.* 11.2). The author of Acts followed in Josephus's footsteps, calling the Pharisees a *hairesis* (Acts 15:5, 26:5), employing that same term for the Sadducees (Acts 5:17), as well as for the Nazoreans, i.e. the early Christians (Acts 24:5). Acts is also the first text from which one can learn that *hairesis* might be used in a pejorative sense: Paul, defending himself before Felix, explained that he followed the Way, which enabled him to worship the God of his fathers, believing everything laid down by the law or written in the prophets. Nevertheless, others called this way a *hairesis* (Acts 24:14).

The terminology of the Greek authors, as just summarized above, was intended to make these groups comprehensible to their readers, in the context of the intellectual framework within which the Jewish groups were presented. Not surprisingly, the terms in Hebrew, which

---

[6] For Josephus's account of John the Baptist, and the crowds which gathered about him, see *Ant.* 18.116–119. Josephus related his experience with Bannus in *Life* 11–12. Josephus is our only source concerning Bannus and he did not indicate the number of followers assembled around this leader.

the groups employed for themselves were different. The Qumran community called itself a יחד, a term frequently found in the Manual of Discipline, emphasizing its communal nature, as an association whose members "ate together, prayed together and decided together (1QS vi, 3)." Implicit in eating, praying and deciding as a community were other aspects of life, such as the transfer of property of members to the יחד.[7] A competing group, called in Qumran texts by the code name Ephraim,[8] was organized as an עצה, or as a בנמת (4QpNah iii, 7). These were established social structures: עצה reflected the sense of a group united around some agenda, practical and ideological, and was a word the Qumran sectarians also employed for their own institutions, as in the frequent conjunction עצת היחד (e.g. 1QpHab xii, 4). בנמת went back to the Neo-Babylonian term *kiništu/ kinaštu*, "the collegium" of a temple.[9]

Rabbinic sources employed the word כת for any number of different sorts of groups, from those gathered in the Temple courtyard to offer Passover sacrifice (*mPes.* 5:7), to the ancient Israelites at the Red Sea (*yTaan.* 2.5.65d), the ministering angels (*GenR* 8.5, Theodor-Albeck, 60),[10] robbers (*LevR* 9.8, Margaliot, 186), as well as righteous men (*bShabb.* 104a). Nevertheless, the term could also be used in an explicitly pejorative context – applied to the phenomenon under discussion in this book – utilized for the twenty four heretical groups into which Jews were supposedly divided on the eve of the destruction, according to R. Yohanan (*ySanh* 10.6.29c).[11]

---

[7] An ostracon recording one such transfer has recently been found and published. See F.M. Cross and E. Eshel, "Ostraca from Khirbet Qumrân," *Israel Exploration Journal* 14 (1997), 17–28.

[8] In the view of many scholars this code name stands for the Pharisees. See D. Flusser, "Pharisees, Sadducees and Essenes in Pesher Nahum," in M. Dorman et al. (Eds.), *Essays in Jewish History and Philology in Memory of Gedaliahu Alon* (Jerusalem, 1970), 136–137 [in Hebrew]. This paper also exists in German as "Pharisäer, Sadduzäer und Essener im Pescher Nahum," in K. Grözinger (Ed.), *Qumran* (Darmstadt, 1981), 121–166.

[9] See M. Weinfeld, "The Origin of the Apodictic Law," *Vetus Testamentum* 23 (1973), 74–75.

[10] In addition to the conventional reference, for those rabbinic works for which there is a critical edition the name of the editor and page in the edition are cited throughout.

[11] On the interpretation of this passage as refering to the Second Temple era see S. Lieberman, "New Light on Cave Scrolls from Rabbinic Sources," *Texts and Studies* (New York, 1974), 199, esp. n. 69.

What Is a Sect?

Modern scholars have tended to disregard the terms employed by Josephus, Philo and Qumran, and adopt the terminology of sectarianism for at least some of these groups, a usage which will be followed in this study. In employing the term sect scholars intend to evoke its etymology, indicating that there was some sense in which these movements *cut themselves off* from the larger institutions of their society. Accordingly, every small religious movement is not a sect: some measure of deliberate self definition over and against others is required.

The more precise meaning of a term such as sect, when employed by social scientists or historians, depends to a great extent on the examples chosen to determine the paradigm. The fragmented saint cults of contemporary Muslim North Africa, which flourish in the Atlas Mountains, studied by Gellner, are enmeshed in the social order, make the greatest concessions to it, and promote the integration of individuals into that order. The local unitarian and united central tradition, which governs their lives, by contrast, is more severe and demanding, and promotes divisiveness. If these saint cults were taken as the model of sectarianism, Gellner asks, what sort of definition would result? Sects would be defined as groups devoted to fostering harmony between their members and the social order![12] Indian sectarianism offers another model. As explained by Dumont, Indian sectarianism is based on renunciation of participation in a hierarchical social order.[13] A sectarian of this sort rejects the social order by refusing to accept its limitations. Sectarianism of this type would be of little use in understanding groups in less hierarchical societies. These two instances are to be contrasted with the church/sect patterns familiar from western Christianity, which have been studied at length by historians and social scientists, virtually the mirror image of the North African picture presented by Gellner.[14] In the west, sects promote divisiveness, while larger movements such as churches are devoted to integration of their members in the social order.

---

[12] E. Gellner, *Saints of the Atlas* (Chicago, 1969), 11. For similar reflections on the significance of the choice taken as paradigmatic see S. Fraade, "Ascetical Aspects of Ancient Judaism," in A. Green (Ed.), *Jewish Spirituality – From the Bible through the Middle Ages* (New York, 1986), 253–257.

[13] L. Dumont, *Homo Hierarchicus – The Caste System and its Implications* (Chicago/London, 1980, 3rd edition), 184–191.

[14] See L. Dawson, "Church/Sect Theory: Getting it Straight," *North American Religion* 1 (1992), 6–7.

In light of these difficulties, a universal definition of sectarianism, applicable to all cases, is not the objective here.[15] The models of sectarianism proposed by social scientists (which rarely if ever exist in disorderly reality)[16] only have heuristic value in research such as mine. I will adopt a usage of the terms sect and sectarianism which originates in the classic studies of Weber and Troeltsch, and which begins by insisting on the voluntary nature of sectarianism, and on sects as protests against the practice and beliefs of the rest of society.[17] These characteristics, however, are not sufficient for a useful definition of sectarianism, as voluntary groups of protest can be of many sorts, and something further should distinguish sects. The definition should include the practical consequences drawn by sectarian voluntary associations of protest. A direction in which to look is suggested by a comment of M. Douglas: "any sect tends to define

---

[15] Cf. Dawson, "Church/Sect Theory," 5–28. Compare Talmon, "Qumran Studies," 6, who would deny the use of the term "sect" for even the group he calls the "Community of the Renewed Covenant," of which one center (in his opinion) was at Qumran. In Talmon's view, there must be a normative version of a religion for dissenting sects to be possible. But is any version of a religion ever as normative as it would like? I would argue not, and if not, sectarianism would then never be present, according to Talmon, clearly an impossible situation. Against Talmon see also B. Wilson, *Religious Sects: A Sociological Study* (London, 1970), 22–25 who notes that it is misleading to insist that sects depend on an antithetical relationship with normative churches for their existence. Compare my definition of sect, below, which focuses on boundary marking against other members of one's own group as the defining characteristic of a sect, and thus does not require the existence of a normative version of the religion in order to permit the emergence of sectarianism.

[16] Few real movements, if any, fit solely into one category or other, and virtually all display features of several types at any one time and/or over the course of their history, as they respond to different situations. See further S. Talmon, "The Emergence of Jewish Sectarianism," in *King, Cult and Calendar* (Jerusalem, 1986), 99: "While . . . typology in essence may be upheld in theory, more attention should be given to *Mischtypen* which in actual reality constitute the majority of cases." See also J. Gager, *Kingdom and Community* (Englewood Cliffs, 1975), 68–69. Even Dawson, "Church/Sect Theory," 13,18–19 concedes that Weber never meant his ideal types to be more than devices intended to facilitate comparative analysis.

[17] In stressing the opposition of these groups to prevailing views, I mean to take advantage of the insights of R. Stark and W. Bainbridge, *The Future of Religion: Secularization, Revival and Cult Formation* (Berkeley, 1985), 23. Note, however, that sects of the type I am considering were not truly revolutionary (cf. Hill's analysis of the Ranters, in C. Hill, *The World Turned Upside Down: Radical Ideas during the English Revolution* [London, 1972], 184–230): they did not mean to overturn the established society. Rather, these sectarians, as will be stressed throughout this study, were integrated into the social order at the same time as they were criticizing it. Their devotion to the values of the larger society was extreme, leading them to separate themselves from those who did not live up to the practices and beliefs which they felt were dictated by true allegiance to the common values.

itself by purity rules."[18] I would therefore define a sect as a *voluntary association of protest, which utilizes boundary marking mechanisms – the social means of differentiating between insiders and outsiders – to distinguish between its own members and those otherwise normally regarded as belonging to the same national or religious entity.* Ancient Jewish sects, accordingly, differentiated *between Jews who were members of their sect and those not.*

This definition posits some degree of dissent against those being marked off as outsiders, and/or against the mainstream institutions of the society of the time. That mainstream is most conveniently represented in the ancient Jewish cases by the Temple in Jerusalem, and by the policies of those responsible for its practice.[19]

The realms of life in which these boundaries were drawn can vary from one sect to the other. The boundary marking of ancient Jewish sects, as will be demonstrated in the rest of this book, concentrated on food, dress, marriage, commerce and worship, with virtually all groups having regulations concerning food. In some groups these boundaries were also reinforced by constant self admonition, ensuring that members did not slip into the defiled ways of those outside.

A consideration of the place of boundary defining mechanisms in the lives of non-sectarian Jews can help clarify their role in the experience of ancient Jewish sectarians. Ordinary Jews employed boundary marking mechanisms in realms of life such as food, marriage and worship to distinguish between themselves and non-Jews. These were the practices which anti-Jewish authors considered xenophobic, which the decrees of Antiochus IV were intended to abolish (1 Macc. 1:44–50), and which more sympathetic outsiders tried to understand (e.g. Hecataeus of Abdera on Jewish marriage customs).[20] Ordinary Jews,

---

[18] M. Douglas, "Afterword," in J. Neusner, *The Idea of Purity in Ancient Judaism* (Leiden, 1973), 141.

[19] My definition should be compared with that proposed by S.J.D. Cohen, *From the Maccabees to the Mishnah* (Philadelphia, 1987), 125–127. While the emphases are different – I stress the voluntary nature of sectarianism a bit more, as well as the role of boundary marking as creating a new variety of outsider, while Cohen underscores the sectarian claim to absolute truth – the agreement between our definitions is very substantial. Cf. Schiffman, *Reclaiming*, 72–73, who defines a sect as a "religious ideology that may develop the characteristics of a political party in order to defend its way of life." Cohen, Schiffman and I share the concern to define sect in such a way as to apply to the full range of Jewish groups known from the Second Temple period.

[20] See M. Stern, *Greek and Latin Authors on Jews and Judaism* (Jerusalem, 1974–1984), #11, 8, 1.29.

in sum, observed Biblical purity regulations more or less strictly. As
the Rabbis noted:

> We recognize of them (the people of the second Temple period) that
> they labored in the Torah, and were scrupulous (in observing) the
> commandments and concerning tithing, and that they had every good
> way of life (*tMen.* end = *yYoma* 1.1.38c).

This rabbinic memory is confirmed, at least in part, by finds of ritual
baths and of stone vessels of the Second Temple period. These baths
and vessels (found all over ancient Palestine, and not necessarily in
exclusively priestly contexts) were important and often essential means
to facilitate a life of purity.[21] Observing purity rules was not what
made ancient Jewish sectarians special: rather, it was employment of
purity mechanisms as a means of expressing disapproval of the life
of one's neighbor. As the rabbinic text quoted immediately above
continues: if Jews of the Second Temple era were so virtuous why
then was the Temple destroyed? It offers, as one answer among others,
that catastrophes befell Jews of those times because they hated each
other so passionately. An ancient Jewish sectarian of the more extreme
type might therefore be denounced in terms derived from a derogatory seventeenth century definition of "Puritan," as someone who
loved God with all his soul, and hated his neighbor with all his heart
(below, Appendix, at n. 41).

As another comparison of sectarian and non-sectarian Jews, priests,
born into their status, also kept themselves apart from other Jews and
had special regulations to ensure their sacred status. They did so,

---

[21] E.P. Sanders, *Judaism: Practice and Belief 63 BCE–66 CE* (London/Philadelphia,
1992), 222–229. On ritual baths found in excavations see further E. Regev, "Ritual
Baths of Jewish Groups and Sects in the Second Temple Period," *Cathedra* 79 (5756),
3–21 [in Hebrew], who argues for their division into three categories: priestly,
Pharisaic, and ordinary. The latter are by far the most common. On stone vessels in
the Jerusalem area see J. Cahill, "Chalk Vessel Assemblages of the Persian/Hellenistic
and Early Roman Periods," *Qedem* 33 (1992), 190–274. On the connection between
stone vessels and purity observance see *ibid.*, 233–234, based on the conclusions of
I. Magen, *The Stone Vessel Industry in Jerusalem during the Second Temple Period* (Jerusalem,
1988), 109 [in Hebrew]; see also E. Regev, "The Use of Stone Vessels at the End
of the Second Temple Period," in Y. Eshel (Ed.), *Judea and Samaria Research Studies,
the 6th Annual Meeting (24 March 1996)*, forthcoming [in Hebrew]. I would like to
thank Mr. Regev for sharing with me the results of his research prior to its appearing in print. On the general allegiance of most ancient Jews to a life of the law, and
to some measure of scrupulousness in observing the law see also A.I. Baumgarten,
"Qumran and Jewish Sectarianism during the Second Temple Period," in M. Broshi,
S. Japhet, D. Schwartz and S. Talmon (Eds.), *The Scrolls of the Judean Desert: Forty
Years of Research* (Jerusalem, 1992), 145–146 [in Hebrew].

however, not as a matter of choice but of birth, and with the full consent of society, as its embodiment of holiness. In other respects, however, Jews were equal, not marked off in principle from one another. As Douglas remarks:

> In this religion persons of one class do not defile persons of another class by coming into contact. Many of the levitical rules of defilement support the moral code, but there is nothing that supports social stratification.[22]

Ancient Jewish sectarians were therefore different in two senses. First, unlike priests, as Philo rightly emphasized,[23] they chose their way of life. Next, they turned the means of marking separation normally applied against non-Jews against those otherwise regarded as fellow Jews, as a way of protesting against those Jews, and/or against Jewish society at large. As a result of these actions all Jews were no longer on the same footing: *sectarian Jews treated other Jews as outsiders of a new sort.*

The full implications of this definition for understanding the nature of ancient Jewish sects remain to be worked out in the pages that follow.[24] For those who seek modern examples of the pattern I have in mind, to help clarify its significance at the outset, I would point to the ultra-orthodox leader Asher Zelig Margalioth of Jerusalem, whose writings were studied by Y. Liebes.[25] Margalioth insisted that free-thinking Jews were not to be called to the Torah. One was to have no commercial dealings with them, and if a member of one's family lapsed into heresy all contact was to be cut off with that person. Finally, and most telling of all for my purposes, if one such free-thinker wanted

---

[22] M. Douglas, "Atonement in Leviticus," *Jewish Studies Quarterly Review* 1 (1993/94), 113–114.

[23] Even though he had not read Weber or Troeltsch.

[24] In proposing the definition I have suggested I believe it applicable to more cases than just the ancient Jewish ones to be analyzed below. See further the discussion at the end of this chapter, and the Appendix. Nevertheless, I do not aspire to any universality, as should be clear from the discussion of Gellner and Dumont, above at nn. 12 and 13. If my definition does not illuminate some other Jewish, Christian, Muslim or Eastern instances I would not consider that a flaw in the conception. Thus, unlike Stark and Bainbridge, *Future of Religion*, 448, I would not seek data for ancient China, to allow a test of my findings against empirical evidence from so distant a time and place. On the place of boundary marking among ancient Pauline Christians see W. Meeks, *The First Urban Christians – The Social World of the Apostle Paul* (New Haven, 1983), 97–107.

[25] Y. Liebes, "The Ultra-Orthodox Community and the Dead Sea Scrolls," *Jerusalem Studies in Jewish Thought* 3 (1982), 137–152 [in Hebrew].

to join "Israel," i.e. ultra-orthodox Judaism of Margalioth's style, he needed to be ritually re-circumcised: to such an extent did Margalioth apply to free-thinking Jews rules normally reserved for non-Jews. In a similar vein, Moshe Lilienblum testifies that at least some Rabbinic authorities of the nineteenth century insisted that if a woman encountered a heretic when returning from the ritual bath, she must re-immerse herself.[26] This ruling is based on an old custom, going back to medieval times, that a woman should be careful not to meet certain undesirable animals or people on the way home from the ritual bath, lest her children turn out equally unsuitable.[27] The transfer of this practice to heretics marks their exclusion from the community, as that community was defined by the Rabbinic authorities who were the source of Lilienblum's report. More recently, Israeli newspapers report a new manifestation of the ultra-orthodox campaign against television. In one cemetery, a section is set aside by them for those who adhere to their life-style, and do not own television sets. When it was discovered that one woman buried there had in fact owned a television set a wall was built around her grave, so as to separate it off from the others.

---

[26] M. Lilienblum, *Autobiographical Writings* (Jerusalem, 5730), 1.182–187 [in Hebrew]. I owe this reference to the kindness of Dr. S. Feiner.

[27] The notion that a woman returning from the immersion which renders her fit for resuming sexual activity is in a particularly vulnerable position – hence can be influenced for good or evil by those whom she meets – is an old one. One cause of this vulnerability may be obvious: under conditions of the time, with immersion performed in a more or less public place, these women were likely naked (see Tosafot on *bBM* 84a, commenting on *bPes.* 111a).

The sense of being exposed and susceptible to outside influences at that moment is reflected in the Rabbinic story that R. Yohanan would sit outside the ritual bath, so that he would be the first person women would see, so that they would have sons as learned in the Torah as he (*bBer.* 20a; *bBM* 84a). On the other side of the coin, Eleazar b. Judah of Worms (c. 1165–c. 1230), in his *Sefer ha-Rokeah*, notes the custom that if a woman returning from immersion encountered a dog her children will be ugly, if a donkey, they will be stupid, and if an *am haaretz* they will be likewise. On the other hand, if she met a horse they will be beautiful and speak well. Note that these consequences are not connected to the *kashrut* status of the animals involved: dogs, donkeys and horses are all equally non-kosher. Rather, it is the ugliness of a dog, the stupidity of donkeys, and the strength and grace of horses that determines the outcome. See B.S. Scheerson (ed.), Eleazar of Worms, *Sefer ha-Rokeah* (Jerusalem, 5727), #317, 202. I owe this information to the help of Elisheva Baumgarten. This background helps explain Lilienblum's report. The Rabbinic authorities insisted that the woman who met a heretic when returning from the ritual bath re-immerse herself so that the effect of meeting the heretic when first going home be nullified, so that when she finally went home and resumed sexual activity she would not bear children in the likeness of the heretic.

Those who travel on El-Al airlines will understand the aptness of the definition proposed above when they remember that a number of different *kashrut* supervisions are available for meals served there. Sometimes, alas, a passenger who has requested supervision A, receives a meal under supervision B. In most instances, that passenger will refuse to eat the food, treating it as if it were *not kosher at all.* That passenger is giving explicit expression to the gap which she or he has imposed voluntarily between those Jews who insist on supervision A and those who will only eat food prepared under supervision B.[28]

Varieties of Sectarianism

In the body of this book I intend to show the ways in which Sadducees,[29] Pharisees, Essenes, Qumran, Fourth Philosophy, and the followers of John the Baptist or of Bannus – to mention the most obvious examples – were all sects within the meaning of the term as I have defined it.[30] In order to achieve this objective the definition of

---

[28] Many of these disagreements go back to the introduction of special procedures of ritual slaughtering by Hassidic groups, on which see C. Szmeruk, "The Social Significance of Hassidic Shekhita," *Zion* 20 (5715 C.E.), 47–72 [in Hebrew].

[29] The Sadducees pose a major problem for the study which follows. Our information on them is so limited that only rarely can they be discussed in terms of the definitions or historical explanations to be offered. Nevertheless, they must be included within the compass of ancient Jewish sects, as Josephus listed them with Pharisees, Essenes and Fourth Philosophy as part of the same cultural, religious and social phenomenon.

The Samaritans are also outside the framework of the discussion of this book, and hence mentioned infrequently. Samaritan secession may belong to the forerunners of sectarianism, as argued below, and the little known of their interactions with Jews fits well into the definition of sectarianism proposed. According to John 4:9, "Jews have no dealings with Samaritans," to the extent of not asking a Samaritan for a drink of water. Nevertheless, once Samaritans had erected their own Temple, and accepted a version of the Bible which supported that action, they had gone beyond the reformist/introversionist categorization proposed below. Thus when Jews would not ask Samaritans for a drink of water, it is not clear whether these actions are to be classified as their xenophobia towards non-Jews (cf. Juvenal, *Satires* 14.104 = Stern, *Greek and Latin Authors* #301), or as an indication of sectarianism. Ben Sira's denunciation of the Samaritans, as a foolish people that dwells in Shechem, that is no nation (50:25–26), reflects this same difficulty of classifying the Samaritans as Jews or as non-Jews. Cf. Cohen, *Maccabees to the Mishnah*, 169–170, who proposes a definition of sectarianism slightly different than I do, above n. 19, and accordingly includes the Samaritans within the compass of Jewish sectarianism.

[30] Those loyal to the Temple at Leontopolis might have been a sect, as I choose to employ the term. Alongside the grudging acknowledgement of the legitimacy of sacrifice at Leontopolis accorded by the Rabbis, *mMen.* 13:10, we also learn that in

sect/sectarianism suggested has been conceived so as to allow considerable room for variation in the degree of separation from other Jews, or opposition to prevailing views, a group must have demonstrated in order to be considered a sect.

I have taken this path because I am well aware that not all the ancient Jewish groups just listed were the same. Thus, without pre-empting too much of the detailed discussion to follow, virtually all scholars[31] recognize that a pre-eminent characteristic of the Qumran community was its close to total rejection of everything connected with the way the Temple of its day was being run. All would see the Qumran division of the world into sons of light vs. sons of darkness as indicative of an extreme position, which brooks no compromise, and has culminated in separatism. The Qumran community, insisting on a fully common life, is a classic example of a "greedy" institution, demanding total loyalty and absorbing all of its member's identity, to borrow the terminology and summarize the analysis of the sociologist Lewis Coser.[32] This "greediness" is indicative of a turning into itself so complete that little if anything outside remains

---

the view of the Rabbis, priests who served at Leontopolis were ineligible to serve at Jerusalem. These priests, as the Mishnah makes explicit, were thus similar in status to those who had served in pagan temples. Perhaps if we had more information we could describe other ways in which those loyal to Leontopolis and Jerusalem employed boundary marking mechanisms against each other. On the other hand, Leontopolis may have been small enough and far away enough, off the beaten track, to have been ignored, and for there to have been little boundary marking in either direction between its loyalists and other Jews.

If the disqualification known to the Rabbis was in force at the time, the account in Josephus, *Ant.* 13.354–355 – according to which a member of the reigning priestly family at Leontopolis used his influence with the Ptolemaic Queen Cleopatra III to convince her to restore Jannaeus as ruler in Jerusalem – is particularly poignant. It might be another example of the "inelegant landings," conclusions not quite consistent with our logic which abound in reality, discussed below, Introduction, at n. 40. On the incident at the time of Cleopatra III as a whole see M. Stern, *Studies in Jewish History – The Second Temple Period* (Jerusalem, 1991), 119–120 [in Hebrew].

[31] For the most prominent exception to this consensus see H. Stegemann, "The Qumran Essenes – Local Members of the Main Jewish Union in Late Second Temple Times," in J. Barrera and L. Montaner (Eds.), *The Madrid Qumran Congress: Proceedings of the International Congress on the Dead Sea Scrolls, Madrid, 18–21 March 1991* (Leiden, 1992), 1.83–166. I have discussed Stegemann's conclusions as some length in A.I. Baumgarten, "Josephus on Essene Sacrifice," *Journal of Jewish Studies* 45 (1994), 173, 183. In my view, Stegemann must pervert the meaning of Josephus's comments on the Essenes in order to portray them as the main Jewish group, eliminating by problematic exegesis all signs of tension between the Essenes and those who ran the Temple.

[32] See L. Coser, *Greedy Institutions: Patterns of Undivided Commitment* (New York, 1974), esp. 103–116.

worthy of favorable notice. Movements of this sort should be contrasted with the Pharisees, who did divide themselves off from other Jews on some matters, but for whom the walls which separated them from other Jews were less high, and much more permeable. The Pharisees remained loyal to the Temple, in spite of the shifts in control that institution underwent over time, which must have affected Temple practice. They participated in the life of the Hasmonean and Herodian court, to the extent of eating at a dinner party hosted by the king, according to a famous story in Josephus, *Ant.* 13.289 and *bQid* 66a. They had lives as individuals, and had not sacrificed all their identity to a "greedy" institution.

If groups as diverse as Qumran and the Pharisees are all called sects, how should the variation between them just outlined be expressed? A brief return to the world of social scientific theory will provide the concepts necessary to resolve this issue: B. Wilson's distinction between "reformist" and "introversionist" sects is most helpful. One should classify Sadducees and Pharisees as reformist sects, while the Qumran Covenanters would fit Wilson's category of introversionist.[33] That is the former hold hopes of reforming the larger society, and have not given up on it or renounced it totally, still perceiving themselves as members of the whole. At times during the era to be considered, in fact, both Pharisees and Sadducees succeeded in controlling the Temple (the Pharisees at the beginning of the reign of John Hyrcanus and at the time of Salome Alexandra, the Sadducees at the end of the reign of Hyrcanus and during the rule of Alexander Jannaeus). The introversionist sort of sect, by contrast, has so finally rejected the institutions of the society as a whole as to turn in on itself completely, and to rank those outside its bounds as irredeemable. While movements of both sorts insist on the rightness of their way, social relations between members of reformist sects and those outside its limits are more open than those between members of introversionist sects and the larger society. Hence the divergent behavior of members of ancient Jewish sects, as outlined above.

---

[33] See B. Wilson, *Magic and the Millennium* (London, 1973), 18–26. For the same conclusion concerning the Pharisees, as a reformist sect according to Wilson, see A.J. Saldarini, *Pharisees, Scribes and Sadducees in Palestinian Society: A Sociological Approach* (Edinburgh, 1988), 286. For the Pharisees as a sect see also Cohen, *Maccabees to the Mishnah*, 162. In reaching this conclusion Cohen, Saldarini and I disagree with those scholars, such as E.P. Sanders, *Paul and Palestinian Judaism* (London, 1977), 425–426, who would deny the use of the term sect for the Pharisees.

There are, admittedly, other ways of classifying these groups. Thus, to take one example, the reformist/introversionist sect division adopted here corresponds well with the distinction between party and sect proposed by Sanders.[34] It reflects equally the categories of reformist movement/sect suggested by Watson.[35] In a less precise way, it coheres with the distinction between reformist and revolutionary movements proposed by Hobsbawm.[36] In spite of the terminological differences, there is close agreement between the various systems in their description and assessment of the phenomena.

What are the relative advantages of one system of nomenclature over another? Why should one system be preferred to another, particularly if these are nothing more than varying ways of describing the same set of circumstances? Some choice between these options, however, must be made, and one system adopted as the basis of discussion in this book, if only in order to facilitate the presentation of its argument. I have chosen to employ the terms in the way outlined above because, as will be argued more fully below, there was a fundamental similarity in the nature of the different movements: I see them as alternate responses to basically the same set of dilemmas raised by a new age, with a continuum of greater or lesser opposition to the changing practices in force in Jerusalem along which groups could and did move. As such, I take what united these groups to be at least as important as what divided between them, hence I prefer a terminology which reflects that similarity as well as the differences. Defining sect in such a way that one can employ that term for all the various movements, while acknowledging that they were of different sorts, some reformist others introversionist, seems the most accurate way to reflect the situation that obtained in antiquity in the terms employed.

There was one additional aspect of ancient Jewish sects subject to variation – an internal one. The extent of animosity between any group and other Jews could change over the course of the life of a group, sometimes becoming greater at other times less.[37] As Temple practice, a primary standard against which sectarians defined themselves, was

---

[34] See Sanders, *Paul and Palestinian Judaism*, 425–426.

[35] See F. Watson, *Paul, Judaism and the Gentiles – A Sociological Approach* (Cambridge, 1986), 38–48.

[36] E.J. Hobsbawm, *Primitive Rebels* (New York, 1959), 10–12.

[37] I have discussed this point at length, with reference to the work of Stark and Bainbridge in Baumgarten, "Rule of the Martian," 182–183.

subject to change over time,[38] the attitude of sect members towards the Temple might shift accordingly. At least two of our groups, Pharisees and Sadducees, controlled the Temple at different moments prior to its destruction: when they ran Jewish life, their animosity towards its central institutions must have been nil. Finally, Temple policy could also help construct the identity of groups, in response to their being designated deviant by those in charge there.[39] Sectarian identity was not set, for the ages, in stone. A group might begin as reformist, become more introversionist, and then move to yet a third stance. Nor can the possibility of "inelegant landings," combinations of attitudes and positions awkward by our logic, be excluded, particularly at times when the muddle seemed great and clarity remained to be achieved.[40]

JEWISH SECTS ARE PECULIAR TO CERTAIN TIMES

The phenomenon of sectarianism within Judaism of antiquity has received detailed scholarly attention, many monographs and articles having been devoted to analysis of the sources, or to treatments of individual groups.[41] Fundamental to this study, however, is an approach

---

[38] Thus, at a minimum, Josephus informs us of the events which led Hyrcanus to desert the Pharisees for the Sadducees, which culminated in his banning Pharisaic practice, *Ant.* 13.288–298, as well as of the restoration of the Pharisees on the accession of Salome Alexandra, *Ant.* 13.408. The desire to explain this change is behind the account in Rabbinic sources, *bQid.* 66a.

[39] See *tBer.* 3.25 and the comments of S. Lieberman, *Tosefta Kifshuta Zeraim* (New York, 1955), 1.53–54. See now also D. Flusser, "Some of the Precepts of the Torah from Qumran (4QMMT) and the Benediction Against the Heretics," *Tarbiz* 61 (5752), 333–374 [in Hebrew].

[40] I have discussed one such outcome in Baumgarten, "Josephus on Essene Sacrifice," 182–183: the very same Essenes who were excluded from the Temple continued to send it gifts, and perhaps to pay the Temple tax.

The insistence on a willingness to encounter disorderly reality, as represented by thinkers or groups which appear incoherent and inconsistent when judged in the light of our expectations, or by our logic, should be compared with Hill's stance as described and analyzed by M. Fulbrook, "Christopher Hill and Historical Sociology," in G. Eley and W. Hunt (Eds.), *Reviving the English Revolution – Reflections and Elaborations on the Work of Christopher Hill* (London/New York, 1988), 45 and M. Heinemann, "How the Words got on to the Page: Christopher Hill and Seventeenth Century Literary Studies," in Eley and Hunt, *Reviving the English Revolution,* 85–86. See also Hill's own defense of his position, C. Hill, "The Burden of Proof," *Times Literary Supplement,* November 7, 1975, 1333. The modern world too, we should remember, abounds in examples of incoherence between culture and class: think of radical chic, or of middle class socialists.

[41] See, for example, the bibliography in E. Schürer, *The History of the Jewish People*

which underlies it. Sects are always a possibility within a religious tradition and, according to Stark and Bainbridge, are ever-present.[42] I would argue, however, that even if sects are chronic, it is only rarely in religious experience that sectarianism comes to dominate a society, to the extent it did in Second Temple Judaism, as evidenced by the excursuses Josephus wrote. The phenomenon may in fact be endemic,[43] but its capture of the leading role in a culture is restricted to relatively rare moments. To focus attention on ancient Judaism, while groups flourished in the two hundred years prior to the destruction of the Temple by the Romans, nothing is known of similar splits in the many centuries between the destruction and the early Moslem period, which saw the rise of the Karaites.[44]

I would not want my description of the rise and fall of sectarianism among Jews to cause me to be classified among the naive believers in a primitive orthodoxy, from which sectarianism was a deviance. Such primitive orthodoxies are usually little more than illusions promoted by successful religious movements as a means of denouncing dissidents.[45] In that sense, sectarianism is not any more normal or abnormal than the leadership of the established authorities. Nevertheless, the pre-eminence of sectarian movements in the Second

---

in the Age of Jesus Christ, Revised and Edited by G. Vermes, F. Millar & M. Black (Edinburgh, 1979), 2.381–2; 555–558.

[42] Stark and Bainbridge, *Future of Religion,* 114. The studies collected in this volume occupy a most distinguished place in recent sociological analysis of sectarianism. Thus J. Simpson, "The Stark-Bainbridge Theory of Religion," *Journal for the Scientific Study of Religion* 29 (1990), 369 calls their analysis of sects and cults "the enduring heart of the matter."

On the permanence of sectarianism in human societies, and the error in accepting the perspective of the established authorities and viewing sects as deviant see also M. Douglas, "Radical Dissent, Religious Minorities and Incipient Sectarianism in the Social Sciences," paper read at Pinkhos Churgin Memorial Program, *Application of the Social Sciences to the Study of Judaism in Antiquity,* Bar Ilan University, November 1996.

[43] For a parallel use of the distinction between social phenomena considered endemic versus those which are epidemic see Hobsbawm, *Primitive Rebels,* 5. Hobsbawm applies this notion throughout his study of various movements, attempting to identify the circumstances which bring an endemic possibility to become epidemic. As should be clear from the discussion of the perspective of Hill and Scholem in n. 124 below, I would not want the endemic/epidemic analogy to lead to the consideration of sectarianism as a social disease.

[44] For a provocative analysis of the absence of sectarianism in the aftermath of the destruction of the Temple see S.J.D. Cohen, "The Significance of Yavneh: Pharisees, Rabbis and the End of Jewish Sectarianism," *Hebrew Union College Annual* 55 (1984), 27–54.

[45] In general see the comments of M. Douglas, *How Institutions Think* (London, 1987), 94–95:

Temple period is a special circumstance requiring a special explanation.

Put in these terms, the crucial question to be asked concerning the sects of Second Temple Judaism is why these groups attained the position they reached, at the time they did? What was it about the social, political and religious reality of that era which led to the known results? I intend my analysis to follow in the footsteps of a comment on the Puritan saints by M. Walzer, who understands them as a:

> group of men, hardened and disciplined by an ideology, decisively challenging the old order, offering their own vision as an alternative to traditionalism and their own persons as alternatives to traditional rulers.[46]

Walzer continues with a remark decisive for the intellectual foundations of this book:

> men are open to ideological discipline only at certain moments in history. Most often, they are immune, safe from whatever it is that inspires self-discipline and activism, disdainful of enthusiasm.[47]

That there was once a period of unquestioned legitimacy is the idea that our institutions use for stigmatizing subversive elements. By this astute ploy, the idea is given that incoherence and doubt are new arrivals, along with tramcars and electric light, unnatural intruders upon the primeval trust in the idyllic small community. Whereas it is more plausible that human history is studded all the way from the beginning with nails driven into local coffins of authority.

For a discussion of these principles in terms of the groups which flourished in the historical period which is the focus here see S.J.D. Cohen, "A Virgin Defiled: Some Rabbinic and Christian Views of the Origins of Heresy," *Union Seminary Quarterly Review* 36 (1980), 1–11.

[46] M. Walzer, *The Revolution of the Saints* (Cambridge, 1965), 19.

[47] *Ibid.* My approach should be compared with that of C. Liebman, "Extremism as a Religious Norm," *Journal for the Scientific Study of Religion* 22 (1983), 75–86. As his title indicates, Liebman sees religious extremism as the "normal" phenomenon. In his view, it is religious moderation which requires special explanation. In my opinion, the main flaw in Liebman's approach is that he does not allow sufficient room for apathy or indifference on the part of the dominant majority and hence does not realize that extreme activity is typical of marginal groups, particularly those living in unusual times. When the groups which set the standards for large parts of a society are swept away by religious extremism that remains an event requiring special explanation. For a critique of Liebman from another perspective see J. Cumpsty, "Glutton, Gourmet or Bon Vivant: A Response to Charles S. Liebman," *Journal for the Scientific Study of Religion* 24 (1985), 217–221. Cumpsty's response is based in large part on the argument that there is a recognized boundary beyond which one is clearly located in the lunatic fringe, which people are normally loath to cross. When large numbers move into the lunatic fringe that is therefore an event requiring special explanation, and not the norm. I find it hard to endorse or adopt Cumpsty's critique because of my reluctance to categorize and hence dismiss groups as belonging to the lunatic fringe. See further below, n. 124.

I will therefore be asking what was special about those moments in
Second Temple Jewish History which led at least some people to
make the commitments which produced the known result – the flourishing of sectarianism. In a sense, I will often be working backwards,
from the consequences to an attempt to understand the causes (a
standard technique in the dialectic of historiography). To quote Walzer
again, "hindsight, for all its dangers, is here a form of insight."[48]

WHEN DID ANCIENT JEWISH SECTARIANISM FLOURISH?

To pursue this approach, a determination of the period when sectarianism originated and flourished in Second Temple Judaism is critical:
it is crucial to ascertain which era's political, social and religious
realities must be analyzed as the context for the birth of the phenomenon and its culmination. This task, however, is not as simple as it
might seem, for scholars have seen the emergence of the Jewish groups
introduced above as part of the experience of times ranging from
the mid-fifth century BCE to the first century CE, from Ezra and
Nehemiah to the destruction of the Temple by the Romans. To further
complicate the question, there is a good deal of justification for the
earliest possible dates, as well as for the latest suggested ones: the
books of Ezra and Nehemiah portray a significant dissension among
Jerusalem Jews, with a lively (often harsh) debate taking place between
proponents of alternative interpretations of their religion.[49] At least
one of Nehemiah's actions against an opponent fits perfectly the
definition of sectarianism offered at the outset. Tobiah was a good
Jew in the eyes of other Jews (he was married into the family of the
High Priest – 13:4), but Nehemiah considered him an outsider, repeatedly branding him the Ammonite slave (e.g. 2:10). On the practical
level, Nehemiah treated Tobiah's possessions as a source of impurity, hence when he expelled these effects from the Temple he had
the room purified (13:8–9).[50] At some time after Ezra and Nehemiah,

---

[48] Walzer, *Revolution of the Saints*, 149.
[49] See e.g. J. Blenkinsopp, "A Jewish Sect of the Persian Period," *Catholic Biblical
Quarterly* 52 (1990), 5–20; P.D. Hanson, *The Dawn of Apocalyptic – The Historical and
Sociological Roots of Jewish Eschatology* (Philadelphia, 1983, 2nd edition). See also
A. Rofé, "The Beginnings of Sects in Post-Exilic Judaism," *Cathedra* 49 (1988), 13–
22 [in Hebrew]. Note also the belligerent tone of self justification in Nehemiah's
memoirs, e.g. 5:14–19, a sign of the vehemence of the polemical interaction.
[50] The significance of this action was noticed already by Smith, "Dead Sea Sect,"
353. Smith calls Nehemiah's deed the founding of a new religion.

perhaps at the time of Alexander the Great, perhaps a century or so later, the Samaritans emerged as a distinct entity worshipping the God of the Hebrew Bible, and claiming descent from Jacob (even if Jews would deny them that status).[51] At the other extreme, there can be no doubt that Christians, the Fourth Philosophy and the Zealots[52] were products of the first century CE.

The last events listed above, however, will not be the center of attention in this book, which will disregard the sects which definitely emerged in the first century CE, in the aftermath of the Roman conquest of Palestine. Instead, this study *will concentrate on the Pharisees, Sadducees, Essenes and the Qumran community*. The reasons for adopting this focus are straightforward: the causes for the rise of the sects which emerged in the first century CE are fairly clear, intimately connected with the imposition of direct Roman rule,[53] while explanation of the circumstances which led to the emergence and flourishing of Pharisees, Sadducees, Essenes and the Qumran community, as will be explained more fully below, is a significant historical question, worthy of extended consideration.

Even concentration on Pharisees, Sadducees, Essenes and the Qumran community, unfortunately, will not resolve the chronological problem. While Josephus's excursuses on the groups are situated at a point in his narrative in the early first century CE, he says explicitly in the digression in *Ant.* 18 that the groups he described existed

---

[51] See F. Dexinger, "Limits of Tolerance in Judaism: The Samaritan Example," in E.P. Sanders (Ed.), *Jewish and Christian Self Definition, Volume Two: Aspects of Judaism in the Graeco-Roman Period* (London, 1981), 88–114, 327–338. This conclusion is now the subject of much discussion, as a result of the new evidence acquired thanks to the excavations of Magen. See further H. Eshel, "The Prayer of Joseph, A Papyrus from Masada and The Samaritan Temple on *ARGARIZIN*," *Zion* 56 (5751), 125–136 [in Hebrew]; A. Crown, "Redating the Schism between the Judaeans and the Samaritans," *Jewish Quarterly Review* 82 (1991), 17–50; H. Eshel, *The Samaritans in the Persian and Hellenistic Periods: The Origins of Samaritanism* (Dissertation, The Hebrew University, 1994) [in Hebrew]; H. Eshel, "Wadi ed-Daliyeh Papyrus 14 and the Samaritan Temple," *Zion* 61 (5756), 359–365 [in Hebrew].

[52] I follow M. Smith, "Zealots and Sicarii: Their Origins and Relations," *Harvard Theological Review* 64 (1971), 1–19 and M. Stern, "Zealots," *Encyclopedia Judaica Yearbook, 1973* (Jerusalem, 1974), 135–152 in identifying the Fourth Philosophy with the Sicarii and in distinguishing between the latter and the Zealots.

[53] I would argue that the notions of holiness expounded by Jesus and elaborated by his disciples were a result of the collapse of established ways of achieving holiness, a failure directly connected with the breakdown of the assumptions underpinning the established order in the aftermath of the Roman conquest of Palestine, made acute for Jesus by the arrest and execution of his former master, John the Baptist. Full scale presentation of this thesis is left for some other occasion.

"from the most ancient times."[54] The position of the excursuses in the narrative is therefore of no consequence for an attempt to date the origins of the groups. Indeed, the remark that they existed "from most ancient times," indicates that Josephus had no explicit information on when they had arisen. Some modern scholars have seen the origins of these groups at the time of Ezra and Nehemiah, while others have argued for dates in the mid to late third century BCE.[55] Josephus (*Ant.* 13.171–173), however, first mentions Pharisees, Sadducees and Essenes at the time of Jonathan (152–142 BCE), the younger brother of Judah Maccabee. This would place the beginnings of these movements in the aftermath of Hasmonean assumption of the high priesthood.[56] Consistent with this view would be the opinion of scholars such as Marböck who argue that Ben Sira (who wrote in Jerusalem ca. 180 BCE) lived at a time before the phenomenon of sectarianism became widespread.[57]

---

[54] *Ant.* 18.11.

[55] See e.g., Smith, "Dead Sea Sect," 350–355; L. Schiffman, "Jewish Sectarianism in Second Temple Times," in R. Jospe and S. Wagner (Eds.), *Great Schisms in Jewish History* (New York, 1981), 4 [note, however, an apparent shift in Schiffman's opinion, in the aftermath of 4QMMT, as expressed in *Reclaiming*, 83–95]; R. Beckwith, "The Pre-History and Relationships of the Pharisees, Sadducees and Essenes: A Tentative Reconstruction," *Revue de Qumran* 11 (1982), 3–46; D. Dimant, "Qumran Sectarian Literature," in M. Stone (Ed.), *Jewish Writings of the Second Temple Period – Apocrypha, Pseudepigrapha, Qumran Sectarian Writings, Philo, Josephus* (Philadelphia, 1984), 542–547; Talmon, "The Emergence of Jewish Sectarianism," 192; Talmon, "Qumran Studies," 14–18.

[56] In support of this conclusion I would note the comment of A. Momigliano who sees the martyrdoms of the Maccabean era as a necessary predisposing factor for the emergence of sectarianism. See A. Momigliano, *Alien Wisdom: The Limits of Hellenization* (Cambridge, 1975), 100–101: "where there is martyrdom, there is right to secession." In a similar vein compare Douglas, *How Institutions Think*, 80: "The competitive society celebrates its heroes, the hierarchy celebrates its patriarchs, and *the sect its martyrs* (emphasis mine)."
On the meaning of the Josephus passage contrast S. Mason, *Flavius Josephus on the Pharisees* (Leiden, 1991), 197–202, esp. his conclusion, 199: "the view that [Josephus] is trying here to date the origins of the schools does seem to be a natural interpretation of the introductory phrase," with Saldarini, *Pharisees*, 115–116. Cf. the approach of P. Schäfer, "Der vorrabinische Pharisäismus," in M. Hengel & U. Heckel (Eds.), *Paulus und das antike Judentum* (Tübingen, 1992), 134, who raises the possibility that Josephus's mentioning the three groups at the time of Jonathan may have no connection with any aspect of their history, but may have occurred as a result of other reasons.

[57] See J. Marböck, "Das Gebet um die Rettung Zions Sir 36, 1–22," in J. Bauer and J. Marböck (Eds.), *Memoria Jerusalem – Freundesgabe Franz Sauer* (Graz, 1977), 94. For similar arguments see L. Levine, "The Political Struggle between the Pharisees and Sadducees in the Hasmonean Period," in A. Oppenheimer, U. Rappaport and M. Stern (Eds.), *Jerusalem in the Second Temple Period – Abraham Schalit Memorial Volume* (Jerusalem, 1980), 64–65 [in Hebrew]. Cf. Rofé, "Beginnings," 17–22.

This conclusion would seem to be reinforced by evidence such as the Pharisaic list[58] in *mAbot* 1, and its parallel in *Abot de-Rabbi Natan A* Chapter 5 (Schechter, 26), whose chronological implications I have discussed in detail elsewhere.[59] Sadducees and Boethusians, according to that list, began in the generation of the students of Antigonus of Socho, that is two generations after Simon the Righteous (the contemporary of Ben Sira in the first quarter of the second century BCE), that is sometime after the mid second century BCE.

Archaeological evidence concerning the Qumran community provides another indication of the date of the beginnings of this sect. The settlement at Qumran had its origins during the reign of John Hyrcanus (135–104 BCE) and flourished in particular in the reign of his son Alexander Jannaeus (103–76 BCE). Its message must have been particularly effective and attractive at that time, as the major expansion of the site at Qumran attests.[60] The group, however, must have existed (in Jerusalem, one supposes) prior to its departure for Qumran. It is difficult to know just how much time to allow for the pre-Qumran phase of the community. Some scholars see the pre-history of the community as extending back to the late third century BCE, or as resting on Babylonian foundations.[61]

The pre-history is, however, alluded to at the beginning of the Cairo Damascus Document (= CD, now also known, of course, from numerous manuscripts found at Qumran).[62] It tells of a decisive

---

[58] As noted below, n. 109, I find it hard to accept Rabbinic evidence as a direct source of information on the Pharisees. Nevertheless, it seems clear that the list in *mAbot* 1 is Pharisaic, in spite of the fact that it has undergone some subsequent revision to reach us in the form in which it is found now. See further the discussion in A.I. Baumgarten, "The Pharisaic *Paradosis*," *Harvard Theological Review* 80 (1987), 63–77.

[59] A.I. Baumgarten, "Rabbinic Literature as a Source for the History of Jewish Sectarianism in the Second Temple Period," *Dead Sea Discoveries* 2 (1995), 52–56.

[60] In archaeological terms, this is the transition from period Ia to Ib. See further R. De Vaux, *Archaeology and the Dead Sea Scrolls* (Oxford, 1973, 2nd edition), 3–5.

[61] For the case for the third century origins of the group see F. García Martínez and A.S. van der Woude, "A 'Groningen' Hypothesis of Qumran Origins," *Revue de Qumran* 14 (1990), 537. For the argument for Babylonian roots see P.R. Davies, *Behind the Essenes* (Atlanta, 1987), 35–36.

[62] The exact relationship between CD and the Qumran community remains unclear: multiple copies of CD were found in Cave 4 at Qumran, and works exist such as 4Q265, which straddle CD and 1QS (and accordingly dubbed 4QSD). While these facts indicate that CD was an integral part of the life of the Qumran community, CD envisages a way of life not always consistent with that emerging from other texts found at Qumran. A particularly important difference concerns the attitude towards the Temple and participation in its sacrifices, on which see P.R. Davies,

moment in the rise of the group dated 390 years after the Babylonian exile, ca. 196 BCE on the assumption that their chronology agreed with ours.[63] The dating of several manuscripts found at Qumran also indicates that the community's pre-history went back to the late third or very early second century BCE. Some key proto-Qumranian works are dated from that time, such as sections of 1 Enoch, one manuscript of which found at Qumran was copied ca. 200 BCE, hence the work as a whole must have been composed even earlier.[64] The notion that the roots of the Qumran community go back to the late third or early second century BCE is thus incontestable.

To summarize, the sources relate contradictory indications for the date of the rise of the groups which are the subject of this book – from hoary unspecified antiquity to Ezra and Nehemiah, down to the mid second century BCE, with an important moment around the turn of the third century BCE – yielding significant disagreement in the chronological conclusions reached by modern scholars. The price paid for this uncertainty has been ineffective attempts to explain the connection between the origins of ancient Jewish sectarianism and any of these time periods. Thus consider the following comment by S. Talmon:

> The situation changed radically when in 163 BCE the Hasmoneans re-established Jewish political sovereignty for one hundred years, after which time, Rome subjugated the Jewish state. *It is precisely during this*

"The Ideology of the Temple in the Damascus Document," *Journal of Jewish Studies* 33 (1982), 287–301. The literary and manuscript evidence, however, leaves little doubt that CD had a central place in the life of the Qumran sect, in spite of the disparities noted. The way in which these differences are to be explained awaits detailed study, of the sort begun by J. Baumgarten, "The Cave 4 Versions of the Qumran Penal Code," *Journal of Jewish Studies* 43 (1992), 268–276. For the status of the question on CD see L. Schiffman, *Law, Custom and Messianism in the Dead Sea Sect* (Jerusalem, 1993), 21–31 [in Hebrew].

[63] See A. Laato, "The Chronology of the Damascus Document of Qumran," *Revue de Qumran* 15 (1992), 605–607. Of course, there is no assurance that their chronology was the same as ours, but lacking further evidence the assumption is unavoidable. On this point see further P.R. Davies, *The Damascus Covenant* (Sheffield, 1982), 6. For one indication of the perils of calculating ancient dates note Josephus's comment that Aristobulus I became king (104–103 BCE) four hundred and eighty one years after the return from the Babylonian exile (*Ant.* 13.301). This is about fifty years too much, by our standards. Compare the alternate date for the kingship of Aristobulus I, *War* 1.70, where this event is placed four hundred and seventy one years after the return, only about forty years too much by our calculations.

[64] See e.g. J. VanderKam, *The Dead Sea Scrolls Today* (Grand Rapids, 1994), 38. This consideration is crucial for Beckwith, "Pre-History."

"Hasmonean Century" that the Commune of the Qumran Covenanters flourished . . .
No definite correlation between the status of political independence and the specific
mode of Qumran secession can be readily established (emphasis mine).[65]

In other words, while the community at Qumran flourished in a
specific period, Talmon is unable to explain those facts in their chronological context.[66] Nor is this view unique to Talmon, the contradictory chronological indications have led Y. Sussmann to be reluctant
to draw historical conclusions concerning the background against which
to place the Qumran sect.[67]

SECTARIANISM: ANTECEDENTS, FORERUNNERS AND
FULL FLEDGED FORMS

At the very end of his posthumous book *The Jews in the Greek Age*,
E. Bickerman offered the following observation:

> As Vico observed more than two centuries ago, people accept only the
> ideas for which their previous development has prepared their minds,
> and which, let us add, appear to be useful to them.[68]

Successful ideas or institutions, as sociologists of knowledge have taught
us, rarely (if ever) spring full-born into the world. They have a history,
which recounts the extent to which they were considered useful by
people of different eras. That extent changed, perhaps as the idea or
institution was modified, perhaps as circumstances made the idea or
institution more appealing, perhaps both. While infinite divisions are

---

[65] Talmon, "The Emergence of Jewish Sectarianism," 192.

[66] For this reason among others, Talmon therefore antedates the emergence of
the community to the beginning of the second century BCE, *ibid.*, although its roots
stretch back to the First Temple period, Talmon, "Qumran Studies," 15.

[67] Y. Sussmann, "Research on the History of the Halacha and the Scrolls of the
Judean Desert," *Tarbiz* 59 (5750), 38, n. 120 [in Hebrew].

[68] E.J. Bickerman, *The Jews in the Greek Age* (Cambridge, 1988), 305. In a similar vein
compare C. Hill, *The Intellectual Origins of the English Revolution* (Oxford, 1965), 1–3:

> Ideas do not advance merely by their own logic. . . . The logical implications of
> Luther's doctrine could not be realized in practice in England until political
> circumstances – the collapse of the hierarchy and the central government –
> were propitious. Ideas were all important for the individuals whom they impelled
> into action; but the historian must attach equal importance to the circumstances
> which gave these ideas their chance.

On the place of ideas and ideology in explanations of the rise of ancient Jewish
sectarianism see further the discussion at the end of Chapter Four.

possible, it seems convenient to divide the course of a successful idea
or institution into vague antecedents, forerunners, maturity, and after-
effects. What separates any one stage from the others is the extent to
which the idea or institution served as a basis for social cohesion
and action. This determination is only possible with the benefit of
hindsight: a historian must first know when full maturity was reached,
and only then can the story be organized in a meaningful way. Then
the vague antecedents become clear, the period in which the idea or
institution only seemed useful to a small group of people, often viewed
with benign disdain by their fellows. Then the forerunners emerge in
their full clarity, as a time when some social cohesion has been generated around the idea or institution, but it was still not a social
force on a fully meaningful level.[69]

The remarks in the preceding paragraph are based on the analysis
of the history of Zionism offered by Jacob Katz,[70] in turn dependent
on the work of his teacher Mannheim.[71] I suggest that Katz's approach
can provide the key to making clearer sense of the data on ancient
Jewish sectarianism. In addition, adopting this strategy will help avoid
falling into the generic fallacy, in which determination of the point
of origin is taken to be the most important question of all, and hence
is sometimes the sole objective of scholarly endeavor.

The first task, if one is to apply Katz's method, is to establish the
moment of full maturity. In the case of ancient Jewish sectarianism,[72]
I propose that two factors must converge in order to reach that point
of social effectiveness: (1) there must be more than one group; and
(2) at least one group must have taken its own position seriously
enough to secede from the mainline institutions. The first condition
insists that the question was widely felt, that there was more than
one competing answer, before concluding that sectarianism had
reached full utility. The second condition demands a willingness to

---

[69] On the phenomenon of precursors in general see the discussion and bibliography
in Douglas, *How Institutions Think*, 60–90.

[70] J. Katz, "In Clarification of the Term 'Forerunners of Zionism,'" *Jewish Eman-
cipation and Self-Emancipation* (Philadelphia, 1986), 104–115. I would like to thank Dr.
S. Feiner for calling this important study to my attention. For another study by
Katz of the maturing of a phenomenon under the proper circumstances see below,
Chapter Six, n. 5.

[71] See K. Mannheim, "The Problem of Generation," *Essays on the Sociology of Knowledge* (London, 1952), 276–320.

[72] At the risk of belaboring the obvious, in some other case of sectarianism full
maturity might be determined by other criteria.

risk one's social position and station in the name of sectarian commitment, before deciding that sectarianism was fully mature. Both conditions together are necessary as proof of the meaningful social consequences needed to confirm full fledged sectarianism.

Viewed in these terms, ancient Jewish sectarianism can only be considered fully formed from the Maccabean era onwards. It is first then that we hear of more than one group (Pharisees, Sadducees and Essenes mentioned by Josephus at time of Jonathan, *Ant.* 13.171–173; Pharisees and Sadducees in conflict at time of John Hyrcanus, *Ant.* 13.288–298). The secession of the Qumran community, as related in 4QMMT, apparently also took place at that time.[73]

Nehemiah, therefore, was a vague antecedent of ancient Jewish sectarianism. While he had built a coalition in support of his platform it was *ad hoc* and of little lasting effect. Few people saw his reforms as of value, and they likely lapsed after his second term, as they had in the period between his two terms. His attempts to consider rivals as outside the bounds of the Jewish people did not prevail.[74]

Works such as the early sections of 1 Enoch or the book of Jubilees fall into the category of forerunners. They are the focus of some social action, in response to the new situation created by the encounter with Hellenism. They lead more or less directly to the Qumran community, as attested by fragments of the works in their library and the citation of Jubilees in the Damascus Document (CD xvi, 4). Nevertheless, works such as Jubilees have not yet generated true social effectiveness. Can one confidently write of a community behind the Enoch literature, or Jubilees?[75]

A similar conclusion is appropriate for the stage of sectarianism represented in the opening sentences of the Damascus Document. At that point in the history of the movement, to the extent that one existed, its members only recognized that they were not fulfilling the law properly, and did not yet know the right path. They were like

---

[73] The significance of Samaritan secession, whenever it took place (see above, Introduction, at n. 51) for this argument is difficult to determine. Perhaps it would fit in among the forerunners of ancient Jewish sectarianism, when there were still few groups on the scene. In any case, the Samaritans pose a dilemma for consideration under the rubric of the definition of sectarianism I have proposed, as their status as members of the Jewish people is disputed (see above n. 29).

[74] On the proto-sectarianism (his term) of Nehemiah see also Cohen, *Maccabees to the Mishnah*, 138–141.

[75] On 1 Enoch see J. Collins, *The Apocalyptic Imagination* (New York, 1984), 56–63. On the question of a community round Jubilees see *ibid.*, 67.

blind people, feeling their way in the dark, until their eyes were opened and the world illumined by the Teacher of Righteousness.[76] All this is appropriate to the status of forerunners.

Full maturity will require one further transformation – Maccabean high priesthood and the events culminating in the achievement of independence under the Maccabees. These tipped the balance, making the ideas associated with sectarianism seem useful to a truly wide circle of people, a role they were to retain down to the destruction of the Temple by the Romans.[77] The full array of reasons for which the balance was tipped at that time remain to be elaborated in the chapters that follow. For present purposes, however, it is sufficient to note the series of rapid changes in Jewish life, a breakdown in the old order, which took place at the time. These include: (1) the encounter with Hellenism; (2) the persecutions of Antiochus IV, changing the terms of close to four hundred years of control of Jews and Judaism by different world empires;[78] (3) the cooperation of at least some of the traditional leaders with those persecutions; (4) the successful revolt against Antiochus IV and his decrees;[79] (5) the rise of a new dynasty of high priests, soon to be followed by the achievement of political independence – the last four events on this list having taken place over a quarter of a century.

A poignant indication of the breakdown of the old order is suggested by Ben Sira 50:24, according to the Hebrew version:

> May His love abide upon Simon, and may He keep in him the covenant of Phinehas; may one never be cut off from him; and as for his offspring, (may it be) as (enduring as) the days of heaven.

---

[76] One is entitled to wonder whether the people who lived at that stage of the evolution of the Qumran movement would have agreed to the description of them in CD as blind men, groping for the truth, but not yet finding it.

[77] Then circumstances changed, so as to lead to the waning of sectarianism and the transformation of what had once been competing groups into explicit winners and losers. The prime case of transformation within Judaism must be that of the Pharisees, who become the Rabbis, after 70. A different sort of transformation changed the nature of the early Christians.

[78] The terms go back to the Persian Empire and were copied virtually without change by Alexander the Great and his successors. For an example of the old arrangement see Ezra Chapter 7.

[79] This fact does not necessarily require us to believe that any of the later groups emerged from the ill defined group of Hasidim who played a role in the rebellion against Antiochus's decrees, as has sometimes been suggested. See P.R. Davies, "*Hasidim* in the Maccabean Period," *Journal of Jewish Studies* 28 (1977), 127–140 and Sussmann, "Research," 43.

Ben Sira, who wrote in the first quarter of the second century BCE, represented traditional values in the attitudes displayed here. He regarded Jewish life as it existed under the reign of Simon as the virtually complete embodiment of the nation's highest aspirations, as the flowering of all God's works in creation during human history.[80] He put his trust in the hands of the descendants of his hero, Simon son of Onias, praying for their loyalty and continued rule as priests. Yet, within a few decades after his death, some of the progeny of Simon were among the "hellenizers" in Jerusalem; others of his offspring were to leave Jerusalem and found the "House of Onias," in service of the Ptolemies, at Leontopolis in Egypt.[81] The priests in charge in Jerusalem were to be the Maccabees. One indication of the gap between Ben Sira's expectations and the reality which ensued has been noted by Di Lella and Skehan:[82] when Ben Sira's grandson translated his ancestor's work into Greek he changed the meaning of 50:24, rendering it "May He entrust to us His mercy, and let Him deliver us in our days." This was done, Di Lella and Skehan suggest, so as to avoid embarrassing his grandfather in the eyes of later readers, who would have been aware of the painful contrast between the original author's hopes and events as they had unfolded. All this is explicit indication of the rapid change which took place in the space of two generations, between Ben Sira and his grandson, thus providing a crucial contingency necessary for the emergence of sectarianism.

It is these connections between context and consequences, from the forerunners in the pre-Maccabean era to the waning of sectarianism in the aftermath of the destruction of the Temple, which the historian should seek to establish and elucidate. Special emphasis must be given, however, to the moment of full maturity, at the time of Maccabean victory, without which ancient Jewish sectarianism might have died still born. The question to which this book will be devoted

---

[80] For a full discussion of this aspect of Ben Sira see B. Mack, *Wisdom and the Hebrew Epic* (Chicago/London, 1985). See also the discussion below, Chapter Five, at nn. 63–67, of Ben Sira's aspirations for the annihilation of the enemies of Israel, as expressed in Chapter 36 of his work.

[81] The history of this house is discussed several times by Josephus. See *War* 7.421ff.; *Ant.* 12.387f.; 13.62ff.; 20.236. On this event see F. Parente, "Onias III's Death and the Founding of the Temple of Leontopolis," in F. Parente and J. Sievers (Eds.), *Josephus and the History of the Greco-Roman Period – Essays in Memory of Morton Smith* (Leiden, 1994), 69–98.

[82] A. Di Lella and P. Skehan, *The Wisdom of Ben Sira* (New York, 1987), 554. See also Mack, *Wisdom and the Hebrew Epic*, 180.

can therefore be specified more precisely: *without losing sight either of the forerunners or of the aftermath, what are the connections between the context of the Maccabean era and the consequences – the flourishing of Pharisees, Sadducees, Essenes and the Dead Sea Scrolls Sect?*

The State of the Question – A Survey

The recognition that there might be some association between the rise of the sects, whose history is my subject, and the events of the second century BCE has been fairly widespread. Nevertheless, this perception has remained vague, lacking specific content, leading to the sort of comment quoted from Talmon above.

In addition to the reasons discussed in previous sections of this chapter, one further reason the perception has remained vague may be connected with the focus of attention of many studies of the social history of Second Temple Judaism. In these works, Jesus and the movement to which he gave birth are the principal matter under investigation.[83] Accordingly, events of the Maccabean era, such as the emergence of Pharisees, Sadducees, Essenes and the Dead Sea Scrolls Sect are often treated as preparation for discussion of the essential question (in the minds of these scholars, at the very least).[84] While perceptive comments are made in these works, they are inevitably brief and not fully elaborated. Thus, to take Theissen's presentation as an example,[85] he devotes a few pages to the Maccabean period, proposing that the encounter with Hellenism was crucial to the emergence of sects in that time:

---

[83] See for example I. Zeitlin, *Jesus and the Judaism of his Time* (New York, 1988), 16–17, 22, 28; G. Theissen, *Sociology of Early Palestinian Christianity* (Philadelphia, 1978), esp. 84–93; R. Horsley, *Sociology and the Jesus Movement* (New York, 1989).

[84] At the risk of belaboring the obvious, scholars differ in their assessments of the questions which are worth asking and deserve extensive answers. No one scholar need be bound to the agenda of another. Nevertheless, the choice of topics a historian deems worthy of investigation is one of the most revealing self-disclosures which can be made.

[85] The choice of Theissen as an example for extended discussion is not arbitrary. His book has been characterized as "the most influential sociological study of earliest Christianity to date;" Horsley, *Sociology and the Jesus Movement*, 9. Horsley provides an extensive critique of Theissen's work, but it is a critique more concerned with the interpretation of Jesus and his movement, as opposed to my interest in the Maccabean era.

Thus the attempt to preserve the cultural identity of Judaism [in the face of Hellenistic civilization, a superior alien culture] by intensifying the norms of the law leads to schism.[86]

Theissen is thus a spur to the scholar whose focus is on the Maccabean era.[87] In particular, Theissen's comments force me to ask why many peoples encounter superior alien cultures, yet not all these contacts result in sectarianism. Theissen serves to highlight the question of what was special about the Jewish encounter with the superior alien culture that led to the known results.

The situation is analogous in the case of Saldarini.[88] His account also concentrates on the first century CE and explicitly attempts to set Pharisees, Scribes and Sadducees within the context of first century CE Judaism in the *Roman* period (the era when these groups form part of the background to the gospels). Not surprisingly, his interest in the circumstances which brought these groups into existence is limited, and his comments restricted to a few remarks on the Hellenization of the Maccabees leading the Pharisees to seek "a new communal commitment to a strict Jewish way of life, based on adherence to the covenant."[89]

In contrast to Theissen and others, my choice of topic is different: I view events of the Maccabean era as the principal subject requiring explanation.[90] My analysis begins with the commonplace of scholarship

---

[86] Theissen, *Sociology*, 86. Theissen describes a process which he sees as leading to intensifying norms of observance of the law. I take this to be another way of characterizing the more general process I call the narrowing of limits of tolerance, discussed at the end of the next chapter.

One of Theissen's merits is in making explicit a point concerning the connection between Hellenism and the rise of ancient Jewish sectarianism, somewhat more diffuse in M. Hengel, *Judaism and Hellenism – Studies in their Encounter in Palestine in the Early Hellenistic Period* (Philadelphia, 1981), esp. 224–227.

[87] My comments are not intended to minimize the significance of the encounter with Hellenism as part of the explanation of the results. Other cases of sectarianism have shown the possible importance of the meeting of a native culture with that of colonial conquerors as a factor in the flourishing of religious groups. See e.g. S. Arjomand, "Social Change and Movements of Revitalization in Contemporary Islam," in J. Beckford (Ed.), *New Religious Movements and Rapid Social Change* (Paris, 1986), 89 & 91. I object to turning the encounter with the foreign culture into the beginning and end of the explanation of the rise of these groups. See further Chapter Two, below, where I discuss the impact of Hellenization at length.

[88] Saldarini, *Pharisees*.

[89] *Ibid.*, 95. See also his remarks, *ibid.*, 59.

[90] As a period of renewed Jewish independence, the Maccabean period is the subject of a virtually permanent fascination on the part of Israeli audiences, both popular and academic.

that religious movements tend to proliferate in conditions of rapid social change,[91] an idea applied by scholars to any number of cases across human history and in the present. Many of these applications, however, are lacking: they do not specify the kinds of movement which proliferate at times of rapid change, nor do they elucidate the aspects of rapid change which account for that proliferation. They do not clarify the mechanisms by which rapid social change affects religious change. These criticisms are drawn from J.A. Beckford, who notes the need for a deeper sociological understanding of religious movements of the present, suggesting that these are important questions which need to be answered.[92] Beckford's insistence on specificity applies equally to interpretations of groups of the past. The brief explanations of the origins of Pharisees, Sadducees, Essenes and the Dead Sea Scrolls Sect offered by Theissen and Saldarini as part of their introductions to the main subjects of their studies cannot but be found wanting by these standards.

In that sense, E.P. Sanders's discussion of these issues is far more detailed and complex.[93] While his principal intention, as indicated by the title of his book, is to discuss the period from 63 BCE to 66 CE, Sanders addresses the question of what issues generated parties in

---

[91] I strongly prefer the terminology of rapid social change to that of deprivation, or relative deprivation. The latter were once seen as virtually the all purpose explanations of a wide variety of social phenomena. See e.g. C. Glock and R. Stark, *Religion and Society in Tension* (Chicago, 1965), 242–259. More recent research has raised significant doubts about the adequacy of these explanations. See B. Wilson, *The Social Dimensions of Sectarianism* (Oxford, 1990), 218. See also R. Stark and W. Bainbridge, "Networks of Faith: Interpersonal Bonds and Recruitment to Cults and Sects," *American Journal of Sociology* 85 (1980), 1377–78. Replicating the research and conclusions of L. Gerlach and V. Hine, "Five Factors Crucial to the Growth and Spread of a Modern Religious Movement," *Journal for the Scientific Study of Religion* 7 (1968), 27, Stark and Bainbridge argue that interpersonal bonds and networks are at least as significant as relative deprivation in explaining who joins a cult or sect, and who does not. For a position close to mine see R. Wuthnow, "World Order and Religious Movements," in E. Barker (Ed.), *New Religious Movements: A Perspective for Understanding Society* (Toronto, 1982), 49–51. Wuthnow suggests that the emergence of new religious movements is correlated with changes in the larger world order. Cf. J. Duhaime, "Relative Deprivation in New Religious Movements and the Qumran Community," *Revue de Qumran* 16 (1993), 265–276 who notes objections to placing great emphasis on relative deprivation as an explanation for the emergence of sectarianism but who nonetheless continues to invoke it as the key to unlocking virtually all mysteries. The supposed role of relative deprivation in sparking millennial movements will be discussed in detail below in Chapter Five, at nn. 31–41.

[92] J.A. Beckford, "Introduction," in Beckford, *New Religious Movements*, xii.

[93] Sanders, *Practice and Belief*, 13–29. For similar statements of the issue see Cohen, *Maccabees to the Mishnah*, 161, and Schiffman, *Reclaiming*, 65–81.

Judaism of the second century BCE as a subject worthy of lengthy discussion, and not just as part of the backgrounds to the career of Jesus. He surveys the history of the period from Alexander the Great to Salome Alexandra, considers the role of Hellenization, and places extensive emphasis on the importance of the rise of the Hasmoneans as a new high priestly dynasty. Attitudes towards this new leadership, both as high priests and as military rulers, played a crucial role in the emergence of parties, in his view.

Nevertheless, even Sanders's approach does not seem to do justice to the intricacy of the issues. One aspect of Sanders's suggestion builds on a conclusion first proposed by A. Geiger. In Geiger's view, the Hasmonean dynasty deposed the old Sadoqite priestly families, but succeeded fairly quickly in reconciling the former office holders to their rule, so that these Sadoqites became the nobility of the new court, as the Sadducees.[94] This idea was then expanded by Cross, when Qumran texts such as The Damascus Document and the Manual of Discipline also allocated an important place in the leadership of that community to the Sadoqite priests. As stated by Cross:

> the ancient Zadokite house gave way to the lusty, if illegitimate Hasmonean dynasty. Essene origins are to be discovered precisely in the struggle between those priestly houses and their adherents.[95]

The Qumran-Essenes (identified with each other by Cross) represented the unreconciled Sadoqites, who should be contrasted with those who had been co-opted by the regime and become the Jerusalem Sadducees, and with the non-priestly Pharisees. Here is a parade case of attitudes towards the new dynasty leading to the emergence of groups.

While some doubts were expressed concerning this conclusion by scholars such as Liver,[96] it was widely accepted, and apparently serves as a foundation for Sanders's conclusions. In recent years, however, in particular since Sanders completed writing his book, significant reasons for doubting this approach have been raised. New texts from Cave 4 have taught us that the attitude of the Qumran community

---

[94] A. Geiger, *Urschrift und Ubersetzungen der Bibel in ihrer Abhänglichkeit von der innern Entwicklung des Judentums* (Frankfurt, 1928, 2nd edition), 101–102; *Judaism and its History* (New York, 1952), 102–103.

[95] F.M. Cross Jr., "The Early History of the Qumran Community," in D. Freedman and J. Greenfield (Eds.), *New Directions in Biblical Archaeology* (Garden City, 1971), 81.

[96] J. Liver, "The 'Sons of Zadok the Priests,'" *Revue de Qumran* 6 (1967/70), 27–30.

towards the Maccabean dynasty was not as hostile as once perceived.
On the other side of the coin, the place of the Sadoqite priests as
leaders of Qumran is no longer as certain as it once seemed.[97] It is
therefore difficult to employ Qumran attitudes towards the Hasmonean
house as the point of departure for understanding the origins of the
Qumran group.[98] If even the most prominent case of sectarianism as
a result of political conflict is now in serious doubt, much room for
other explanations remains.

Another focus of historical inquiry directly connected with the
questions being asked in this book has been research into Qumran
origins, which has already entered the discussion immediately above.[99]
That topic has attracted more than its share of scholars, as well as
its share of cranks.[100] Theories of Qumran origins have recently been
multiplying as mushrooms after the rain.[101] Nevertheless, the results
are not as satisfying as one might wish. Qumran texts abound in
vague code-words, alluding to people and events in ways scholars
cannot always identify precisely.[102] There is an almost never-ending
discussion concerning the identity of the "wicked priest," with virtually every known priest from the second century BCE to the destruction of the temple having been proposed for that role.[103] The same

---

[97] See G. Vermes, "Preliminary Remarks on Unpublished Fragments of the
Community Rule from Qumran Cave 4," *Journal of Jewish Studies* 42 (1991), 250–
255. See now also A.I. Baumgarten, "The Zadokite Priests at Qumran: A Reconsideration," *Dead Sea Discoveries*, forthcoming, and below. Chapter One, n. 6.

[98] I have discussed this matter at length in Baumgarten, "Crisis in the Scrollery,"
399–405.

[99] For a survey of research see P.R. Callaway, *The History of the Qumran Community: An Investigation* (Sheffield, 1988).

[100] At one point in 1991 tabloid newspapers sold at supermarket checkout counters
in North America proclaimed that the Dead Sea Scrolls revealed a cure for AIDS.
On a more serious level, in dealing with new texts, surrounded by mystery and
occasional scandal due to delays in full publication, the normal scholarly mechanisms of sanction against those who hold bizarre views have been ineffective. Every
Qumran scholar likely has a private list of others holding views not worthy of serious discussion, who nevertheless persisted in diffusing these theories, uncorrected by
the criticism to which their ideas were subjected. This situation has prevailed since
the founding generation of Qumran studies.

[101] See my summary of these views and their significance in Baumgarten, "Crisis
in the Scrollery," 406–407.

[102] The only contemporary figure, definitely known to us from some other source,
explicitly mentioned in the *pesharim* is Demetrius King of Greece = Demetrius III of
4QpNah i, 2.

[103] Some have proposed that the "wicked priest" was a generic term for all the
Hasmonean rulers. See A.S. van der Woude, "Wicked Priest or Wicked Priests?
Reflections on the Identification of the Wicked Priest in the Habakkuk Commentary,"

is true for other figures or episodes alluded to in the various *pesharim*. Opponents are regularly denounced, but are rarely if ever named in ways which make their identity explicit beyond doubt to us. The difficulties in the one explicit chronological indication we are given, locating a moment in the past of the group 390 years after the Babylonian exile, have been noted above (n. 63). This assertion is therefore not as useful as it might seem for reconstructing the history of the Qumran sect. Theories of Qumran origins might thus help illuminate the more general phenomenon of ancient Jewish sectarianism, but the light they have cast thus far has been dim and irregular.

THE WAY TO BE TAKEN

If one hopes to advance further, attention must first be concentrated on the Maccabean age as a worthy object of study in and for itself.[104] The appeal to rapid change at that time as an explanation of the results is acceptable as a point of departure, but as Beckford and others have shown, more extensive specificity of interpretation is necessary. That will be possible only if new sources of insight can be found. I propose to turn to two. First is the text from Qumran known as 4QMMT.[105] In this source a member of the community explains to a representative of "official" Judaism why he (and his group) have seceded. Scholars can now read the self-description and justification of a group of sectarians, written at a crucial moment in its history. This should give us an important advantage in seeking to comprehend the phenomena. One benefit of 4QMMT has already been

---

Journal of Jewish Studies 33 (1982), 349–359. Even more despairing is the position of Davies, *Behind the Essenes*, 28, who denies all reality to an historical individual called the Wicked Priest.

[104] The Maccabean era, in particular the period after the purification of the Temple, is now beginning to get more of the scholarly attention it deserves. See e.g. J. Sievers, *The Hasmoneans and their Supporters* (Atlanta, 1990); D. Mendels, *The Rise and Fall of Jewish Nationalism* (New York, 1992). See also the essays collected in H. Eshel and D. Amit (Eds.), *The History of the Hasmonean House*, (Jerusalem, 1995) [in Hebrew].

[105] For the early public discussion see E. Qimron & J. Strugnell, "An Unpublished Halakhic Letter from Qumran," *Israel Museum Journal* 2 (1984–85), 9–12; *Id.*, "An Unpublished Halakhic Letter from Qumran," *Biblical Archeology Today: Proceedings of the International Conference on Biblical Archeology Jerusalem, April 1984* (Jerusalem, 1985), 400–408. See also L. Schiffman, "The New Halakhic Letter (4QMMT) and the Origins of the Dead Sea Sect," *Biblical Archaeologist* 53 (1990), 64–73; Sussmann, "Research" 11–76. See now E. Qimron and J. Strugnell, *Discoveries in the Judean Desert X, Qumran Cave 4. V – Miqsat maase ha-Torah* (Oxford, 1994).

reaped in the discussion above: the secessionist point it records served as a meaningful indicator of when sectarianism reached full maturity, and helped arrange the history of antecedents and forerunners in greater clarity. Other texts from Qumran will also be of assistance in our endeavor, as they supply additional first hand evidence of how one group of sectarians saw themselves and presented their positions.

This approach may be criticized by some as being excessively dependent on too atypical a group of sources, the writings of the Qumran community. How can the larger phenomenon be understood properly when leaning heavily on texts written by a group extreme even by the standards of its own time, who left the major centers of Jewish life for the desert? What can these cranks and crackpots teach about sectarianism within the society at large? I would offer two complementary responses to this possible objection. First, my research has shown that the pool of terms used by groups of that era to describe themselves was quite small and that there was a significant overlap between the terms used by different groups. It seems as if there was a competition between groups which had the right to appropriate these favorable terms for itself.[106] This was but one aspect of the fundamental similarity between groups alluded to above in determining the way in which the terms sect and sectarian are employed in this book, and to be discussed in greater detail below (Chapter One, at nn. 60–66). This similarity was both halachic and conceptual.[107] The different groups thus inhabited the same intellectual and religious universe of discourse, and it is therefore legitimate to use one to interpret the other. This conclusion supports a more general one: what makes groups extreme is not that they originate on some different planet than their contemporaries, but that they are willing to take certain opinions current in their world to their logical ends, even if these are quite radical. The members of these groups do not necessarily hold essentially different views on the issues of the day; rather, they do not shirk from drawing the full consequences of these positions,

---

[106] See Baumgarten, "Qumran and Jewish Sectarianism," 141–146.

[107] See Sanders, *Paul and Palestinian Judaism*, 419–430. Sanders's conclusions have been subject of controversy. See the critique by J. Neusner, "The Use of the Later Rabbinic Evidence for the Study of Paul," in W.S. Green (Ed.), *Approaches to Ancient Judaism Volume II* (Chico, 1980), 43–64 and Sanders's response, "Puzzling out Rabbinic Judaism," *ibid.*, 65–80. In spite of the criticisms directed against his work, the existence in Ancient Judaism of the common patterns of thought which Sanders calls "covenantal nomism," or "common Judaism" seems assured.

even if these consequences seem to demand far-reaching measures. In that sense, rather than being misleading, extreme groups can function as an especially effective source of insight into the principles motivating a society: in them one can see written clearly notions which are less distinctly expressed in other sectors.[108]

Second sources of new insight to be utilized are analogous situations in other times and places. Sects, as noted at the outset, are specific to certain periods in Judaism, but such groups are also found scattered across the history of other religions and cultures. I have deliberately chosen to employ as analogies examples in which sectarianism expressed itself by voluntary boundary marking, so as to retain a basic similarity to the Jewish instances which are the focus of this study. The ways in which each of the cases employed for comparative purposes conforms to the basic pattern of sectarianism will be noted in the paragraphs which follow.

These analogous examples, I believe, can teach us much about Second Temple Judaism, a period for which there is little extensive documentation (of Pharisees, Sadducees, Essenes and the Dead Sea Scrolls Sect the only group whose sources can be read directly is the Qumran covenanters).[109] Comparative history, as Marc Bloch taught historians,[110] is always potentially rewarding, but also an uncertain intellectual enterprise.[111] This is particularly the case when the comparison is of the sort stigmatized by Bloch as being in the "grand manner," between societies that were not in some geographic and/or chronological proximity to each other.[112] Nevertheless, the insight

---

[108] See e.g. the comments of C. Hill and G. Scholem discussed in n. 124 below.

[109] The picture improves a bit if one enlarges the chronological limits and includes the early Christians. Assigning the different apocryphal and pseudepigraphal works to known groups is no longer as well regarded a scholarly enterprise as it once was.

Some may be surprised that I do not include Rabbinic literature as a whole as a source of *direct* information derived from the Pharisees. I do so because I do not believe Pharisees and Rabbis to be identical, some transformation having taken place in the shift from the Pharisees, being one competing sect among many, to the status of the Rabbis. Literary-critical work of isolating the Pharisaic strata in Rabbinic literature must be undertaken to recover the Pharisaic foundations of Rabbinic Judaism. This work should now be aided significantly by new Qumran evidence, such as 4QMMT.

[110] M. Bloch, "A Contribution Towards a Comparative History of European Societies," *Land and Work in Medieval Europe, Selected Papers by Marc Bloch* (Berkeley, 1967), 44–81.

[111] For one especially successful application of these techniques see R. Syme, *Colonial Elites* (Oxford, 1958).

[112] Bloch, "Comparative History," 47–48.

to be gained from such comparisons in the "grand manner" is often indispensable,[113] hence the risk seems worth taking. Thus, in turning to analogies – even ones far removed in time and place from Second Temple Judaism – I hope that they make *suggestions* which will help illuminate what is hidden in the ancient Jewish case.[114] Let me stress: I am *not* engaged in a full-scale systematic comparative history, but merely hoping for insight from analogies. Yet, even in invoking these analogies I intend to be sensitive to similarities as well as differences.[115]

One set of analogies on which I have drawn occasionally is the era in which the Karaites and other groups emerged. As movements which grew within Judaism several centuries after the period being studied here, they and the Rabbinites engaged in much boundary marking against each other, most prominently in food rules and worship (the calendar).[116] In turning to the Karaites a further word of caution and explanation is needed. Some scholars have seen a secret underground connection between the sects of the Second Temple era and the Karaites, and have suggested a direct line of inspiration from the earlier groups to the later. In looking to the Karaites and other movements of their period I am not thereby

---

[113] See W. Sewell Jr., "Marc Bloch and the Logic of Comparative History," *History and Theory. Studies in the Philosophy of History* 6 (1967), 214–215.

[114] In general, when an analogy has played a crucial role in sparking my thinking on a topic it will be discussed at the appropriate point in the text. When, however, the analogy's role was to support a conclusion which I had already reached on other grounds it is mentioned in the notes. In that sense, the distribution of references to analogies is intellectually autobiographical.

[115] See Bloch, "Comparative History," 58–67, and nn. 120–121 below.

[116] See the provisions of Karaite-Rabbinite marriage contracts, attempting to regulate differences in the realm of food and calendar, as discussed by M.A. Friedman, *Jewish Marriage in Palestine: A Cairo Geniza Study, II, The Ketuba Texts* (Tel Aviv/New York, 1981), 2.290–301. These divergences in behavior did not prevent Karaite-Rabbinite marriages, as indicated by the Geniza contracts just mentioned. The reality of Karaite-Rabbinite marriages should be contrasted with the blanket statements of authorities such as Qirqasani (See B. Chiesa and W. Lockwood, *Yaqub al-Qirqasani on Jewish Sects and Christianity* [Frankfurt, 1984], 144) that Jews and Karaites did not marry each other. Disorderly reality, that refuses to conform to our attempts to systematize it, rears its head again.

As one further mark of the disorderliness of reality, these Karaite-Rabbinite marriages required each side to respect the practices of the other concerning food laws and the calendar. As a final indication that calendar differences were not so insurmountable, when Maimonides and his court forbade Jews to marry Karaites, they did not mention food laws or the calendar as the offending behavior, as one would expect on the basis of Qirqasani. Rather, they focused on Karaite interpretations of laws of sexual impurity. On this point see M. Cohen, "Maimonides' Egypt", in E. Ormsby (Ed.), *Maimonides and his Time* (Washington 1989), 30–31.

agreeing with this conclusion.[117] Rather, as just noted above, I am interested in using the context in which these groups arose as evidence for the *phenomenon* of sectarianism.[118]

A second set of analogies, to which I have resorted much more frequently, consists of the case of sectarianism in sixteenth and seventeenth century England. This choice has been motivated by a number of considerations. First, boundary marking was present in these instances. As Christopher Hill noted:

> excommunication was one of the principal activities of the early sects. The maintenance of internal purity disrupted unity: [but] without internal purity, survival as a sect was impossible.[119]

Second, the British sectarians came from roughly the same social background as the ancient Jewish ones, the middling sort and better, as will be discussed in detail in Chapter One, below. Third, although these sectarians were Christians, they were Bible crazy, devoting much of their energy to understanding the Biblical text and its practical implications for everyday individual life, as well as for the political and religious life of the nation. The Bible was thus a driving force behind these movements, making them very much like the Jewish groups who are our main concern.[120]

The British groups will prove to be a particularly rich lode to mine for insight for two further reasons: they flourished in an age when printing had become widespread, hence there are abundant primary sources on which to base conclusions. Finally, there are numerous excellent studies, written by historians sensitive to social, political and religious issues, asking questions of the broadest scope, devoted to understanding these examples.[121]

---

[117] On this point see further H. Ben-Shammai, "Methodological Remarks Concerning the Relationship Between the Karaites and Ancient Jewish Sects," *Cathedra* 42 (5747), 69–81 [in Hebrew].

[118] An important difference between the sects of the Karaite period and those of the Second Temple era should be stated at the outset: regionalism seems to have played an important role in the emergence of the groups of the later period. On this point see the discussion by S. Baron, *A Social and Religious History of the Jews* (New York, 1957), 5.179–182. There is no information about the role of regionalism as a factor in the rise of the sects of the Second Temple era.

[119] Hill, *World*, 378. See further the Appendix below.

[120] As these British groups were Christian, the Bible for them included the New Testament, while the Bible of the Jewish groups was limited to the Hebrew Bible. Throughout this book, the term Bible will follow the usage of ancient Jews and mean the Hebrew Bible.

[121] Let me state a number of obvious differences between the cases: (1) an extensive

A third set of analogies, invoked when appropriate in the argument below, is suggested by contemporary Jewish life, particularly in Israel. The place of voluntary boundary defining mechanisms in modern Jewish life was noted above, in introducing the definition of sectarianism. Moreover, Jews of our day have achieved political independence after many hundreds of years of subjugation to various empires and kingdoms, and after several centuries of life as a minority in western democracies. Their experience may therefore teach us something about the responses of Jews of the Maccabean era, who achieved independence after approximately four hundred and fifty years of subjection to world empires.[122] All historians are taught the dangers of anachronism, which should make one leery to apply experience based on the present to the past.[123] Nevertheless, as has often been recognized, the present can suggest important conclusions for understanding the past, which would not have occurred otherwise, if employed carefully.[124]

---

economic, social and intellectual revolution was taking place in Britain, while the extent of whether such a revolution took place in the period between Alexander and the Seleucid conquest has been much debated. For different views see Hengel, *Judaism and Hellenism*; J. Goldstein, "Jewish Acceptance and Rejection of Hellenism," in E.P. Sanders (Ed.), *Jewish and Christian Self Definition Volume Two: Aspects of Judaism in the Graeco-Roman Period* (London, 1981), 64–87, 318–326; L. Feldman, "How Much Hellenism in Jewish Palestine?" *Hebrew Union College Annual* 57 (1986), 83–111, a perspective expanded in *Id., Jew and Gentile in the Ancient World* (Princeton, 1993), 3–44; Bickerman, *The Jews in the Greek Age*; (2) Voluntary groups of the Puritan period were quite rigorously egalitarian, while the Qumran sect – the best known group to concern us – was a mixture of egalitarianism and hierarchy; (3) Determinism was a crucial belief for Calvinists and for those at Qumran. Nevertheless, it helped fuel a revolution that achieved considerable success in one instance, but was the belief of a marginal group in the other.

In the pages that follow, as references make clear, my debt to the example of Christopher Hill and to other historians of the "Past and Present" School is substantial. To the extent possible, given the nature of the surviving sources for Second Temple Judaism, I would like to offer a grand interpretative scheme, addressing one of the larger questions of the history of those times.

[122] For our purposes, the difference between four hundred fifty and two thousand years is immaterial. Both periods cover much more than many generations, making the reacquisition of independence after so long a time a significant event.

[123] See e.g. Bickerman, *Jews in the Greek Age*, ix: "The author has labored to evade the two worst pitfalls of historiography: nationalism and anachronism."

[124] I take this to be one of the principal arguments of E.H. Carr, *What is History* (Baringstoke, 1987, 2nd edition). From among the examples Carr cites one, that of Mommsen, strikes me as particularly significant. Mommsen's *History of Rome* elaborates a grand explanatory scheme for understanding the history of the republican period, especially its waning days. This insight, Carr argues, came to Mommsen as a result of the era in which he lived. Mommsen's time, however, provided no such key for comprehensive explanation of the imperial period. Carr continues: "Surprise has

To summarize, the objective of this book is to explain the rise of Pharisees, Sadducees, Essenes and the Qumran community against the background of Second Temple Judaism, and especially their flourishing during the Maccabean era, in as explicit detail as possible, by taking advantage of the direct testimony afforded by 4QMMT and of what can be learned from other instances of sectarianism.

"An Interpretation"

Implicit in the discussion above is one point which I would like to make explicit in concluding this chapter. I have called this book *The Flourishing of Jewish Sects in the Maccabean Era: An Interpretation*. In choosing

---

often been expressed that Mommsen failed to continue his history beyond the fall of the republic. He lacked neither time nor opportunity nor knowledge (*ibid.*, 31)."

Carr, however, does not find Mommsen's failure to write a comprehensive account of the imperial period surprising. What Mommsen lacked for the imperial period, Carr concludes, was a vision of the past illuminated by insights derived from the issues of the present. For an impassioned dissent against Carr, in the name of historical objectivity, see J.H. Hexter, *Doing History* (London, 1971), 77–106. In spite of my agreement with Carr, a careful historian should beware lest contemporary insights and commitments predominate, to the extent of losing sight of the "otherness" of the past. See further below, at n. 128.

The connection between past and present in historical research is also one of the recurring themes in the studies of Christopher Hill. Note for example his comment in C. Hill, *Change and Continuity in 17th Century England* (New Haven, 1991, 2nd edition), 284:

> That is why history has to be rewritten in each generation: each new act in the human drama necessarily shifts our attitude towards the earlier acts. . . . We ourselves are shaped by the past; but from our vantage point in the present we are continually reshaping the past which shapes us.

or C. Hill, *World*, 15–16:

> History has to be rewritten in every generation, because although the past does not change the present does; each generation asks new questions of the past, and finds new areas of sympathy as it re-lives different aspects of the experiences of its predecessors. . . . Each generation, to put it another way, rescues a new area from what its predecessors arrogantly and snobbishly dismissed as "the lunatic fringe" . . . Historians, in fact, would be well advised to avoid the loaded phrase, "lunatic fringe". Lunacy, like beauty, may be in the eye of the beholder. There were lunatics in the seventeenth century, but modern psychiatry is helping us to understand that madness itself may be a form of protest against social norms, and that the "lunatic" may in some sense be saner than the society which rejects him.

For a discussion of Hill's latter point – that the historian's task is to understand extremists, not merely to dismiss them as psychopathic – compare G. Scholem, *The Messianic Idea in Judaism* (London, 1971), 85–86.

the subtitle, in particular, I wish to emphasize the tentative and some-what speculative nature of the venture. This is *An Interpretation*, which I hope will be judged successful, not *the* explanation. As such, missing links in explicit proof for points in the chain of arguments are inevi-table, and the available evidence may sometimes be stretched thin. Nevertheless, as this is *An Interpretation*, I will feel free to suggest con-nections between ideas, or explanations for which there is no confirma-tion in the ancient sources, utilizing the techniques discussed above. I take this risk because, in the words of C. Hill,

> The attempt to see connexions is hazardous and may lead to mistakes. But these can be corrected. Failure to look for connexions leads to barrenness, myopia, blinkers.[125]

In proposing conclusions not found in the ancient sources, in suggesting explanations of events, even when the actors in those events, or our only sources concerning them, did not explain things in the same way, I will be following in the path set down by Morton Smith in his work on Jesus:

> Trying to find the actual Jesus is like trying, in atomic physics, to locate a submicroscopic particle and determine its charge. The particle can-not be seen directly, but on a photographic plate we can see the lines left by the trajectories of larger particles it put in motion. By tracing these trajectories back to their common origin, and by calculating the force necessary to make the particles move as they did, we can locate and describe the invisible cause.[126]

---

[125] C. Hill, "Partial Historians and Total History," *Times Literary Supplement*, Novem-ber 24, 1972, 1431.

[126] M. Smith, *Jesus the Magician* (New York, 1978), 6. This view of historiography goes back to Thucydides, who felt free to disregard explanations of the causes of the Peloponnesian war put forward at the time in order to offer what he felt was the "true" but unspoken reason. It is a fundamental feature in the approach of Christopher Hill (above, n. 124). On this aspect of Hill's work see M. Finlayson, *Historians, Puritanism and the English Revolution: The Religious Factor in English Politics before and after the Interregnum* (Toronto, 1983), 27. Finlayson's critique of Hill as a doctrinaire Marxist, *ibid.*, 27–31 strikes me as exaggerated, hence unfair. An even more extreme dissent concern-ing the merits of Hill's work is J.H. Hexter, "The Burden of Proof," *Times Literary Supplement*, October 24, 1975, 1250–1252. For a more favorable evaluation of Hill's approach to writing history see the essays collected in Eley and Hunt, *Reviving the English Revolution*. My position on the freedom of a historian to suggest explanations not in the ancient sources should be compared with the similar one stated by Meeks, *First Urban Christians*, 5–7.

History, as Smith concedes, is not physics, and results of such historical work can never claim more than probability. But, as Smith concludes, quoting Bishop Butler, "probability is the very guide of life."[127]

In the end, a work such as this book is also inevitably personal and as much an expression of its author as of anything else, even more so than would be the case in a less speculative endeavor. I have therefore allowed the present in which I live to generate questions and to create commitments which motivate my research. Nevertheless, I have tried not to forget that the past was different than the world in which I live, so that contemporary understandings and personal commitments will not run amuck.[128] Finally, this book has been written in the conviction expressed by Seneca, that the person who hopes the truth can be found, *and therefore dares to act accordingly, and does not cease to ask questions*, is likely to make the greatest contribution to its discovery.[129]

---

[127] Smith, *Jesus the Magician*, 6.

[128] For one especially effective reminder of the "otherness" of the past, that we are not free to understand it however we will, see Hill, *Change and Continuity*, 104:

> Words change their meanings in ways which trap the historically unwary. . . . When the poet William Alabaster looked forward to hearing in heaven the singing of "Archangels, angels, virgins and professors", he was not paying tribute to the academic profession. And when Henry Vaughan sweetly sings "How fair a prospect is a bright backside" he means only that it is nice to have a little garden.

These circumstances prevail in all languages, but are especially prominent in modern Hebrew, revived as an invented tradition by the *Maskilim* at the close of the eighteenth century, and then adopted by the Zionist movement. Speakers of modern Hebrew, who have direct access to the oldest layer of sources in their language without recourse to translation, must beware lest they forget that the words they use in certain senses have different meanings in the Biblical text. See E.Y. Kutscher, *A History of the Hebrew Language* (Jerusalem/Leiden, 1982), 200.

If accurate understanding requires sensitivity to the changing meaning of words, the basic building blocks of communication, how much more so larger cultural constructions. Respect must be given to the difference between the world of some culture in the past and the concerns of the modern scholar. For a critique of one work, flawed in the opinion of the author of the critique, in that the author of the work maintained virtually no distance between his own commitments and the subject, see J. Harris, "The Circumcised Heart," *Commentary* 99 (June 1995), 57–60.

[129] Seneca, *Nat. Quaest.* 6.5.2.

CHAPTER ONE

SETTING THE STAGE

A Social Description of Ancient Jewish Sectarians

Before undertaking more detailed discussion, several introductory points need treatment. One of the useful foundations for a better appreciation of the reasons for the emergence and flourishing of groups is a description of the size and composition of their membership. Such an analysis is impossible for Sadducees, Pharisees, Essenes and the Dead Sea Sect, the movements to be considered in this study, if the picture is restricted to data concerning the Maccabean period, as information about their size and composition for that era is nonexistent. The effort has repaid so handsomely in other cases, however, such as Meeks's analysis of the early Christians,[1] that it seems worth coming as close as one can to a social description of the movements who are the subject of this book. Accordingly, I will utilize evidence from the period of the formation of these groups *up to* the destruction of the Temple.

Concerning the size of the different groups our sources contain few indications; nevertheless, the general picture is clear. Josephus writes that there were six thousand Pharisees who refused to take an oath at the time of Herod,[2] and he and Philo agree that the Essenes

---

[1] Meeks, *First Urban Christians*, 51–74. Cf. the effort to describe the men of Qumran, more theological in outlook than the social description to follow, by F. García Martínez, "The Men of the Dead Sea," in F. García Martínez and J. Trebolle Barrera, *The People of the Dead Sea Scrolls – Their Writings, Beliefs and Practices* (Leiden, 1995), 31–48.

[2] *Ant.* 17.42. This low number has caused some difficulty for those who believe that the Pharisees "controlled" Jewish life. See e.g. H. Mantel, "The Sadducees and Pharisees," in M. Avi-Yonah & Z. Baras (Eds.), *Society and Religion in the Second Temple Period. World History of the Jewish People Volume VIII* (New Brunswick, 1977), 117, who argued that these were six thousand *heads of households*, thus increasing the total number of Pharisees. This increase, however, is not really significant when viewed against the background of the total population. An alternative is to argue that six thousand Pharisees refused to take the oath, but there were more members of the group. This, however, goes against the sense of the comment in Josephus, which implies that there were six thousand Pharisees in all. The passage in Josephus causes a different sort of difficulty for Ellis Rivkin. The Pharisees are portrayed most unfavor-

numbered four thousand.[3] The community of Qumran proper might have reached four hundred members, but was likelier smaller, between one hundred and two hundred fifty.[4] The early Christians, in spite of exaggerated accounts in the Book of Revelations (7:4; 14:3), probably were no more than a thousand in any of the first generations, spread over Palestine and the diaspora.[5] The aristocratic Jerusalem Sadducees[6] cannot have been a large group.[7] The total figures for known group membership, therefore, do not reach twelve thousand.

---

ably here, a conclusion Rivkin resists at all costs, hence he takes the extreme step of denying that these six thousand were Pharisees at all. See further A. Baumgarten, "Rivkin and Neusner on the Pharisees," in P. Richardson (Ed.), *Law in Religious Communities in the Roman Period* (Waterloo, 1991), 113–114.

At the level of detail with which this study is concerned, Josephus's evidence fits remarkably well into the structure of Jewish sectarianism, as known from other sources. Of course, he wrote ethnography about these picturesque people (the Essenes, in particular), skewed to the interests of non-Jewish readers, or to fit his apologetic purposes, but his account of the details of their lives still rings true. This conclusion emerges with special force throughout this chapter, and even more so in the next. For that reason, I have regularly accepted his evidence as reliable. See G. Baumbach, "Schriftstellerische Tendenzen und historische Verwertbarkeit der Essenerdarstellung des Josephus," in C. Thoma, G. Stemberger, and J. Maier (Eds.), *Judentum, Ausblicke und Einsichten, Festgabe für Karl Schubert zum siebzigsten Geburtstag* (Frankfurt, 1993), 23–51, esp. 49–51. Cf. R. Bergmeier, *Die Essener-Berichte des Flavius Josephus* (Kampen, 1993); T. Rajak, "Cio che Flavio Giuseppe vide: Josephus and the Essenes," in Parente and Sievers, *Josephus and the History of the Greco-Roman Period*, 141–160. A similar analysis and conclusion have led me to accept New Testament accounts of the Pharisees as reliable evidence for the behavior of members of the group, even if not as trustworthy for events in the life of the historical Jesus. In spite of the denunciations of the Pharisees which are rife in passages such as Mt. 23, the reformist nature of the group shines through. For a corresponding approach to New Testament evidence on the Pharisees see J. Neusner, *From Politics to Piety – The Emergence of Pharisaic Judaism* (Englewood Cliffs, 1973), 67–80.

[3] *Ant.* 18.21; Philo, *Quod Omnis Probus* 75.

[4] See de Vaux, *Archaeology*, 86. See further M. Broshi, "The Archeology of Qumran – A Reconsideration," in D. Dimant and U. Rappaport (Eds.), *The Dead Sea Scrolls – Forty Years of Research* (Leiden/Jerusalem, 1992), 113–114.

[5] On the growth of Christianity, analyzed on the basis of several independent criteria see R. Stark, *The Rise of Christianity – A Sociologist Reconsiders History* (Princeton, 1996), 4–13.

[6] How far should scholars go in revising their picture of the Sadducees in the light of the overlap of at least some Qumran laws with those identified as Sadducean by the Rabbis? Additional incentive for such a reassessment may be provided by the place of the Sadoqite priests in texts such as 1QS and CD. For earlier statements of my view see A. Baumgarten, "Rivkin and Neusner on the Pharisees," 111–113; "Who were the Sadducees? The Sadducees of Jerusalem and Qumran", in I. Gafni, A. Oppenheimer and D. Schwartz (Eds.), *The Jews in the Hellenistic-Roman World – Studies in Memory of Menahem Stern* (Jerusalem, 1996), 393–412 [in Hebrew]. See, however, the discussion in the Introduction, at nn. 96–98.

[7] See Josephus's remark on them *Ant.* 18.17: "There are but few men to whom this doctrine has been made known."

Even if allowance is made for error and for the fact that there were many other smaller groups concerning which little information at all, and even less concerning the number of their members has reached us,[8] these figures must be put in the context of a total Jewish population in Palestine for the period of at least five hundred thousand, sometimes estimated at as high as two million.[9] Membership in sects was therefore definitely a minority activity.

Not enough is known about the background of those few who elected to be active in such groups. The scanty evidence, however, suggests that they must have been primarily males. One group of Essenes, according to Josephus, was exclusively unmarried males;[10] other Essenes married to beget children,[11] but one may wonder whether these wives were considered members of the group. Only men were buried at the main cemetery at Qumran, while the bodies of women were found in extensions of the main cemetery and in secondary cemeteries.[12] Wives and children born to group members were obliged to follow the rules of the group, according to CD vii, 6–9. Rules for picking wives are given in fragments of CD known

---

[8] On the proliferation of groups and sub-groups in Second Temple Judaism see S. Lieberman, "The Discipline in the So-Called Dead Sea Manual of Discipline," *Journal of Biblical Literature* 71 (1951), 206–7. The disciples of the hermit Bannus or of John the Baptist are examples of the sorts of movements of which only a few details are known, hence for which even a guess at their size is impossible.

[9] See M. Avi-Yonah, "Historical Geography," in S. Safrai and M. Stern (Eds.), *The Jewish People in the First Century Volume One* (Assen, 1974), 109. For a more recent discussion, reaching a conclusion of about one million, on the basis of the grain-growing capacity of the area, see M. Broshi, "Western Palestine in the Roman-Byzantine Period," *Bulletin of the American Schools of Oriental Research* 236 (1979), 6–7.

[10] See *War* 2.120; *Ant.* 18.22; Pliny, *NH* 5.73 = Stern, *Greek and Latin Authors* #204.

[11] *War* 2.160–161.

[12] De Vaux, *Archaeology*, 58. I have discussed the implications of the Qumran cemeteries for the issue of whether those at Qumran married in "Rule of the Martian," 189–191. I proposed there that perhaps many of those at Qumran deferred marriage in the unredeemed world, in the hope of soon living in the perfect unions possible only after the end of the then current evil age. A minority of the community, however, could not maintain this standard and therefore married in the here and now, rather than sin. For a similar suggestion see also Fraade, "Ascetical Aspects of Ancient Judaism," 268–269. Since proposing this way of resolving the apparent contradiction in the data I have learned of at least one millenarian group whose members refuse to marry until the cosmic redemption will be complete. See the discussion of the Spanish peasant movements in Andalusia in Hobsbawm, *Primitive Rebels*, 60, 84.

On women in the Qumran literature, in general, see now Schiffman, *Reclaiming*, 127–143.

from Cave Four (e.g. Fragment D^c Fragment 1, i, 12–15),[13] and a list of those with whom marriage was forbidden is known, 4Q340,[14] but it is not clear that these wives were full fledged members of the sect. Crimes against parents are mentioned in a passage from 4Q270 recently discussed by J. Baumgarten.[15] That text explains(?) the lighter punishment inflicted on those who commit some crime against the mothers[16] as due to the fact that "mothers do not have authority(?) within the [congregation]."[17] If this interpretation of this difficult text is correct,[18] it would support the argument above that women were not perceived as full fledged members of the community described in CD. Given the priestly nature of the Jerusalem Sadducees and their intimate connection with the Temple, one would not expect to find women among their ranks, while all of the known Pharisees were men. Among groups which arose in the first century CE, John the Baptist and Bannus seem to have had only male followers; the Fourth Philosophy was also apparently male (although women numbered among those who died at their stronghold of Massada), as were the Zealots. The followers of Jesus and other early Christians were both male and female.[19] The relatively minor place occupied by women in most of these movements would accord well with their concern for purity.

In geographical terms, it may be significant that one member of each of the two earliest Pharisaic pairs was not from Jerusalem (Yose b. Yoezer of Zeredah and Nittai the Arbelite), while one was.[20] The Sadducees known to us from Josephus and the New Testament had their center of power in the Temple. Sadoqite priests, presumably

---

[13] See B. Wacholder and M. Abegg, *A Preliminary Edition of the Unpublished Dead Sea Scrolls, The Hebrew and Aramaic Texts from Cave Four, Fascicle One* (Washington, 1991), 23.

[14] See further M. Broshi and A. Yardeni, "On Nethinim and False Prophets," *Tarbiz* 62 (5753), 45–50 [in Hebrew].

[15] A fragment of CD from Qumran Cave 4 = D^e Frag. 11, Column i, 13–15, analyzed among others by J. Baumgarten, "Cave Four Versions," 268–276. See further Wacholder and Abegg, *Preliminary Edition, Fascicle One*, 46.

[16] For that crime against fathers, the offender is expelled for life; against mothers, a ten day suspension suffices.

[17] J. Baumgarten, "Cave 4 Versions," 270.

[18] On the difficulties in the text see esp. *ibid.*, 270, n. 10.

[19] Christianity, however, was something of an exception to the patterns of ancient Jewish sectarianism, a point which would require a separate monograph to discuss in full, hence the different role of men and women as members of early Christianity is no surprise.

[20] The connection between sectarian activity and urbanization will be discussed more fully below, in Chapter Four.

originally from Jerusalem, played a particularly dominant role at one moment, at the very least, at Qumran.[21] To the extent that the Temple was the main focus of sectarian interest, as will be discussed further below, Jerusalem must have been the center of sectarian activity.[22] Nevertheless, Judah the Galilean (or more accurately the Golanian) the founder of the so-called Fourth Philosophy was from Gamla, an urban center in the Golan.[23] As such he may be indicative of the spread of sectarianism to areas outside Jerusalem in the first century CE, in the aftermath of the Roman conquest, a time when (according to the gospels) Jesus encountered Pharisees there (see above, n. 22). According to Josephus, the Essenes had centers in every town.[24] These were therefore urban movements, with a particular concentration in Jerusalem, a concentration which may have abated with the passage of time.

Names are an important cultural marker, hence worthy of attention in the attempt to characterize the membership of sects. The names of the earliest Pharisees preserved in the list of the chain of tradition in *mAbot* 1 are all either Hebrew, Aramaicizing or Aramaic, except for two which are Greek (Antigonus and Abtalion). The Qumran members known by name from 4Q477, the "Rebukes of the Overseer" are all Hebrew (Yohanan, Hananiah ben Sim[on] and Hananiah Notos), but the latter Hananiah's epithet, Notos, is Greek.[25] The names of the Qumran members in the Cross-Eshel ostracon (Introduction, n. 7) are also semitic. This would suggest that those involved in sectarian activities were taken from among those less rapidly acculturated in the changing world after the conquests of Alexander.[26]

Did one have to be a priest to join these groups? In some groups more likely yes, such as the Jerusalem Sadducees. In others, such as

---

[21] On the place of the Sadoqites in Qumran see above, n. 6.

[22] First century sources, especially the New Testament, mention Pharisees in the Galilee, and Pharisees who come from the diaspora. On the possible significance of these sources see Saldarini, *Pharisees*, 291–297.

[23] See *Ant.* 18.4. The implications of Judah's origins have been interpreted to suggest different conclusions by Smith and Stern in the studies cited above, Introduction, n. 52.

[24] *War* 2.124. Cf. Philo *Hyp.* 11.11; *Quod Omnis Probus* 76.

[25] See E. Eshel, "4Q477: The Rebukes of the Overseer," *Journal of Jewish Studies* 45 (1994), 116, 121. Cf. M. Broshi, "A Day in the Life of Hananiah Notos," *Alpayim* 13 (5757), 130–132 [in Hebrew] who prefers understanding the epithet as meaning "bastard."

[26] See L.I. Rabinowitz, "Names, In the Talmud," *Encyclopedia Judaica* 12.807. On names as a cultural marker see Meeks, *First Urban Christians*, 55–63.

Qumran, according to 1QS, leadership roles (but not membership) were restricted to priests. In the case of the Pharisees, priestly descent does not seem to have been as important. The Pharisaic chain of tradition in *mAbot* 1 does not mention that any of the members of the pairs were priests. Josephus writes, for example, that two of the Pharisaic members of the delegation sent to challenge his rule in the Galilee were laymen (*Life* 196–198).[27]

The terms of admission to Qumran make it clear that new members were expected to have some property which they would commingle with that of the community,[28] but it is not clear how substantial those assets usually were. In the case of the ostracon, recently published by Eshel and Cross (Introduction, n. 7), these assets were considerable, and included a house and its boundaries, as well as olive and date (trees?), and a slave. This property was likely well above average. Men with and without possessions, according to Josephus, joined the Essenes.[29]

These few clues, in spite of their vagueness, when taken together with the numbers discussed above, suggest that members of these groups were men likelier to come from the economic, social and educational elite – the "middling sort" (to the extent that there was such a class in antiquity)[30] and better – who could afford the "luxury" of indulgence in affairs of the spirit, and who had sufficient background to become sensitive to and interested in issues of a certain character, appropriate to their status.[31] These were people well integrated into

---

[27] On conflict between priests and Pharisees see below Chapter Three, at n. 16.

[28] The nature of Qumran "communism" has been the subject of much scholarly discussion. See esp. C. Rabin, *Qumran Studies* (New York, 1957), 22–36. Compare Schiffman, *Reclaiming*, 106–112. Communism was a regular feature of hellenistic utopias, on which see further D. Mendels, "Hellenistic Utopias and the Essenes," *Harvard Theological Review* 72 (1979), 212.

[29] *Ant.* 18.20.

[30] On the question of whether there was anything like a modern middle class in the world of antiquity see Saldarini, *Pharisees*, 36.

[31] I believe it would be an error to restrict membership in these groups to true aristocrats. These would likely have been too few to supply the number of members attested in our sources, hence I have described the members as coming from the "middling sort" and up. This conclusion is reinforced by the research of Ginzberg and Finkelstein on the Pharisees. While their economic and social analyses are not as much in favor today as in a previous generation, their work retains some validity; it proves that at least some Pharisees reflected the social perceptions of the middle classes in their halachic positions. Cf. Cohen, *Maccabees to the Mishnah*, 172 who is not interested in the social standing of the members of the sects: it is their status as an elite that interests him. But to what extent could people be part of an elite without enjoying a higher social standing?

the social structure, among its natural leaders, while also open to the possibility of criticizing it, and thus harboring a potential for disobedience.[32] They were thus well positioned to become sectarians of the reformist or introversionist kind, either working to change the culture from a position of advantage, and sometimes even succeeding in achieving dominance, or being the most obstinate opponents of the establishment. For these reasons, in spite of the loyalty at times more than merely residual commanded by the Temple, and in spite of the small size of the sects, the activity of these groups was so significant a part of Jewish life of that period,[33] and they were accorded the prominence given them by Josephus, the point of departure of this study.

To put this point in other terms, literacy need not have been an absolute requirement for membership; nevertheless, it would certainly have been useful, and at Qumran it was more or less assumed. Qumran possessed a large library, with multiple copies of key works, suggesting that these texts were much read. According to the Qumran scrolls there was always to be someone engaged in searching and interpreting the Bible.[34]

Estimates of literacy can thus give us a clue of the number of potential members of sects. Literacy, however, was not that widespread: one approximation puts it at three percent of the population, and even if it is acknowledged that nearly all women were illiterate and one concludes that six percent of men could read,[35] that still

---

[32] For this aspect of seventeenth century British sectarianism see P. Collinson, *The Religion of Protestants* (Oxford, 1982), 149–150, 177–178, 187–188.

[33] For a similar analysis of the role of sectarians as a small but decisive elite working in the context of a significant residual loyalty to the Anglican church see B. Reay, "Radicalism and Religion in the English Revolution: An Introduction," in J.F. McGregor and B. Reay (Eds.), *Radical Religion in the English Revolution* (Oxford, 1984), 9–10.

[34] See 1QS vi, 6. The long room called the *scriptorium* by the excavators may well have served this purpose. From this perspective it would be closer in function to a *bet midrash*. In other words, the real purpose of this room at Qumran may not have been as a place for copying texts, but as one for studying them. As those at Qumran believed in ongoing revelation there must be someone constantly engaged in study of the Biblical text so as to serve as a potential receiver of that revelation, whenever it should come. It would be tragic from their perspective should God send some fresh revelation and there be no one ready to receive it at the time. Perhaps, then, regular study took place in the so-called *scriptorium*. Concerning the debate about the purpose of this room see already de Vaux, *Archaeology*, 29–33. For a consideration and critique of recent theories see R. Reich, "A Note on the Function of Room 30 (the 'Scriptorium') at Khirbet Qumran," *Journal of Jewish Studies* 46 (1995), 157–160.

[35] M. Bar Ilan, "Illiteracy in the Land of Israel in the First Centuries CE," in

leaves the members of groups (who were almost exclusively male in any case, as discussed above) as a minority in the nation.[36]

These conclusions are confirmed by the cases of which a few more details are known.[37] Josephus writes of himself as having tried out the schools of Pharisees, Sadducees and Essenes, before spending three years with Bannus in the desert, and before making his final decision to join the Pharisees.[38] Josephus himself was from Jerusalem, of a priestly family, well connected with the local elite, related on his mother's side to the Hasmonean house.[39] Even if his exaggerated self praise is discounted substantially,[40] his economic, social and educational level should have been far above average.[41]

Much the same emerges from descriptions of Simon b. Gamaliel I, a leading Pharisee of the era immediately prior to the destruction of the Temple. His father, Gamaliel I, had been a member of the Sanhedrin in Jerusalem, where Pharisees and Sadducees sat, according to Acts 5:33–34. Simon himself was described by Josephus as coming from a very illustrious family (*Life* 191), and as one of the

---

S. Fishbane (Ed.), *Essays in the Social Scientific Study of Judaism and Jewish Society, Volume II* (New York, 1992), 54–55.

[36] These conclusions agree well with the results of W.V. Harris, *Ancient Literacy* (Cambridge, 1989). On ancient Jewish literacy compare Harris's remarks, *ibid.*, 281–2: "The mirage of mass literacy in first century Judaea, which would be very much at odds with what we know of Greek literacy, begins to fade."

The closest ancient analogues of Jewish sectarians were members of philosophical schools and doctors. Thus, the Greek terminology used by Josephus for discussing the Jewish groups has its origins in the world of philosophy or medical groups (with *hairesis* being the most obvious example). Members of philosophical schools and doctors, however, usually could read, as noted by Harris, *ibid.*, 82. In my opinion this increases the likelihood that their equivalents among Jews, the members of sectarian groups, were also largely literate.

[37] I am deliberately not employing Paul as a paradigm for these purposes, and considering Josephus as our only example. For a consideration of whether Paul should be viewed as a typical Pharisee see Saldarini, *Pharisees*, 134–143. Paul's excellent educational background – evident throughout his letters – may, however, be typical of that of a usual member of a Jewish group.

[38] *Life* 10–12. The difficulties in this account have received excellent discussion by S. Mason, "Was Josephus a Pharisee? A Reexamination of *Life* 10–12," *Journal of Jewish Studies* 40 (1989), 31–45.

[39] See *Life* 2. When visiting the ruins of the luxurious homes of priests uncovered in the Herodian quarter of Jerusalem, I always imagine Josephus wandering around there. Even if he did not live in one of these grand places two thousand years ago, his cousins or uncle must have.

[40] For an example of such self glorification see *Life* 8–9.

[41] If this conclusion is accepted the analogy between ancient Jewish sectarians and one group of early Puritans would be especially close. See C.H. Garrett, *The Marian Exiles* (Cambridge, 1966, 2nd edition), 40–41.

leaders of outstanding reputation, whose arguments against the pro-
letarian Zealots were supported by Gorion, son of Joseph, son of
Gorion (Joseph son of Gorion, along with Anan son of Anan, had
been selected for "supreme control" of the revolt, *War* 2.563), and
by the most eminent of the High Priests, including Anan son of Anan,
the Sadducee (*War* 4.159–161).[42]

Finally, along these lines, the sectarian author of 1QH wrote of
himself as having given up a life involved in the "roaring of peoples,"
and "the tumult of kingdoms when they assemble (1QH vi, 7)." That
is, the author had renounced a life of political activity, which would
otherwise have been his portion, in return for his allegiance to the
Qumran sect, and his belief that he now shared a common lot with
the angels who served God's presence (1QH vi, 13). Such political
activity would normally be a role reserved for those better educated
and of more substantial means (see Ben Sira 38:33, 39:4).

Nor should these conclusions be surprising. Membership in sectarian
groups of the second Temple period should have only interested a
small minority of the nation, most of which would have been relegated
into the category of the "people of the land," or of the "naive" by
those who had chosen to join sects.[43] Indeed, these terms employed
for the non-sectarian majority constitute proof that members of sects

---

[42] In setting the question to be addressed in this study in the Introduction, at
n. 52, I excluded the groups such as Christians, Fourth Philosophy and Zealots
from its scope. As argued there, this was because the latter movements were born
and flourished in the age of Roman conquest, while Sadducees, Pharisees, Essenes
and the Dead Sea Sect had emerged and prospered at an earlier juncture in history, in response to other circumstances. The analysis just completed supplies an
additional reason for the focus proposed. Whatever the social composition of Christians, Fourth Philosophy and Zealots may have been (on the dispute concerning the
latter two see Introduction, n. 52), they were *not* movements of the middling sort
and better, drawn from the ranks of the local elite: Sadducees, Pharisees, Essenes
and the Dead Sea Sect were composed of a different class of people. Perhaps, as
the end of the Second Temple period drew near, this distinction became less sharp:
Pharisees were then to be found in the Galilee (see above, n. 22), and the Fourth
Philosophy was co-founded by a Pharisee, but the elitist nature of Pharisees, Sadducees
and Essenes still pervades Josephus's comments.

[43] The first of these terms appears in Rabbinic texts, and may go back to Pharisaic usage. In the original context the distinction is between *haverim* (whoever these
may have been, and whatever may have been the relationship between the latter
and the Pharisees), and the "people of the land." The second term is one of the
Qumran designations for the misguided masses who have been led astray by the
truly evil rulers of the nation. These "naive" are entitled to a special privilege according to Qumran speculation. They will have the opportunity to recognize the truth
of Qumran ways at the end of days and thus participate in at least some of its
blessings. See further 1QSa.

regarded themselves as standing above society as a whole, thus confirming my conclusion that this was, in fact, their position.

The main benefit of the social description attempted in the preceding pages is in supplying an orientation for the effort to follow. Ancient Jewish sectarians, it should now be clear, were *not* lower class dissidents, shunned by the ruling powers.[44] They were not an alienated and underemployed intelligentsia, searching for a place in society, of the sort posited by some historians as comprising the members of other sectarian moments.[45] This analysis also raises a question concerning the account of Pharisees as a retainer class, in the service of the ruling groups, as suggested by Saldarini.[46] Ancient Jewish sectarians were, however, elitist. The reasons for the appearance and maturity of movements such as Pharisees, Sadducees, Essenes and the Dead Sea Sect to be proposed below will thus have to be appropriate to the status of their members, and will have to take account of their members's role as guardians of the local order, of their desire to see that world perfected, as well as of their potential for protest and dissent when others seemed to be failing at that task.

SECTARIAN OPTIONS

One further generalization is suggested by Josephus's account of his own experience, and while this conclusion cannot be proven beyond doubt, it remains most appealing. Josephus, as noted above, recounted that he spent a year learning the doctrines of Pharisees, Sadducees and Essenes, before his three years with Bannus and before making his final choice to live as a Pharisee. Scholars have regarded this account with some skepticism: to begin with, Josephus's claim to have chosen the Pharisees as a youth is borne out by little in his actions during most of his life. The declaration of having been a Pharisee seems, therefore, to be a late in life conversion, at the best.[47] Furthermore, scholars are concerned that this passage as a whole might be

---

[44] Cf. the sectarian group of the Persian period of which we learn from III Isaiah, and the discussion in Blenkinsopp, "Jewish Sect," 7–11. Cf. also the emphasis on lower class nature of Christian sectarian movements through the ages, which goes back at least as far as the writings of Troeltsch.

[45] Cf. Collinson, *Religion of Protestants*, 179.

[46] Saldarini, *Pharisees, passim.*

[47] Perhaps the choice of the Pharisees was factual, but was a necessary but regrettable concession made by Josephus, as suggested by Mason, *Josephus*, 342–356.

tainted both by Josephus's usual self exaltation and by a *topos* familiar from ancient autobiography in which the author asserts that he
learned all that there was to learn from all schools and sources.[48] In
spite of these doubts, I find Josephus's account of his past believable
and potentially revealing for the experience of others. *Topoi*, we should
remember, derive their power because they describe a usual experience. There may thus be reason to doubt whether Josephus's career
followed every detail of the typical pattern which he claimed, but
there is no reason to doubt that the pattern which Josephus claimed
to have followed, *of having tried out several groups before making a final
choice*, was typical.

In support of this conclusion I would note that experiences such
as Josephus's are common in other sectarian environments. Consider
the following:

> Given this breakdown of confidence on the one hand, and the preva-
> lent millenarian enthusiasm on the other, it is hardly surprising that
> men and women faced with an unprecedented freedom of choice, passed
> rapidly from sect to sect, trying all things, finding all of them wanting.
> Again and again in spiritual autobiographies of the time we read of
> men who passed through Presbyterianism, Independency and Anabap-
> tistry before ending as Seekers (. . .), as Ranters (. . .), or as Quakers.[49]

---

[48] See S.J.D. Cohen, *Josephus in Galilee and Rome: His Vita and Development as a Historian* (Leiden, 1979), 106–107.

[49] Hill, *World*, 190–191. See also B. Reay, "Quakerism and Society," in McGregor
and Reay, *Radical Religion*, 143. According to Reay, the Quakers, when they entered
an area, sometimes carried lists of advanced separatists residing there who were
most likely to be receptive to the Quaker message. Reay discusses this point in
greater detail in his monograph *The Quakers and the English Revolution* (London, 1985), 17.
If further proof of this idea is needed it can be found in the accounts of the
figures studied by J.F.C. Harrison, *The Second Coming: Popular Millenarianism 1780–
1850* (New Brunswick, 1979), many of whom passed through any number of groups
before making their final choice. See for example the story of John Ward, *ibid.*,
152–154, or the comment of John Greenleaf Whittier quoted by Harrison, *ibid.*,
191–192: "These modern prophets . . . speak a language of hope and promise to
weak, weary hearts, tossed and troubled, who *have wandered from sect to sect*, seeking in
vain for the primal manifestations of the divine power (emphasis mine)."
See also the summary in H. Schwartz, *The French Prophets: The History of a Millenarian
Group in Eighteenth-Century England* (Berkeley, 1980), 217–219.
This pattern of trying out various possibilities before settling on a final choice
remains true even if the arguments of J.F. McGregor (and others) that Ranters and
Seekers existed as organized movements more in the minds of heresiologists than in
reality is valid. See J.F. McGregor, "Seekers and Ranters," in McGregor and Reay,
Radical Religion, 121–139, and the review of the subject in E. Thompson, "On the
Rant," in Eley and Hunt, *Reviving the English Revolution*, 153–160.

Ultimately, it may be impossible to determine whether Josephus was telling the whole truth when he stated that he had tried out several groups before making his final decision. Nevertheless, I would argue that this was a fairly common phenomenon.[50]

Sects, I would further suggest, were well aware of the fact that many who came to join would not necessarily remain, but move on elsewhere. This, in my view, is one effective meaning of the regulations of the *haverim* (whether or not they were the Pharisees, as has been discussed by scholars at great length) and at Qumran, according to which one was not accepted as a full fledged member of the group at the outset but had to undergo a process of admission lasting several years;[51] the Essenes, according to Josephus,[52] had a similar system. Both the group and the prospective candidate needed that time to decide if, in fact, they were right for each other. From an ideological point of view, the Qumran evidence indicates that the covenanters found a way to explain to themselves the awkward fact that many more might come than would persist. According to the doctrine of predestination it was easy to understand that all those who left before becoming full fledged members had simply not been chosen by God from the outset for the rare distinction of being taught by God, through His direct revelation.[53]

Awareness of the phenomenon of movement from one group to another underlines the importance of the oaths taken by incoming

---

Empirical studies of contemporary movements confirm this conclusion. See R. Balch, "When the Light Goes Out Darkness Comes: A Study of Defection from a Totalist Cult," in R. Stark (Ed.), *Religious Movements: Genesis, Exodus and Numbers* (New York, 1985), 10, 38–39. See also E. Barker, "People Who do not Become Moonies," in Stark, *Religious Movements*, 74. For discussion of this point from a theoretical sociological perspective see G. Schwartz, *Sect Ideologies and Social Status* (Chicago, 1970), 215. See also Stark and Bainbridge, *Future of Religion*, 272–273.

[50] As very partial support for the conclusion that choices were often not final note the case of Paul and Sadoq the Pharisee (co-founder of the Fourth Philosophy according to Josephus, *Ant.* 18.4), both of whom began as members of one group, but ended in another. Too much reliance should not be put on these examples, however, as Paul may be atypical (see above, n. 37) and the differences between the Pharisees and the Fourth Philosophy may not have been that great. As Josephus remarked (*Ant.* 18.23), the latter agreed with the former in all respects, the only difference being that the members of the Fourth Philosophy had a passion for liberty that was almost unconquerable. On people who vacillate between choices in political-national terms see E. Gellner, *Nations and Nationalism* (Oxford, 1983), 46.

[51] For a discussion of the sources on Qumran and the *haverim* see Lieberman, "Discipline," 199–206.

[52] *War* 2.137–142.

[53] See CD xx, 1–8.

members among more introversionist movement such as the Essenes (*War* 2.139–142). Since the new member was accepting a way of life devoted to a "greedy" institution, and one that called for substantial sacrifice, he needed to ratify his new status by an oath (it is no accident, in my view, that there is no information on oaths taken by incoming Pharisees, members of a more moderate, reformist group).[54] These oaths were "tremendous," binding for life, and hence intended to discourage further exploration of alternative options. For this reason they were only administered after the candidate had proven himself worthy during the preceding three year trial period. Similar vows were taken by the new member at Qumran (1QS v, 8).

Awareness of the existence of "floaters" also helps another aspect of the evidence take on greater meaning. Two regulations in 1QS treat the problems raised by unfaithful members who wished to return to the fold (unfaithful members who never wished to return posed no equivalent problem, hence did not merit discussion). According to 1QS vii, 18–25, unfaithful members who had been part of the sect for less than ten years were allowed the option of rejoining, and of undergoing the process of acceptance over again, while unfaithful members of long-standing were never allowed to rejoin.[55] Similar provisions can be found in *tDemai* 2:9 (Lieberman, 70) concerning a lapsed *haver*:[56] some authorities would allow him to resume his former status, depending on the gravity of his sins, but R. Meir would never permit this. What realities lie behind these discussions? Where have these unfaithful members been in the interim between their times as members of the Qumran group or as *haverim*? What were they doing when they were "walking after the hardness of their heart (1QS vii, 18, 22)?" At least two possibilities exist: perhaps these wayward members renounced all forms of sectarian activity during that interim period, or perhaps they spent it with some other group. The second possibility, of course, accords well with the existence of the "floaters."

---

[54] Note that even if Pharisees are identified with *Haverim*, there is no clear indication that admission to the *Havurah* was accompanied by an oath. See further Lieberman, "Discipline," 200.

[55] See the detailed discussion in Schiffman, *Law, Custom*, 240–267. There are similar regulations, but less detailed, in CD xx, 1–8. As we have no evidence to prove this scenario, I cannot explore the possibility that some apostates in a position of leadership may have helped themselves to the community's assets on departure. If there were such instances, the blow would not only have been one of morale, but also financial. See further S.J. Stein, *The Shaker Experience in America* (New Haven, 1992), 143–148.

[56] On this point see further Lieberman, *Tosefta Kifshuta, Zeraim*, 1.214.

Further support for this conclusion comes from 1QH vi, 3–7, in which the author thanks God for having saved him from the assembly of evil and the congregation of wickedness, and for having brought him into the counsel of the sons of His truth. The evildoers from whom the author was saved were organized into a formal group, as the terms for them indicate ("assembly," "congregation").[57] I suggest that the author saw himself as having been saved from these evil organizations in the sense that he once was a member of these groups, but now believed that he had found the truth in Qumran. Here too, the texts would reflect the phenomenon of the "floaters" which has been under consideration here.[58]

Did these "floaters" ever make a final choice? Perhaps that was not determined until the day of their death, when further changes were no longer possible. In any case, to the extent that they made long-term commitments, it should not be expected that these were taken only on the basis of ideology, halacha, or theology, as there was so much common ground on these matters from one movement to the next (see below). Rather, interpersonal relations with the group whose members they found most congenial must have played a part.[59]

Variations on the Same Theme

The reasons for the phenomenon of movement from one group to another are not hard to discover. Above all, in spite of their mutual hostility, and in spite of the contrast between the height of the purity walls groups erected around themselves – some reformist, others introversionist – there was not that much difference in world outlook

---

[57] See 1QH ii, 22.

[58] Our understanding of the phenomenon must also include the account in Josephus, *War* 2.143–144 of expelled Essenes who remain loyal to their old way of life to the point of starvation, who are ultimately reaccepted by the group. At Qumran too, members were warned not to have any dealings with expellees. This stands in contrast to our expectation that those who had been thrown out might be more than happy to renounce all connection with the way of life promoted by their former group. In fact, as contemporary research has shown, the process of joining a group involves stages of bridge building between one's old and new identity, while there are stages of bridge burning which are inherent in the process of defection. Indeed, the difference between bridge building and burning may be largely semantic. Whatever the case, instances of the co-existence of old and new ways, which are hard to explain rationally, are common in both transitional stages. See further Balch, "Defection," 13, 45; Barker, "People who do not Become Moonies," 87.

[59] See Stark and Bainbridge, *Future of Religion*, 101.

or fundamental ideology between the groups. This aspect of ancient Jewish sects is confirmed by my analysis of the different terms used by groups in their self description, in which (in spite of our very limited knowledge of how they would have described themselves) a number of terms keep appearing. There seems to have been a limited pool of words with good overtones to which many groups tried to attach themselves, and claim as their own. Thus the assertion of zeal in observing the law was shared by Jewish-Christians, Zealots, Qumran covenanters and, perhaps, the Pharisees. The claim to being separatists was shared by Pharisees and those at Qumran, and the claim to accuracy in observing the law (*akribeia*) by those same two groups, at the very least.[60] As Sussmann has noted, there was also a significant overlap in the halachic terminology employed by the movements.[61] The law as observed by one group was not that different from the way it was fulfilled by others, similarities which contemporary scholars are hard pressed to explain: halachic positions turn out to be far from distinct to each of the sects.[62] Covenantal nomism, as Sanders has suggested, supplied the theological basis on which all groups were erected.[63] Given these similarities – all were offering more or less the same merchandise, to put the point in commercial terms – it should not be surprising that a person considering joining a group did not necessarily know at the outset that only one group was appropriate for him. Those interested felt the need to "shop around." Indeed, when viewed in the light of their fundamental similarity, the mutual hostility of the groups (which might seem to contradict this conclusion) becomes more explicable: because the groups were so similar, and offering more or less the same thing to a relatively restricted pool of people, their mutual hatred makes better sense.[64] Thus the evidence for those who "shopped around" between groups confirms the *fundamental similarity of the different groups of that era.*

---

[60] I summarize here briefly the conclusions of my article "Qumran and Jewish Sectarianism," 141–146. "Preciseness" in religion was one of the rallying cries of the Puritan groups. See W. Hunt, *The Puritan Moment* (Cambridge, 1983), 188.

[61] Sussmann, "Research," 26, 37; See also E. Qimron, "Halakhic Terms in the Dead Sea Scrolls and their Contribution to the History of the early *Halakha*," in *Scrolls of the Judean Desert*, 128–139 [in Hebrew].

[62] Compare the different efforts of Stegemann, "Qumran Essenes," 106–107; J. Baumgarten, "The Disqualification of Priests in 4Q Fragments of the 'Damascus Document,' A Specimen of the Recovery of pre-Rabbinic Halakha," *Madrid Qumran Congress* 2.510–513.

[63] See the discussion in the Introduction, at n. 107.

[64] In Puritan Britain the competition between groups – in spite of their similarities – sometimes had a boomerang effect. As Hill writes, *World*, 191:

That basic correspondence between groups must also be explained: I propose that the best historical explanation is that all were competing answers to the same sets of questions raised by the circumstances of their era. The phenomenon of rival solutions arising at a time of rapid change is a well known one. These opposing responses, as might be expected, tend to recruit from the same pool.[65] In other words analysis of the phenomenon of the "floaters" helps confirm the conclusion that the Jewish sects who are the subject of this book were alternate responses to the issues raised by events culminating in the mid second century BCE, from the encounter with Hellenism to the decrees

> All the leading protagonists seemed equally certain, all appeared to have backing from Biblical texts or from the authority of the spirit within. Many concluded by questioning the value of all ordinances. . . . "When people saw diversity of sects in any place," wrote Richard Baxter, "it greatly hindered their conversion." Many, "would be of no religion at all."

See also C. Hill, *Antichrist in 17th Century England* (London, 1971), 135:

> Gradually social anxiety and a wearied disillusion drove some conservatives to question the whole search for Antichrist . . . Edmund Hall . . . Thomas Hall's, younger brother, wrote in 1653. . . . "Some make Antichrist a state . . . some a particular man, a king, or a general. Others give out that Antichrist is like the philosophers' stone, much talked on but never seen yet or known."

To the extent the sources which have survived allow us to see the world of ancient Jewish sectarianism nothing analogous occurred there: we have no indications of a relativism which reduced all groups to the same level of uncertainty. Later on in Jewish History, in the era which saw the rise of the Karaites, however, there is evidence for such attitudes. The Mishwayh, as reported by Qirqasani, in Chiesa and Lockwood, *Qirqasani on Jewish Sects*, 151 believed that all money was a convenience, hence counterfeit, and none "real." One should therefore adopt the festivals of the community, as a matter of convenience, since no truly accurate way for determining the calendar existed.

Nor does the ancient Jewish material indicate that events caused many to lose their faith entirely, of a widespread corrosive doubt of the sort Hill, *World*, 170–182, 262–268, has shown for seventeenth century Britain. Ancient Jewish sources do, however, show a trace of a breakdown of religious discipline, of the "rusty sword of the church," so visible in Britain of the early modern era (on which see C. Hill, *Society and Puritanism in Pre-Revolutionary England* [London, 1964], 370–374). See *mSota* 9:9 on the abolition of the rite of breaking the heifer's neck when murderers became too numerous, or of ending the ordeal of the *sotah* when adultery became widespread.

[65] See Stark and Bainbridge, *Future of Religion*, 140–141, 143 and 405. They discuss Christadelphians, Adventists and Russellites (of whom the best known are the Witnesses), all spawned in the aftermath of the failure of Millerite prophecy in 1844. These groups invested special effort in directing their messages to the inhabitants of the "burned out" districts in New York and New England, where the disappointment at disconfirmation of Millerite expectations was greatest. The Shakers too, already in existence for several generations at the time of the "Great Disappointment" made special efforts to recruit among ex-Adventists. Long-term retention rates among these new members were not, however, high. Celibacy was a particularly difficult practice for these former Adventists to accept. See Stein, *Shaker Experience*, 209–211. Compare the description of the recruiting practices of the Quakers, above, n. 49.

of Antiochus IV, reaching their climax in the successful rebellion against those decrees and the achievement of political independence.[66]

These arguments allow the setting of the stage for the discussion to follow in one further sense, already alluded to above (Introduction, at nn. 106–108). The extent of our sources for the different sects is very varied. We know a good deal first hand from Qumran, very little first hand about other groups, with the possible exception of the Pharisees. Second hand evidence, from Philo, the New Testament, Josephus or Rabbinic literature is not that extensive, and it too differs in range from one group to the other. The basic coherence of sectarian movements with each other, however, allows greater freedom than might otherwise be justified in applying answers based on the sources of one organization to another.

As Seen by their Contemporaries: Non-Jews

In the previous pages the groups have been described as seen in the light of modern criteria of size and social origin. I would now like to turn to the other side of the coin: how were these movements perceived by their contemporaries, first by non-Jews. Unfortunately, we have little information on this subject, other than Pliny's description of the Essenes. Nevertheless, some insight into this matter can be derived from Philo and Josephus, as their comments on the Jewish sects were written, at least in part, with a non-Jewish audience in mind. Proof of this intention is contained in remarks drawing parallels between Jewish groups and those known in the Greek world (the Essenes were a *thiasos*, according to Philo, *Hyp.* 11,5; they were like the Ctistae among the Dacians, according to Josephus, *Ant.* 18.22; they were similar to Pythagoreans, *Ant.* 15.371; the Pharisees were similar to the Stoics, *Life*, 12).[67]

---

[66] I have discussed the tension between competing answers to the same set of questions from another perspective in A. Baumgarten, "Euhemerus's Eternal Gods: Or, How Not To Be Embarrassed By Greek Mythology," in R. Katzoff, Y. Petroff and D. Schaps (Eds.), *Classical Studies in Honor of David Sohlberg* (Ramat Gan, 1996), 91–103.

[67] I have discussed the implications of the comparisons made by Philo and Josephus in A.I. Baumgarten, "Greco-Roman Voluntary Associations and Jewish Sects," in M. Goodman (Ed.), *The Jews of the Greco-Roman World*, forthcoming. For a slightly different perspective on these issues see S. Mason, "Greco-Roman, Jewish and Christian Philosophies," in J. Neusner (Ed.), *Approaches to Ancient Judaism, New Series, Volume Four* (Atlanta, 1992), 1–28.

To begin with Philo, the comparison of the Essenes to a *thiasos* was explained by Philo as based on the custom of common meals. The Essenes ate together, under religious auspices, as did members of a Greek *thiasos*. This analogy has much to recommend it, as members of a *thiasos* were usually urban and often literate, much like the Jewish sectarians described above, but the Essenes were more than a group that met occasionally for a meal under religious auspices. The Essenes, as will be argued in greater detail below in Chapter Two, could *only* eat food when prepared according to the rules of their order. This pure food could *only* be eaten together with members of their order. Greek private associations had regulations of different sorts, many of which have been profitably compared with those of the Dead Sea Scroll community.[68] None of these associations, however, to the best of my knowledge, erected purity walls between itself and the surrounding culture of the sort put up by the Jewish sects. Philo's comparison of the Essenes to a *thiasos* thus has a certain merit, but it also obscured important differences. Philo's Greek reader would understand that a company of urban men who ate together was under consideration, but that Greek reader might not realize the extent to which this company of men lived their lives by a severe rule, far beyond that known in Greek contexts.

Josephus presented the Jewish groups as philosophies (*War* 2.119; *Ant.* 18.9, 11). In another place he described them as heresies (*Ant.* 13.171), as philosophical groups which have taken an independent course. His comparisons to Ctistae, Pythagoreans and Stoics have been noted above. To the Greek reader all this would suggest a company of men who met together under the guidance of some authority figure to discuss intellectual issues, whose doctrines would be passed down from one generation to the next.[69] While some groups would be active as teachers of those outside their circle, others would not.[70] Like philosophical schools these Jewish movements might be called the "house of X;"[71] even closer to the practice of the schools

---

[68] See in particular M. Weinfeld, *The Organizational Pattern and the Penal Code of the Qumran Sect* (Fribourg, 1986).

[69] Think, for example, of the history of the Platonic academy.

[70] The Cynics were the most notable Greek philosophical movement active in public teaching. Epicureans too were interested in spreading the saving word of their doctrine, if one may judge from Lucretius.

[71] The best examples are the houses of Hillel and Shammai in Rabbinic texts.

was the drawing up of a list of leaders of the movements, as was done by the Pharisees in the passages known as *mAbot* 1.[72]

As in the case of Philo, there is room to protest that Josephus's analogy between Jewish sectarians and Greek philosophers was not quite accurate. No philosophical school with the possible exception of the Pythagoreans imposed food regulations on their members of the sort usual among the Jewish sects. In spite of our quibbles, what would this comparison to the philosophers suggest to Josephus's non-Jewish reader? I propose that they were intended to prepare him for a discussion of a group of literate, urban men, with a clear intellectual agenda. That Greek reader would expect the chief items on this agenda to be matters of belief, and Josephus will not disappoint those anticipations, describing the various Jewish sects mainly in terms of doctrine, rather than halacha. The approximate social standing of a member of a Jewish sect suggested by Josephus's analogy with the philosophers also accords well with the picture drawn above on the basis of other sources.

As Seen by their Contemporaries: Jews

How were Jewish sects seen by fellow Jews? Here Philo and Josephus form a chorus in praise of the Essenes, while Josephus's opinions of the Pharisees have been the subject of extensive discussion.[73] Given the role of boundary marking as the heart of ancient Jewish sectarianism, as was presented in the previous chapter and will be discussed in greater detail in the next, it is reasonable to expect that those excluded by these boundaries would not have relished this status, and would have responded in a hostile manner. Such antagonism towards the Pharisees can be seen in the New Testament, in passages such as Mt. 23, where they are accused above all else of hypocrisy, of preventing others from entering the Kingdom of Heaven, yet not meeting its requirements themselves. The Pharisees claim that they have atoned for the sins of the past, yet their actions are no different. They bind heavy burdens and lay them on men's shoulders,

---

[72] See E.J. Bickerman, "La chaine de la tradition pharisienne," *Studies in Jewish and Christian History, Part Two* (Leiden, 1980), 256–279.

[73] See the summary of scholarship in Mason, *Josephus,* and my summary and critique in "Neusner and Rivkin on the Pharisees," 109–126.

but do not lift them themselves. Even the relatively moderate and reformist boundary marking of the Pharisees evoked this response. If only we could know what Jewish opponents thought of the Essenes or of Qumran!

This information would be particularly interesting because the Essenes and Qumran, required members to merge their property with that of the community. What might the relatives of these Essenes or Qumran sectarians have thought? The property of family members now transferred to the Essene order or the Qumran sect was an asset in which relatives had an interest, which had been harmed by this action. Deeds of this sort might therefore have been resented. Perhaps family members would have believed that their relations had "lost their minds" or been "terrorized" into joining these groups. Perhaps there were attempts by families to free relatives from the clutches of these movements, by force, if necessary. When the author of 1QH ii, 22–23 thanked God for saving him from "violent men," who sought after his life because he clung to God's covenant, was he referring to such an incident? This cannot be proven, but the possibility merits mention.[74]

To the extent that "greedy institutions" tried to devour all the loyalty or identity of their members and divert it from connection with relations – to the extent that the new sectarian "brothers" were more important than "natural" brothers – these suspicions might have been enhanced. Sectarian identity as a new brotherhood, more important that natural relationships, is attested explicitly in our sources. Josephus employed the analogy of kinship brotherhood for the Essenes – *War* 2.120, 122, 127, as did Philo, *Omnis Probus* 79, *Hyp.* 11.2 – and this new kinship superseded natural ties. Essenes, according to Josephus, were allowed to distribute charity freely, as they saw fit, but needed the permission of the leaders of the order to help relatives (*War* 2.134).[75] The same attitude towards family members is exhibited in 1QH ix, 35–36:

> for my father knew me not, and my mother abandoned me to Thee. For Thou art a father to all [the sons] of Thy truth, and as a woman who tenderly loves her babe, so dost thou rejoice in them.

---

[74] For a brief summary and analysis of passages from Qumran texts referring to these violent men see Davies, *Behind the Essenes*, 98–99.

[75] See further 4Q477, frag. 2, ii, 8 in which someone was rebuked for loving his near kin, and the discussion in E. Eshel, "4Q477," 117–118.

The analogy of kinship was also important in Qumran (1QS vi, 10, 22; CD vi, 20; vii, 1–2).[76] The new brotherhood, with all the sons of God's truth, fellow members of the sect, has supplanted previous relationships.

These conclusions are somewhat hypothetical: there is scant confirmation in our sources that indicates that other Jews considered ancient Jewish sects as I have proposed in this sub-section. Nevertheless, attitudes such as I have suggested are part of the way many communistic groups, such as the Shakers, were viewed by outsiders, hence I believe it likely that the Essenes or Qumran evoked similar responses.[77]

The discussion in this section has moved from the ways sects were seen by non-Jews, to the way they were seen by fellow Jewish sectarians, to the impression these groups made on the non-sectarian Jewish majority. Unfortunately, that majority left no sources outlining its opinions, hence any further consideration plunges deeper and deeper into speculation based on analogies. If the Puritan experience is any indication, however, I would suggest that ordinary Jews might have respected the devotion of sectarians, but also resented their exclusivist attitudes somewhat, regarding them with at least some disdain, and believing (1) that sectarian ideas were new-fangled inventions of the minds of their devotees, and (2) that if traditional practice had been good enough for generations past there was no need to change it.[78]

For More Mundane Reasons

A brief digression is necessary here. The principal focus of this inquiry is to explain how and why ancient Jewish sects emerged and flourished at the time they did. From the perspective of the members who populated these movements, the objective is to discover why they joined *for all the right reasons*, out of commitment and devotion to the

---

[76] These texts contradict the argument of Bergmeier, *Essener-Berichte*, 95 that the brotherhood terminology in Josephus was of Pythagorean origin. In the early Church, Paul regularly addressed fellow Christians as "brethren." See Meeks, *First Urban Christians*, 87.

[77] Stein, *Shaker Experience*, 50. Perhaps communistic ancient Jewish groups attempted to deflect hostility by ad hoc decisions to return to natural heirs all or part of the property their relations had deposited on joining. See further *ibid.*, 140.

[78] For a discussion of the Puritan examples see Hunt, *Puritan Moment*, 148–155. While not my topic here, the religious practices and beliefs of that ancient Jewish majority are a subject of great interest, worthy of scholarly attention. See in particular the reconstruction proposed by Sanders, *Practice and Belief*.

way of life and ideology propagated by the sects. Nevertheless, at this juncture, one cannot overlook the indications that there were those who joined groups for more mundane reasons. Their motivations must be presented and analyzed before continuing to attempt to understand those who acted for the right reasons.

The information available concerns the reformist Pharisees, as well as the introversionist Essenes and the Qumran sect, the latter two groups which made extensive demands of their members. The evidence concerning the Pharisees requires a return to Josephus's account of his spiritual and religious career, in *Life* 10–12. After his year exploring the various options and three years with Bannus, Josephus explains that he returned to the city and elected to live as a Pharisee. As understood by Mason, this passage suggests that Josephus chose to live as a Pharisee not out of conviction (according to Mason, Josephus regularly regretted Pharisaic influence, treating their standing as a lamentable fact), but because that was a necessary condition of having a public career in the city. That is, given the position of the Pharisees, if one wanted to be active in politics one had no choice but to be part of their group.[79] If Mason is correct, Josephus's decision was made for less than the best of reasons, yet it would attest to the stature of the Pharisees, and to the sense in which politicians found it necessary to be Pharisees. Whether Mason is accepted or not concerning Josephus, the notion that it paid to be a Sadducee or Pharisee must have been attractive to ambitious young men at times of dominance of these groups, such as the Sadducees during the reign of Alexander Jannaeus or the Pharisees at the time of Salome Alexandra. The dominance of Ephraim = the Pharisees is well described in 4QpNah ii, 9: kings, princes, priests, laymen and converts were all under their sway.[80] At times such as these the attractions of

---

[79] See the preliminary version in Mason, "Was Josephus?" 36–45 and the fuller version in Mason, *Josephus*, 342–356.

[80] At a certain point, later in Christian history, it paid to be a Christian, as the power and influence of the Christian clergy – even to order around Emperors – was evident. On this see M. Smith, "Review of *The Cambridge History of the Bible, Volume I: From the Beginnings to Jerome*," *American Historical Review* 77 (1972), 98, n. 32, commenting on Augustine's claim to have converted as a result of Ambrose's allegories, which revealed the true sense of the texts:

> Can this be true? Augustine was no fool, and Ambrose must also have revealed to an ambitious man, how powerful a bishop could become. Of course we have the *Confessions* to the contrary. But can the passionate published confessions of a professional rhetorician be doubted?

the Pharisees must have been irresistible, even if only for mundane reasons.

As for the Essenes and Qumran, in both these groups, members ate simply (see further the discussion of Essene diet in Chapter Two, at nn. 37–38), but also ate well. The Essene meal included meat and wine (*War* 2.133), while the remains of animal bones at Qumran[81] prove that meat was a part of their diet. Nor is this surprising. The Essenes were engaged in agriculture as a matter of choice (see further Chapter Two below, at n. 65), but these were gifted individuals, far better intellectually endowed than the average farmer working at subsistence agriculture. It is therefore reasonable to conclude that Essene agricultural efforts were rewarded, as reflected in their diet, significantly richer than the minimum standard of the time.[82] Perhaps, thanks to their position, Essenes were able to work the land using more advanced techniques than employed by the ordinary peasant. Much the same should have been true at the Qumran community.[83]

These advantages would have given the Essenes and the Qumran sect an attractiveness which would have been overwhelming at times of crisis. For the Qumran sect, as we learn from 4QpPs[a] iii, 2–5, in days of famine,[84] when the wicked perished, the congregation of God's chosen ones, as well as all those who chose to go out [there], i.e. to the desert, fared well. Characteristically, the prosperity of the chosen ones was explained in these texts in religious terms (in contrast to the material interpretation offered above): keeping the appointed time of fasting gave them the merit, which kept them alive at the time of famine (4QpPs[a] ii, 9–11), enabling the community to appeal to others, who chose to join them at that time, in a way it might not have normally done, and hence a source of pride.

A modern reader may wonder how many of those attracted by

---

[81] These remains of meals have become the basis of the new theory of Qumran origins proposed by J.B. Humbert, "L'Espace Sacré à Qumran," *Revue Biblique* 101 (1994), 161–214.

[82] See M. Broshi, "The Diet of Palestine in the Roman Period, Introductory Notes," *Israel Museum Journal* 5 (1986), 41–56.

[83] Compare a similar but less focused understanding of these facts in D. Flusser, "Qumran and the Famine during the Reign of Herod," *Israel Museum Journal* 6 (1987), 13.

[84] There was one great famine, at the time of Herod, Josephus, *Ant.* 15.299–316, as well as other disasters, such as a violent storm that destroyed all the crops in 65 BCE (*Ant.* 14.28), and a severe famine in the time of the Emperor Claudius (*Ant.* 20.51). According to Flusser, "Qumran and the Famine," 9, the allusions in the Qumran texts cited are to the Herodian famine, and these allusions help prove that Qumran was *not* abandoned for an extensive time in the Herodian era.

Qumran abundance remained, once the famine(s?) abated. The simple but plentiful food of Shaker communities, a result of their technological sophistication and organization, was a source of great appeal to those in need, particularly as winter approached. Yet few of these prospects remained as full fledged members of the order, earning for themselves the derogatory name of "Winter Shakers," or "bread and butter believers."[85]

The situation may not have been different at Qumran. The annual ceremony of membership renewal, prescribed at the outset of 1QS, contains a section denouncing a member who only pretended to be loyal to the community, while harboring doubts and while blessing himself in his heart and believing that "peace will be with me, even though I walk in the stubbornness of my heart (1QS ii, 11–14)." Such a person was cursed even more strenuously than the sons of darkness. While all the different targets of this section of curses cannot be specified, one group might have been those who remained for material reasons, not out of conviction.[86] The curse would have encouraged such people to take the step they were likely planning in any case – to leave the Qumran community.

The evidence is a bit less explicit in the case of the Essenes. They did not rely only on mature volunteers who came to join their group, but also took in other men's children and raised them while still pliable, hoping to mould them in accordance with their principles (*War* 2.120). Perhaps this was a mark of desperation, an attempt to fill the ranks of the group when mature recruits, who came of their own volition, were dwindling. In any case, Essene abundance was being shared with a class of young people – foundlings, orphans, and those whose families could not feed them – which was quite large in antiquity.[87] The dependence of this population on the Essenes would have given its constituents little choice but to follow Essene rules, at least for the time they enjoyed the bounty of the sect.

Here too, a cynical modern reader may wonder how many of these recruits finished their days as Essenes. If Shaker experience is

---

[85] Stein, *Shaker Experience*, 162.

[86] Another possible target: officials planning to abscond with some of the community's assets. Cf. above, n. 55.

[87] Much of the plots of ancient drama revolve around such people, proof that they must have been numerous to form the basis for so many stories. The modern world has come to the point where foundling institutions and orphanages no longer play the role they did.

any indication, they too raised large numbers of foundlings, orphans and those whose parents indentured them to the sect, but the restrictions placed on the lives of members were repelling. The temptations of the world just over the fence (both real and spiritual) often proved irresistible, hence few of these children remained.[88]

This digression on those who joined ancient Jewish sects for more mundane reasons confirms a conclusion already stated above, and of great importance for the argument to follow. It shows the sense in which those who elected to join ancient Jewish sects for the "right reasons" were not misfits or incompetents, seeking compensation for what they lacked in other aspects of their lives. These were proficient and able people, worthy of admiration. Whether Pharisees, Essenes or Qumran sectarians, they were capable of success (political and/or economic) according to the most demanding standards of their time. Qumran and the Essene communities were thus better able to cope with the hardships of life, hence their centers were a haven in times of crisis, or for those in dire need. These natural abilities of sectarians may have been enhanced by the sense of certainty at finding one's way often experienced by those who feel they have come to a safe haven in a stormy sea, but these qualities must have been substantial even before that intensification. Any explanation of the choices made by sectarians "for the right reasons" must respect this assessment of their ability. Deprivation theories of various sorts, once popular candidates for a leading role in such explanations, need no longer apply.[89]

STRUCTURE/CONTINGENCY/CHOICE

Why then did those who joined religious groups such as Pharisees, Sadducees, Essenes and Qumran, for the right reasons, take these steps?[90] Perhaps some of the "wrong" reasons above played a part in

---

[88] Stein, *Shaker Experience*, 162.

[89] Cf. Stark and Bainbridge, *Future of Religion*, 102–106. For an analysis of the background of those who chose to be Shakers, reaching a conclusion consistent with mine above see Stein, *Shaker Experience*, 90–91.

[90] For a general answer to the question of why people join religious sects, but one which overly emphasizes the purely social aspects of the problem see Schwartz, *Sect Ideologies*, 40–41, 53, 215. See also the following selected bibliography listed in chronological order. Gerlach & Hine, "Five Factors," 23–40; C. Redkop, "A New Look at Sect Development," *Journal for the Scientific Study of Religion* 13 (1974), 345–352; J.A. Beckford, "Accounting for Conversion," *British Journal of Sociology*, 29 (1978), 249–262; Balch, "When the Light Goes Out Darkness Comes," 11–63; E.B. Rochford,

their decision, as people rarely do things in an unalloyed fashion. Nevertheless, the focus now is on the salvific motives for their actions. A large number of factors play a role, and lest these become hopelessly jumbled, I propose to divide them along the lines of the categories suggested by G. Almond, those of structure/contingency/choice.[91] This tactic will allow me to draw the picture of these movements in its proper perspective. Those factors which do not require detailed discussion are gathered immediately below. Chapters Two–Six, which follow, are reserved for those explanations which require full-scale consideration.

Structure

First, it is important that the subjects believe they know the right path to take, and that they maintain that they occupy a crucial place in the scheme of things: a "chosen" people must believe it faces a critical choice for sects to emerge. This is obviously the case for the Biblical tradition, and for all religions based on it.[92]

Additional impetus in this direction is given when there is widespread belief that this elect has been the recipient of direct revelation,[93] as

---

"Factionalism, Group Defection and Schism in the Hare Krishna Movement," *Journal for the Scientific Study of Religion* 28 (1989), 162–179; B. Wilson, "Becoming a Sectarian," *Social Dimensions of Sectarianism*, 176–200; L. Dawson, "Reflection on Sociological Theories of Sects and New Religious Movements," Paper presented to the May 1990 meeting of the Canadian Society of Biblical Studies, published in part as Dawson, "Church/Sect Theory," 5–28. I would like to thank Professor Dawson for allowing me access to his unpublished paper. Perhaps the most important treatment of the question both in empirical and theoretical terms is by Stark and Bainbridge, *Future of Religion*.

[91] G. Almond, *Crisis, Choice and Change: Historical Studies of Political Development* (Boston, 1973).

[92] For seventeenth century British groups compare the following remarks by S. Wilson *Pulpit in Parliament* (Princeton, 1969), 20:

> The puritans were English patriots who construed their nation's historical destiny in terms of the biblical drama. England had been the seat of the pure church and the great locus of resistance to Antichrist throughout Christian history. In turn they believed it would be the fountainhead of a purified Europe delivered from the Roman incarnation of Antichristian power.

See further B.S. Capp, "The Fifth Monarchists and Popular Millenarianism," in McGregor and Reay, *Radical Religion*, 179–180; *idem*. "The Political Dimension," in C.A. Patrides and J. Wittreich (Eds.), *The Apocalypse in English Renaissance Thought and Literature* (Manchester, 1984), 95–6. In the case of Ulster sectarianism led by Rev. Paisley the sense of election of the people of Northern Ireland as the great bastion of Protestantism against the evil Papacy is also pronounced. See D. Taylor, "The Lord's Battle: Paiselyism in Northern Ireland," in Stark, *Religious Movements*, 244–245.

[93] The extent to which Jews of antiquity believed that prophecy had ceased in their

this further encourages a sense of distinctiveness and of obligation to act, no matter what the cost.[94] This conclusion too would have been common to many Jews in antiquity. It was enhanced even further by those at Qumran who claimed that they received on-going revelation unique to them, which taught them how to live.

When these fundamental sources are written, the structural circumstances favoring sectarianism are enhanced. For, as suggested by Goody,[95] literate religions are usually religions of conversion, not simply religions of birth. They regularly make exclusive truth claims, encouraging or even forcing others to join their fold: the written text supporting a mindset which strengthens the drawing of sharp boundaries between those in and those out. A slight intensification of this attitude can yield a situation in which these propensities are turned inwards, and thus promote the formation of sects.

Next, there must be something worth fighting over, an issue or focus of attention sufficiently important to merit the dissension to be generated. In the ancient Jewish case this role was played by the temple. For the average Jew – one of the "people of the land," or the duped "naive" noted above – the temple was the main center of loyalty. Not overly interested in the details of ritual followed there, so long as it was in accord with what was known of tradition, the temple was the most important focus of identity.[96] The role of the Temple and its stature are made clear by another source. Simon the Righteous,[97] according to *mAbot* 1:2, stated that the entire world depends on three things: the Torah, Temple service and acts of loving kindness. That is, all of eternity depends on these things and the cosmos would collapse into chaos if they were to end. This is, perhaps, assigning an overly grand role to the sacrificial service performed at a minor temple in a backwoods corner of the Seleucid empire, but it reflects well the position of the Jerusalem Temple in

---

era is open to doubt. Theory and practice do not always seem to have agreed with each other. For my discussion of an aspect of this issue, see A.I. Baumgarten, "Miracles and Halacha in Rabbinic Judaism," *Jewish Quarterly Review* 73 (1983), 238–253.

[94] On this point see further Meeks, *First Urban Christians*, 92.

[95] See J. Goody, *The Logic of Writing and the Organization of Society* (Cambridge, 1986), 4–6.

[96] This explains the fierce determination of leaders of the post–70 period to be identified as legitimate successors to the authority of the temple. See e.g. *mRH* 2:8–9. On the role of the Temple in the "common Judaism" shared by those inside and outside sectarian movements see Sanders, *Practice and Belief*, 45–169.

[97] The identity of this Simon and his date have been the subject of much discussion. I prefer to take him as Simon son of Onias the hero of Ben Sira.

the eyes of Jews. Ben Sira's portrait of Simon son of Onias in all his glory (ch. 50), is yet another indication of the importance of the Temple. From this perspective, I am certain that there were Jews who could not believe that the sun was still rising and setting in the aftermath of the cessation of sacrifice and destruction of the Temple in 70 CE. At the very least, the interlude in offering sacrifices could only be temporary, as it had been at the time of the destruction of the First Temple by the Babylonians.

To these considerations two more should be added. The Jews had only one temple.[98] All stands and falls with the events in that one place, should it be rendered unusable or destroyed. Furthermore, as stated explicitly by Philo (*Spec. Leg.* 1.67) and Josephus (*Ag. Ap.* 2.193), *one* temple is the symbolic expression of belief in *one* God. The central place of that temple may have been enhanced by events of the Maccabean era, from the persecutions of Antiochus IV to policies which may have been instituted by the Maccabees such as the imposition of the half sheqel temple tax, as suggested by Bickerman.[99] Payment of this tax, and especially its use to fund regular public sacrifices, would enhance the sense of identification of all Jews with the Temple. All this, however, makes the Jerusalem Temple a perfect subject for sects to wrangle over. In effect, much of sectarian strife is a fight for control of the Temple. It will be no accident, as will be shown below, that a large number of the points at dispute between the author of 4QMMT and "official" Judaism involve detailed points of law concerning the ritual to be followed in the Temple.[100]

---

[98] For our purposes, the temple at Leontopolis can be effectively disregarded. As has been noted by many scholars, it generated little loyalty, even among members of the ancient Egyptian Jewish community. Their allegiance was to Jerusalem. On Leontopolis see also Introduction, n. 30.

Most Jews saw Samaritans as outside the boundaries of their nation, hence the Temple at Garizim, even for the (short?) duration of its existence, would not have been perceived as a contradiction of the principle that one God had one temple.

The existence of a temple at Araq-al-Emir in transjordan, erected by Hyrcanus son of a Sadoqite priest, *Ant.* 12.222–234, continues to be the subject of doubt. Was it a simple fortress, as described by Josephus, or also a temple, as the archeological remains suggest? See further Hengel, *Judaism and Hellenism*, 1.272–277, and Sanders, *Practice and Belief*, 24.

[99] E.J. Bickerman, "La Charte Seleucide de Jérusalem," *Studies, Part Two*, 75–80. See however, J. Liver, "The Half-Sheqel Offering in Biblical and Postbiblical Literature," *Harvard Theological Review* 56 (1963), 173–198; D. Flusser, "The Half-Sheqel in the Gospels and the Dead Sea Sect," *Tarbiz* 31 (5722), 150–156 [in Hebrew]; Sussmann, "Research," 32–33, n. 91; Sanders, *Practice and Belief*, 156.

[100] Sussmann, "Research," 22, n. 53. As noted by Sussmann, one consequence of

To these points one should add basic theological notions such as a belief in divine reward and punishment and, perhaps, in the ultimate salvation of the world. These too, as will be developed more fully in chapters below, will play their part in moving people to make the commitments which are the subject of this book.

The elements of structure considered above are largely, if not wholly matters of belief. One final aspect, of quite a different order, must be noted in closing this part of the argument. As proposed by M. Weinfeld, the nature of Jewish political life under the world empires, with native kings no longer responsible for performance of the cult, favored the emergence of voluntary groups which took these obligations upon themselves. These circumstances went back at least as far as the time of Nehemiah, when the community of the exiles bound itself by a written covenant to a specific way of observing the laws of the Torah and providing for the Temple (Neh. 10). The foundations were thus laid for voluntary associations to be the means for expression of religious devotion, a result which helped prepare the ground for the emergence of Jewish sects when the time was ripe.[101]

Contingency

Most of the "explanations" of phenomena which are usually offered are on the level of contingency, and Chapters Two–Six which follow all fall in that category. Nevertheless, a few remarks on this group of explanations seem appropriate at this juncture. One aspect of contingency has been noted in passing in the Introduction, at nn. 78–81: the flourishing of sectarianism, to use a slightly crude analogy, is a case of collective national religious, political or social indigestion in the aftermath of rapid change,[102] when the old and the new are still

---

this conclusion is clear: if these disputes go back to the origins of the groups, as 4QMMT indicates, then those sections of the Mishnah which deal with the Temple and its attendant laws of purity are likelier to be the older strata of Rabbinic literature, Sussmann, "Research," 28, n. 74. This would pose a severe question to the system of stratification of Mishnaic law proposed by Neusner, who generally sees the material concerning the Temple and its laws as belonging to later layers of the tradition. See e.g. J. Neusner. *Judaism: The Evidence of the Mishnah* (Chicago, 1981), 45–166; see also Saldarini, *Pharisees*, 213 who follows Neusner.

[101] See Weinfeld, "Apodictic Law," 72–75, and the full-scale exposition in M. Weinfeld, "The Crystallization of the Community of the Exiles (קהל הגולה)," paper read at Pinkhos Churgin Memorial Program, *Application of the Social Sciences to the Study of Judaism in Antiquity*, Bar Ilan University, November 1996.

[102] Caution is necessary here. The human condition is rarely if ever so perfect as

coexisting in an odd but ultimately unstable equilibrium.[103] From that perspective, sectarian agendas for change are a commentary on the ills of their time, as seen by the various groups, and thus can be used to reconstruct the environment in which their members felt themselves to be living.[104] At such a juncture, however, when the old world has been jigged out of place for a sufficient number of sensitive people, and is now inadequate to deal with the situation, alternative, hence competing, new orders emerge, each appealing for allegiance.[105]

From this perspective a comment of Walzer's concerning the experience of Puritan ministers is especially interesting:

> The career of a seventeenth century Puritan minister . . . usually began at one of the universities. . . . It was at school that the saint's spiritual

---

to allow people to believe that they are living in untroubled times. See, for example, the illuminating comment of Hunt, *Puritan Moment*, 131: "Despite the relative paucity of information, it is likely that life in the villages and towns of pre-Reformation Europe was as least as risky and stressful as we imagine ours to be." Change is also constant: as Hunt remarks, *ibid.*: "In the fallen world, communities (patterns of interaction) are endlessly dying and being born." The sort of change sought must be rapid, extreme – even more so than usual – and relatively rare in order to explain the results. I believe it clear that the elements of change in the ancient Jewish case meet that test.

[103] See the incisive comments of B. Reay, "Introduction: Popular Culture in Early Modern England," in B. Reay (Ed.), *Popular Culture in Seventeenth Century England* (London, 1985), 4–6. The account Reay cites of someone reading aloud (the old style) from a printed Bible (the new form) is a particularly powerful representation of this interaction of old and new. See also the account of the mixture of legal forms of acquisition, the "dispositive" twig tied to the "probative" text in the examples cited by B. Stock, *The Implications of Literacy: Written Language and Models of Interpretation in the Eleventh and Twelfth Centuries* (Princeton, 1983), 48.

[104] These comments are inspired by the example of F. Manuel, "Towards a Psychological History of Utopias," in F. Manuel (Ed.), *Utopias and Utopian Thought* (Boston, 1966), 69–100, in his analyses of utopian movements. Manuel shows the ways in which a utopia may be the sharpest expression of the anguish of an age. Sectarian groups, particularly of the introversionist sort, differ from utopian ones in that they have a markedly more aggressive character, lacking the placid or benign nature often characteristic of those dreaming of a utopia.

[105] The process has been well described from a slightly different perspective by Douglas, *How Institutions Think*, 108: "First the people are tempted out of their niches by new possibilities of exercising or evading control. Then they make new institutions, and the institutions make new labels, and the label makes new kinds of people."

In the context of her analysis, Douglas is less concerned with the factors which "tempt people out of their niches," than I am. The competition between alternate institutions and the new men each hopes to make, so important to my endeavor, is not a focus of her interest. For this point see also B. Wilson, *Sects and Society* (Berkeley, 1961), 8.

I discuss the allegiance of members of sectarian groups to old-fashioned ways, as part of their protest against the changes which have befallen them, below, Chapter Two, at n. 65.

struggle and final conversion took place, though more often under the impact of town preaching than university teaching. . . . The curriculum at both Cambridge and Oxford continued through the seventeenth century to follow the old scholastic pattern. . . . It is hard to discover anything in the subject matter of an academic education in the seventeenth century that would have turned a careless young man into an ardent Puritan.[106]

This description is inherently paradoxical: the university years were crucial, yet the curriculum at these institutions was virtually unchanged. How can this be? Perhaps it was at university that the sensitive souls realized – *precisely because the curriculum was unchanged* – that higher education offered no answers to the pressing problems they felt, thus freeing these people to seek other – *less conventional* – answers. Unchanged university education was the straw that broke the camel's back, thus opening the way to innovative thinking.[107]

These answers to the dilemmas of the new situation must be disseminated so they will find their appropriate audiences. The normal means of repression of new ideas – virtually rebellious by definition in traditional societies – must therefore be abated. Only thus can groups have the opportunity to present their message to the public at large. The significance of this factor has been noticed by several authors on Puritanism;[108] its importance for the Jewish case has not been similarly noted. Nevertheless, the history of the period under consideration contains a number of excellent opportunities for new ideas to flourish and not be repressed. The rebels against Antiochus's decrees, living in the forests and forced to resolve points of law by themselves, are one obvious possibility.[109] Another is offered by the time span (virtually a decade) between the death of Alcimus and the rise of Jonathan, close to a decade for which virtually nothing is known about what was taking place in Judea.[110] These may have

---

[106] Walzer, *Revolution of the Saints*, 140.

[107] On the place of universities in patterns of change in England of the seventeenth century see Hill, *Change and Continuity*, 127–148.

[108] See, for example, Hill, *Society and Puritanism*, 497. See further Reay, "Introduction," *Radical Religion*, 10. Reay argues that the suppression of the means of repression was more *de facto* than *de jure*, but this distinction is not crucial; what matters in this case is reality, not the law. One of the four factors cited by Wilson, *Social Dimensions*, 219–221 as favoring development of new religious movements is toleration (the other three are impersonal context of life, literacy and faith healing).

[109] See 1 Macc. 2:29–41 and 2 Macc. 10:6. On this period see Sievers, *Hasmoneans and their Supporters*, 75–77.

[110] On this period see H. Burgmann, "Das umstrittene Intersacerdotium in Jerusalem 159–152 v. Chr.," *Journal for the Study of Judaism in the Persian, Hellenistic and Roman Period* 11 (1980), 135–176.

been the times when new ideas spread readily in ways which previously had been difficult.

Choice

The nature of our evidence is such that little is known about the choices made by groups as collectives. Thus, for those who accept the 'Gronigen' Hypothesis of Qumran origins, a crucial choice was made by the "Teacher of Righteousness" and his followers when they elected to form their own association and depart from what had previously been the Essene fold.[111] To the extent that the founding members of the Qumran settlement chose to go to the desert (rather than having been expelled there), that too was a significant choice. Other important choices were made by members of the Qumran community in the aftermath of the disappointment of messianic prophecy according to 1QpHab, discussed further below, Chapter Five, at nn. 96–99. Some defected, while other remained loyal to the original vision in spite of the disconfirmation.

The principal choice in a sectarian context of which we are aware was not so much collective as individual. It was the one made by a member of a group, which has been discussed at length above: selecting which sect to join. For some, it may have been a never-ending story, as they wandered from one group to another, but if someone were fortunate enough to feel comfortable at reaching the desired goal the effect was dramatic. He would find there a sense of certainty and power which he had not experienced in the prior world of confusion. This aspect of Puritanism and of other movements has been well appreciated by Hill who notes:

> His burden rolled off his back, and he acquired a sense of dignity, of confidence in himself as an individual. . . . Conversion gave a sense of strength too through oneness with a community of like-minded people. . . . This double sense of power – individual self-confidence and strength through unity – produced that remarkable liberation of energy which is typical of Calvinism and the sects during our period.[112]

A similar conclusion has been reached by Gerlach and Hine, who have analyzed the success enjoyed by members of extreme religious groups in the contemporary world after their conversion.[113] I believe

---

[111] See for example the discussion of this point by García Martínez and Van der Woude, "'Groningen' Hypothesis," 537.

[112] Hill, *World*, 154.

[113] Gerlach and Hine, "Five Factors," 35–36. See also Wilson, *Social Dimensions*, 123.

one can reasonably expect much the same to have been true of ancient Jewish sectarians. Pliny the Elder, describing the Essenes, provides one solid clue that this is likely to have been the case, when he writes that those who joined the Essenes did so as "refugees" from the tribulations of their lives, but found true spiritual satisfaction as members of the group.[114]

The sense of certainty noted above can also be attested in Qumran sources. 1QS has a number of passages which describe the confidence of the member that he has found the one and only correct answer to the meaning of his tradition in the Qumran community.[115] Josephus tells us that the Essene punished by his community and whose food supply has been cut off will starve to death rather than eat ordinary food and dishonor his vows (War 2.143). Even Paul, who was to reject his Pharisaic origins, did not do so out of a sense of dissatisfaction with Pharisaism; rather he believed that he had found a more profound truth thanks to the revelation he had received of Jesus.[116] Having been blasted and buffeted about – particularly if he had investigated many possibilities before making his final choice – the full fledged member of a group believed he had finally found a safe harbor.[117]

To conclude the discussion of structure/contingency/choice I would stress one conclusion which recurs often in the preceding pages: the sense in which the issues and concerns noted were ones of special significance to the local elites, whose role as members of Pharisees, Sadducees, Essenes and the Qumran sect runs as a theme throughout this chapter. The sense of election, the concern with the details of Temple worship, the liberty to be free of a life of subsistence agriculture and to choose to join a voluntary sect – all these were appropriate to the life of members of the middling sort and better, and to them in particular.

---

[114] Pliny, NH, 5. 73 = Stern, Greek and Latin Authors, #204. In social scientific terms going to the desert would have been an act of bridge-burning – a declaration of intention of a new way to lead one's life. Such acts often generate power which will express itself in an active and successful lifestyle in the aftermath of conversion. See Gerlach and Hine, "Five Factors," 32.

[115] See e.g. 1QS iv, 2–8.

[116] My debt to K. Stendahl, Paul Among Jews and Gentiles and other Essays (Philadelphia, 1976), and Sanders, Paul and Palestinian Judaism, should be obvious from the formulation. It is from them that I have learned of the sense in which Paul did not "abandon" Judaism because of some "flaw" which he had found in it. Paul's conversion, Stendahl and Sanders insist, must be explained in other terms, as suggested in the text above.

[117] See further 1QH vi, 23–26.

4QMMT AND ITS IMPLICATIONS

To turn to the ancient sources, a clearer notion of the contingent reasons why Jews of the Maccabean era turned to sects is afforded by 4QMMT. It is a letter written by a leader of the Qumran group, early in the history of its existence, explaining why its members chose to secede from "official" Judaism. The letter begins with the Qumran calendar, and 20 disputes on specific points of law follow. These are detailed points of ritual, concentrating on questions of how the temple is to be run.[118] To mention a few examples: (1) what degree of purity is required of the priest who offers the red heifer; (2) can impurity travel *up* a liquid stream and render the (pure) vessel from which it is being poured (into an impure vessel) impure; (3) can blind people and others with handicaps be relied upon to keep themselves sufficiently pure so that they can be allowed to enter the temple?[119] In all these points of dispute, the position being attacked is apparently the one known from later sources as that approved by the Rabbis. An ideological section concludes the letter, in which the author explains that for these reasons he and his friends have elected to secede from "official" Judaism.[120] That is, because they have been unable to change the practice of "official" Judaism on these matters, they would rather reject the whole.

In this context, a rabbinical tradition quoted by Sussmann from *bPes.* 70b is instructive.[121] We learn there of a sage named Judah b. Dorti and his son Dorti who objected to the fact that certain sacrifices were not being offered on the sabbath and therefore withdrew to the south (the desert?). The view espoused by this Judah b. Dorti agreed at least in part with that of Rabbinic law and thus his secession was unlike that of those in 4QMMT, which was completely against the practices known as approved by the later Rabbis.[122] Typologically,

---

[118] Strugnell and Qimron, "Halachic Letter," *Biblical Archeology Today*, 401–402 list twelve of the twenty points of law. Half of these directly concern the temple and priestly offerings, while the other half are on general matters of purity.

[119] In the period prior to the official publication of 4QMMT these examples were known in greater detail from Sussmann, "Research," 11–76, and J.Z. Kapera, "An Anonymously Received Pre-Publication of the 4QMMT," *The Qumran Chronicle* 2 (1990), 1–12.

[120] This was one of the first pieces of information from 4QMMT to be made known prior to official publication of the text. See Qimron & Strugnell, "Unpublished Halachic Letter," *Israel Museum Journal*, 9–12.

[121] Sussmann, "Research," 39.

[122] Judah b. Dorti believed that the *hagiga* sacrifice should be offered on Shabbat.

however, Judah b. Dorti is another example of a person who was so distressed by the mistaken ways in which he believed the Temple to be run that he seceded from it, with all the attendant consequences.[123]

To put the conclusion in terms suggested by F. Dexinger, the *limits of tolerance* of these secessionists are narrow.[124] In social scientific terms, their willingness to tolerate the gap between the ideal and the real is narrow.[125] When temple practice did not follow the law they believed correct they turned their backs on the most central institution of Judaism of their era, and on all Jews who remained loyal to that Temple, rather than tolerate a halacha with which they did not agree. In this sense, 4QMMT, other Qumran texts and additional sources now more clearly understood in light of 4QMMT are explicit confirmation of the views of those who have long seen the law as central to Jewish life, and as the wellspring of the formation of sects, a conclusion already articulated by M. Smith in 1960: "But touch the Law, and the sect will split."[126]

This is consistent with the general principle of the Rabbis (as opposed to those at Qumran) that all public sacrifices should be offered on Shabbat. Nevertheless, as the discussion in the Talmud makes clear, this principle does not apply to the *hagiga*. Thus Judah b. Dorti's position is not quite that of the Rabbis nor that of Qumran, and his views are difficult to fit into any of the known groups. To the extent that our information about him is reliable, he may well have suffered the same fate as later Jewish-Christian groups – being excluded by both sides. See further Sussmann, "Research," 39–40, n. 131.

[123] Judah b. Dorti's position is ambivalent from the perspective of the later Rabbinic tradition. As outlined in the previous note, the Rabbis would have agreed with the principle he upheld, but not its application to the specific case. Accordingly, they viewed his action in seceding unfavorably. See further *bPes.* 70b, and Sussmann's comments, "Research," 39.

The attitude towards the Temple displayed in CD is not completely clear. On the one hand, Mal. 1:10 is quoted: better that the Temple be shut than that it be defiled; nevertheless other passages in CD (xi, 18–xii, 2) legislate for the Temple cult, thus apparently acknowledging its legitimacy. See further above, Introduction, n. 62. For a discussion of the odd position adopted by the Essenes concerning the Temple see above, Introduction, at n. 40.

[124] See F. Dexinger, "Die Sektenproblematik im Judentum," *Kairos* 21 (1979), 273–277; 283–286.

[125] See Gerlach and Hine, "Five Factors," 34.

[126] See Smith, "Dead Sea Sect," 360. It received important additional impetus as a result of J. Baumgarten, "The Pharisaic-Sadducean Controversies about Purity and the Qumran Texts," *Journal of Jewish Studies* 31 (1980), 157–170. The conclusion is now quite widespread. It lies at the foundation of Sussmann, "Research," and has since been taken up by a number of scholars. See e.g. F. García Martínez, "The Origins of the Essene Movement and of the Qumran Sect," in García Martínez and Trebolle Barrera, *People of the Dead Sea Scrolls*, 92. It is fundamental to the approach of Schiffman, *Law, Custom and Messianism*, and *Reclaiming*. See also Cohen, *Maccabees to the Mishnah*, 128–134.

As students of the era we are not obliged to accept the self description of our subjects as the final word.[127] Some scholars have argued, for example, that the "real" reason for Qumran separatism has more to do with the bitter feelings of a group of Sadoqite priests who have been displaced from the centers of power by events. These scholars might claim that all the stress on legal disagreement is mere window dressing, an attempt to cover up the more fundamental problem in the view of those at Qumran: the priests in Jerusalem are usurpers, inherently unqualified to occupy the offices they fill, hence their legal practice must be wrong.[128]

From another perspective, the explanations of Qumran schism in 4QMMT may be excessively simplistic. The overlaps between legal positions of different groups, and the difficulty faced by modern scholars in explaining them have been discussed above (n. 62). At least in part, however, these overlaps have a relatively simple explanation: only a limited number of particular legal options were available in many halachic matters. After one group had forbidden something and a second had permitted it, what choices were left for a third, fourth and fifth group? Yet there were numerous sects, far exceeding the number of possible halachic positions. Of necessity, the choices made by any group overlapped with those of others. If these are the reasons for these overlaps, the selections made by different groups tell us little about their essence or the causes for their emergence.

In addition, however, sometimes the variety of legal positions was internal, within the same group and even the same text. Thus, for example, Sanders noted parallel regulations on the same issues, including a very sensitive matter such as terms of admission to the group, one set of regulations lenient another much more stringent, in 1QS.[129]

This is a conclusion I shared, earlier in my research on the subject. See my remarks in "Qumran and Jewish Sectarianism," 139–141. I now have reason to doubt these conclusions, as expressed first in A.I. Baumgarten, "Review of L. Schiffman, *Law, Custom and Messianism*," *Zion* 58 (5753), 509–513 [in Hebrew]; *Id.*, "Zadokite Priests," forthcoming.

[127] This independence has a long history, going back to Thucydides. See above, Introduction, n. 126 for a fuller discussion of this point.

[128] See for example Theissen, *Sociology*, 39, and many others. As a specific suggestion for understanding the rise of the Qumran sect see the classic statement of this position by Cross, "Early History of the Qumran Community," 81. See, however, the difficulties to this view which have been raised by recent evidence, discussed in the Introduction, at nn. 94–98. For a restatement of this approach see Schiffman, *Reclaiming*, 83–89.

[129] Sanders, *Paul and Palestinian Judaism*, 323–325.

Perhaps, therefore, one should argue that not all legal differences
were equal: when disagreement struck certain subjects, such as the
calendar, that had far more significant consequences for the formation
of groups.[130] Against that conclusion one must note, however, that
a fair number of sects agreed in devotion to the calendar employed
by the Temple authorities, but that did not stop them from disagree-
ing on other matters. Furthermore, where there was a will even calendar differences could be overcome, as in the case of Karaites and
Rabbinites, usually cited as the classic case of separation as a result
of calendar controversy, on the basis of the testimony of Qirqasani.[131]

Another tack might be to follow a more nuanced version of Smith's
hypothesis, as formulated in a second article written at the same
time as the contribution in *New Testament Studies* (above, n. 126), discussed above.[132] In the second study, Smith acknowledged that groups
might disagree internally about points of law, such as in the case of
Rabbinic Judaism in general. Hillelites and Shammaites among the
Pharisees, and the marrying order of Essenes, as opposed to those
who remained celibate (Josephus, *War* 2.160–161), might be other
examples of this pattern, not mentioned by Smith. What made for a
single movement, Smith argued, was agreement on the source of
legal authority.[133] Disagreement on the basis of legal authority was the
key to understanding the growth of groups and their splits from each
other, he proposed.

Nevertheless, even the more nuanced version of Smith's thesis will
not help much. Research on the MSS. versions of the Manual of
Discipline now known from 1QS and from Cave 4 fragments indicates that various formulations of legal empowerment circulated simultaneously at Qumran.[134] Older versions were still being copied after

---

[130] See e.g. Sanders, *Practice and Belief*, 360. I have taken this position in the past.
See e.g. Baumgarten, "Who Were the Sadducees?" 396–405. Cf. however, the discussion below. Thus, I can no longer agree with blanket statements such as that of
Z. Ankori, *The Karaites in Byzantium* (New York, 1959), 293: "Of course, differences
of calendar are hardly the *reason* for secession; rather, they seal the separatist trend
and constitute the group's *final* declaration of self-determination and independence."
  Calendar differences are neither a necessary reason for nor an inevitable expression of separatist trends. They can play either role under the appropriate circumstances, but it is precisely those circumstances which it is the task of the investigator
to discover and comprehend.

[131] See above, Introduction, n. 116 and below, Chapter Two, n. 81.

[132] See M. Smith, "What is Implied by the Variety of Messianic Figures?" *Journal
of Biblical Literature* 78 (1959), 66–72.

[133] Smith, "What is Implied?" 72.

[134] S. Metso, "In Search of the *Sitz im Leben* of the Community Rule," forthcoming

newer redactions had been proposed, each version assigning its own relative weight to different components of the community in establishing normative practice. Disagreements on the source of legal authority were thus as prevalent as disputes on the details of legal practice.

In the end, perhaps another part of Smith's analysis of ancient Jewish sectarianism should be employed to question Smith's conclusions concerning the place of halacha and/or legal authority as generators of sectarian schism. In the second article, just mentioned, Smith argued that the variety of messianic figures in Second Temple Judaism, *a variety often to be found in the very same text*,[135] was so great that messianic eschatology cannot have been the groundspring for the emergence of different groups. As Smith wrote:

> If a group had no single eschatological myth, it cannot have been organized as a community of believers in the myth it did not have.... If the variety of eschatological prediction is any evidence, eschatology was, for the members of these groups, a comparatively arbitrary and individual matter.... Such an arbitrary and individual matter can hardly have been the basis of group organization and practice.[136]

Smith therefore suggested turning to the law and common legal authority as the source of the sectarian impulse, as outlined above, a suggestion which now would seem to be confirmed by the central place of a halachic agenda in 4QMMT.

Nevertheless, as I have tried to show, the nature of legal positions adhered to by the different sects was almost as arbitrary and erratic as their eschatological visions. Even within groups, legal authority was not well defined. The life of the law (by itself) may thus be as ill equipped for the decisive role in explaining the flourishing of sects which Smith would assign it as the messianic hopes, which he argued were inappropriate for the part, and for the very same reason. To the extent that one aims for a comprehensive interpretation of the phenomenon of sectarianism, those factors introduced as part of that

---

in the Proceedings of the 1996 International Dead Sea Scrolls Conference, Provo, Utah, July, 1996, to be edited by E. Ulrich and D. Parry. I would like to thank Dr. Metso for making her paper available to me prior to its appearance in print. See further Baumgarten, "Zadokite Priests," forthcoming.

[135] Smith's prime example is 1 Enoch. See Smith, "What is Implied?" 70. As 1 Enoch is a composite work, it should be noted that the variety Smith discovered exists even within sections of 1 Enoch generally considered as having had some independent and coherent existence prior to their being placed in the current compilation, such as Chapters 37–73, the Book of the Similitudes.

[136] Smith, "What is Implied?" 71–72.

explanation should therefore go beyond the existence of a halachic agenda, a particular calendar, or devotion to specific legal authority. None of the latter lead inevitably to the flourishing of sectarianism. Given the will, there is apparently no dispute on which compromise is impossible, and schism avoided. Lacking that will, any issue can become the trigger for the emergence of groups. What must be discovered are the particular circumstances at the time when sects wax which call forth this result.

It therefore seems best to return to the perspective suggested by the definition of sectarianism proposed in the Introduction. Understanding ancient Jewish sectarianism as voluntary boundary marking on the part of members of such groups, whether reformist or introversionist,[137] we need to discover the complex of reasons for which people elected to make these choices, which separated themselves off from other Jews who were less strict in their observance of the law or who accepted other legal authorities. Remembering the elitist nature of the groups under consideration, as stressed throughout this chapter, the search is for the causes of the cultural wedge inserted by the "better part," or the "few," between themselves and the "greater part," or the "multitude."[138] The contribution of the dynamic between the central institutions of a society and members of sects must also be explored.[139] These issues remain to be elaborated in the chapters which follow.

---

[137] The crucial role of the introversionist sect in rejecting the mainstream first and then being rejected by it was already recognized by Locke. In his *Letter on Toleration*, translated from the Latin by R. Klibansky (Oxford, 1968), 132–133, Locke argues that the civil magistrate ought to use his powers to punish and persecute those who themselves are intolerant. When the intolerant are treated as intolerable the process of their exclusion from the mainstream of society is hastened.

To put this same point another way, G. Simmel, *Conflict: The Web of Group Affiliations* (Glencoe, 1955), 93 writes that "groups in any sort of a war situation are not tolerant." As he explains, that state of war need not be external or physical. It may be internal and entirely imaginary, as suggested by Coser, *Greedy Institutions*, 110: a sect needs internal enemies, even imaginary ones, in order to explain its defeat and rejection at the hands of the larger society. Whether this war is at one extreme or the other – external and physical or internal and imaginary, or someplace in between – matters little. Since an introversionist sect sees itself at war with the mainstream of society and *vice versa*, neither will tolerate the other.

[138] Compare Collinson, *Religion of Protestants*, 235–239.

[139] On persecution as a factor in motivating alienation and promoting separatism see Reay, "Introduction," *Radical Religion*, 12. See further the comments of C. Hill, *The Experience of Defeat* (New York, 1984), 290 who notes that in the conditions after 1660, with the natural rulers restored and Parliament legislating against nonconformists, "religious radicals could only survive by organizing into congregations."

CHAPTER TWO

THE ENCOUNTER WITH HELLENISM AND ITS EFFECTS[1]

DISAPPOINTMENT

The encounter with Hellenism has played an important part in the efforts of scholars to explain the rise and flourishing of Maccabean sectarianism, as summarized in the opening chapter. Nevertheless, their efforts were criticized there as insufficiently specific, in that they did not elaborate the details of the route which led from the encounter with Hellenism to the flourishing of ancient Jewish sectarianism. It is therefore essential to determine, as exactly as possible, the role of this factor in elucidating the known results. To achieve this goal, the account of the relationship between Jews and their surrounding cultures, traced in the opening chapter, must be resumed in greater detail, as must the report of the history of the voluntary boundary marking against Jews considered insufficiently observant, which I have proposed to take as the defining characteristic of ancient Jewish sectarianism.

Nehemiah's campaign against those who did not separate themselves off sufficiently from the neighboring nations was noted in the introduction, as were the difficulties which grew as a consequence of the encounter with Hellenism. Perhaps Hecataeus of Abdera had these events in mind when he explained that Jewish custom was no longer as different from that of other nations as it had once been, as a result of the Jews being subject to foreign rule.[2] The Tobiads, according to the account in Josephus, ate and drank freely at the table of the Ptolemies (*Ant.* 12.173, 187, 211–213). Nevertheless, those who wanted to underscore the rift between Israel and the nations reached a point of notable achievement at the time of Antiochus III, ca. 200 BCE. Antiochus issued a decree at the request of the priests (note that in

---

[1] This chapter takes up themes which I have discussed from the more theoretical perspective of "enclave cultures," in A.I. Baumgarten, "The Food of a Sectarian and its Implications: Finding Oneself in a Sectarian Context," in J. Assmann, A. Baumgarten & G. Stroumsa (Eds.), *Self Soul and Body in Religious Experience*, forthcoming.

[2] Stern, *Greek and Latin Authors*, #11.8.

case the decree was violated the fine went to the priests), which high-lighted the holy character of Jerusalem and the nature of Jewish life there as a whole. As cited by Josephus, *Ant.* 12.145–146:

> It is unlawful for any foreigner to enter the enclosure of the temple which is forbidden to the Jews, except to those of them who are accustomed to enter after purifying themselves in accordance with the law of the country. Nor shall anyone bring into the city the flesh of horses or of mules or of wild or tame asses, or of leopards, foxes or hares or, in general, of any animals forbidden to the Jews. Nor is it lawful to bring in their skins or even to breed any of these animals in the city. But only the sacrificial animals known to their ancestors and necessary for the propitiation of God shall they be permitted to use. Any person who violates any of these statutes shall pay to the priests a fine of three thousand drachmas of silver.[3]

None of these provisions is explicitly mentioned in the Bible. They were all part of an unwritten tradition imposed by priestly fiat. As such, they are among the oldest post-Biblical *halakhot* known.[4] Turning to the contents of this proclamation, lay worshippers, as well as foreigners, were regularly excluded from the most sacred areas of near eastern temples. Impure visitors, native as well as foreign, were not allowed to enter the sacred space of Greek temples, but once purified all could enter. The situation at Jerusalem, however, was unique. Access by the native was restricted, but the foreigner was permanently banned. He could do nothing to purify himself and join the natives inside (as far as the latter were allowed in). Hence the need for a warning inscription, informing the foreigner that no means were available that would allow him to enter.[5]

Furthermore, the priests of the era of the Seleucid conquest applied the principles of separation to the animal world as well. Nothing else can explain their insistence, so puzzling in any other terms, that only sacrificial animals be allowed into Jerusalem.[6]

---

[3] The classic discussion of this passage remains E.J. Bickerman, "Une proclamation seleucide relative au temple de Jerusalem," *Studies, Part Two*, 86–104.

[4] See Bickerman, "Proclamation," 92. See Sanders, *Judaism: Practice and Belief*, 72–76, and J. Klawans, "Notions of Gentile Impurity in Ancient Judaism," *AJS Review* 20 (1995), 285–312. I would like to thank Mr. Klawans for sharing his ideas with me prior to his article appearing in print.

[5] I pass over the extensive discussion in the literature concerning the reasons that foreigners could not enter. See further Klawans, "Notions," 297–299.

[6] See the parallel regulations in 11QT47, and the recent identification of a new passage of that section of the Temple Scroll in E. Qimron, "The Chicken, The Dog and the Temple Scroll – 11QT^c (Col. XLVIII)," *Tarbiz* 64 (5755), 473–475 [in Hebrew].

The turn of events in the years immediately following did not favor those who insisted on the barrier between Jews and non-Jews: the decrees of Antiochus IV took direct aim at the practices which separated Israel off from the nations (1 Macc. 1:44–50). The hellenizers, who collaborated with those decrees (at the very least), also believed that regulations dividing between Jews and others were a source of calamity (1 Macc. 1:11). Perhaps these regulations were especially vulnerable to criticism, because crucial aspects of these rules were not to be found in the Bible. They could thus easily be represented as innovations, subject to reform. Others of these precepts had not been observed by the Patriarchs, Abraham, Isaac and Jacob, and his sons,[7] so their abrogation could be portrayed as a return to the "true" religion of the fathers.[8]

Even the revoking of these reforms by the Seleucid king may not have solved the dilemma. Alcimus – installed as high priest after the repeal of Antiochus' reforms, according to 1 Macc. 9:54–56 – started tearing down a wall in the Temple. This was supposedly an ancient wall, which had been the work of the prophets. The function of the wall which Alcimus tried to remove is not specified, but at least some scholars have concluded that it was the wall which separated off the area prohibited to non-Jews.[9] The effect of Alcimus's actions, had they been completed (according to 1 Macc. he was prevented from accomplishing his intentions by divine intervention), might thus have been to remove a barrier between Jews and non-Jews, and whose legality had once been confirmed by royal decree (Josephus, *Ant.* 12.145–146, above).

Jews loyal to the old order in those difficult times could look back wistfully at the "good old days," before the troubles had overtaken them. Now, however, with even Jews, nominal members of the "children of heaven (2 Macc. 7:34)," destroying boundaries protecting the Jewish people, what course was left to follow? They could honor those, such as Razis of Jerusalem, who when Jews disagreed[10] with

---

[7] Who took foreign wives (e.g. Judah, Gen. 38:2), and who ate gentile food with gentiles (Jacob's sons in Joseph's house, Gen. 43:32; the separation made between diners there was due to *Egyptian* sensibilities).

[8] See E.J. Bickerman, *The God of the Maccabees* (Leiden, 1979), 114.

[9] See the discussion in J. Goldstein, *I Maccabees* (Garden City, 1976), 391–393, who rejects this conclusion.

[10] This is the correct meaning of *amixia*. See B. Risberg, "Textkritische und exegetische Anmerkungen zu den Makkabäerbüchern," *Beiträge zur Religionswissenschaft* 2 (1915), 28–31. I would like to thank Prof. D. Schwartz for calling this article to my attention.

each other concerning their attitudes towards the gentile world, maintained the old standards in their relationships with gentiles. Razis was accused of "Judaism," but was willing to take all risks to preserve it (2 Macc. 14:38). On a practical level, however, these loyalists had to take extreme steps, from armed revolt to restricting the sources of their food in order to avoid defilement. Thus 2 Macc. 5:27 indicated that Judah and his nine companions escaped to the wilderness (the traditional refuge of those on the lam, far from the long arm of the law), where they kept themselves alive as wild animals do. This was not merely a tactical necessity. As 2 Macc. explained: "they continued to live on what grew wild, so that they might not share in the defilement (compare 1 Macc. 1:62–63; compare also the behavior of Daniel and his companions in the king's court, Dan. 1:8)."

Sometime around 160 BCE, 1 Enoch 91:9 proclaimed as its slogan: "all that which is (common) with the heathen shall be sundered." At about the same time, from a similar perspective, perhaps even quoting the Enochic literature known to us as the Epistle of Enoch (1 Enoch 91–108, in Jub. 4:18),[11] the author of the Book of Jubilees attempted a "last stand" on the old national perimeter,[12] restating the need for reinforcing the boundaries between Jews and other nations. He has Isaac warn Jacob:

> Remember my words and observe the commandments of Abraham your father. Separate yourself from the nations, and eat not with them, and do not according to their works, and become not their associate,[13] for their works are unclean, and all their ways are a pollution and an abomination and an uncleanness (22:14–16).

This sense of Jubilees as the final attempt to bolster the external wall is reinforced by the discussion of marriage with foreign men or women in Chapter 30. In a law unparalleled elsewhere, any man who gave

---

[11] On the date of the Epistle of Enoch and the connections between it and Jubilees see Collins, *Apocalyptic Imagination*, 49. On the difficulties in dating this section of 1 Enoch see C. Rowland, *The Open Heaven – A Study of Apocalyptic in Judaism and Early Christianity* (New York, 1982), 252.

[12] On the date of Jubilees see the discussion of O. Wintermute, "Jubilees," in J. Charlesworth, *Old Testament Pseudepigrapha* (New York, 1983–85), 2.35–51.

[13] In the comments below, I take "associate" in a business sense. See K. Berger, *Das Buch der Jubiläen* (Gütersloh, 1981), 437 who translates *Gefährte*. The latter means associate, companion or comrade. It can mean associate in a business sense, someone who shares the *Gefahr*, or risk. This translation may be more problematic than I would like: perhaps the intention was merely social, rather than economic. Such translations have, in fact, been preferred by other translators of Jubilees.

his daughter or sister to a foreigner has committed a capital crime: both he and the bride were to be executed (30:7). Later in that same chapter a different tack was taken against those who married foreigners and thus defiled the nation with a contemptible act. They were to be excluded from the Temple. No sacrifice, holocaust, fat or other offering was to be accepted from them (30:16). Just who these offenders might have been, the author of Jubilees did not specify. Perhaps they came from the nation as a whole, perhaps they were concentrated among the priests. In my view the latter is the likelier alternative, as offering *fat* was normally the prerogative of the priest (see e.g. Ezek. 44:15: the Sadoqite priests who were faithful when the children of Israel strayed – they and only they will minister to God, and offer "*fat* and blood," a verse quoted with favor in CD iv, 1–2). If this interpretation is correct the author of Jubilees was arguing that certain priests who have not remained loyal to the external boundary of the nation in their marriage practices (compare the difficulty posed by the marriage patterns of priests in the days of Ezra and Nehemiah – Ez. 9:1–2 and Neh. 10:28–30, 13:4) were to be disqualified from service in the Temple.[14] Priests who defied these restrictions were forbidden to serve in the sanctuary, an explicit way of marking them off as having forfeited their priestly status.

Separating oneself off from the gentiles was also connected in at least one place in Jubilees with another of the central themes of the book – the solar calendar.[15] In the mind of the author the lunar calendar was associated with the error of the foreign nations. This conclusion had a certain degree of plausibility, as every nation of mediterranean antiquity (but one, Egypt, to be discussed below) set their months by the waxing and waning of the moon.[16] From the perspective of the author of Jubilees, the only way not to forget the feasts of the covenant and to avoid the feasts of the gentiles, with all their errors and ignorance, was to adopt a year of thirty day months (6:32–38).[17] Such was the ancient Egyptian calendar, which consisted

---

[14] J. Baumgarten "Disqualifications," 503–514.

[15] Jubilees also connects the separation from the gentiles with the Sabbath, another focus of attention in the work as a whole (see e.g. Chapter 50). The separateness of the Jewish people is expressed in the uniqueness of their Sabbath observance (2:19).

[16] See E.J. Bickerman, *Chronology of the Ancient World* (London, 1968), 17, quoting Ovid, *Fasti* 3.833: *luna regit menses*.

[17] A similar idea can be found in 4QpHos[a] ii, 16. See the discussion of Jubilees and 4QpHos[a] in light of each other in M. Bernstein, "'Walking in the Festivals of

of twelve months of thirty days plus five supplementary (epagomenal) days.[18] To employ the Egyptian version of the solar calendar, however, would not avoid the error of the ways of the gentiles: that calendar too was tainted with the ignorance of one of the surrounding nations. I therefore suggest that it was no accident that the solar calendar favored by Jubilees consisted of 364 days, twelve months of thirty days each, plus only four epagomenal days, for a total of fifty two complete weeks per year. Loyalty to this calendar, as against that tainted with the error of the gentiles observed by other Jews, was to be a crucial form of boundary marking, to be discussed more fully below.

In the context proposed in the Introduction, these moments are still located among the forerunners of sectarianism. I propose that the decisive moment, which brought about the full fledged phenomenon, came with the victory of the Hasmonean dynasty and their claim for the restoration of traditional rule. The successful revolt of the Maccabees, their assumption of the high priesthood, and the eventual achievement of independence, all raised hopes for a reimposition of boundaries between Jews and non-Jews, restrictions which had suffered so much damage in the preceding decades, in particular. Confirmation that these were the expectations can be found in Maccabean propaganda, which asserted that Judah had fortified Mt. Zion with high walls and strong towers, to keep the gentiles out (1 Macc. 4:60). Simon also worked to achieve these same objectives: Simon established peace, and in his time "every man sat under his vine and his fig tree and there was none to make them afraid (1 Macc. 14:11)." Principal among those "none to make them afraid," were the gentiles, and a zealous hatred of gentiles pervades 1 Macc. as a whole.[19] Furthermore, as the decree affirming Simon's rule asserted, Simon "put the Gentiles out of the country," as well as expel-

---

the Gentiles' 4QpHosea[a] 2.15–17 and *Jubilees* 6.34–38," *Journal for the Study of the Pseudepigrapha* 9 (1991), 21–34. In spite of the similarities between the texts noted by Bernstein, one difference deserves mention: 4QpHos[a] is less explicit. It charges that the opponents of the community make their feasts according to the appointed times of the nations, but it does not contain outspoken comments in favor of a solar calendar of 364 days, as in Jubilees.

[18] Bickerman, *Chronology*, 40.

[19] This disdain towards non-Jews may help explain the response of the gentiles to the decrees of Antiochus IV, which according to 1 Macc. 1:41 and 2:19 also required them to desert their religions in favor of the new religion established by the king. According to 1 Macc. 1:43, "All the gentiles accepted the command of the king." Non-Jews, according to 1 Macc., are so far from real spirituality that they will even give up their own religions at the slightest provocation.

ling the men in the citadel of Jerusalem, "from which they used to sally forth and defile the environs of the sanctuary and do great damage to its purity (1 Macc. 14:36)." Simon, in summary, according to his supporters, continued in the footsteps of his brother Judah, and "built the walls of Jerusalem higher (1 Macc. 14:37)," in every sense of the word.

In fact, however, Maccabean policy concerning the surrounding culture was inconsistent.[20] While on some fronts they opposed practices associated too closely with the surrounding culture, the needs of government playing the international game of politics, required paying the price of adapting to the surrounding culture.[21] The tension between these objectives was present when Jonathan accepted the

---

[20] Compare the two classic studies by E.J. Bickerman, "Genesis and Character of Maccabean Hellenism," *From Ezra to the Last of the Maccabees* (New York, 1962), 153–165 and V. Tcherikover, *Hellenistic Civilization and the Jews* (Philadelphia, 1959), 235–268. See also the recent summary, written from a different perspective than Tcherikover or Bickerman, one that does not demand consistency of the Maccabees in all aspects of their policy, and one less concerned with judging the Maccabean house as a success or failure, U. Rappaport, "On the Hellenization of the Hasmoneans," *Tarbiz* 60 (5751), 447–503 [in Hebrew]. See also T. Rajak, "The Hasmoneans and the Uses of Hellenism," in P.R. Davies and R.T. White (Eds.), *A Tribute to Geza Vermes – Essays on Jewish and Christian Literature and History* (Sheffield, 1990), 261–280.

[21] I summarize here the argument of my essay "The Hellenization of the Hasmonean State," in H. Eshel and D. Amit (Eds.), *The History of the Hasmonean House*, (Jerusalem, 1995), 77–84 [in Hebrew]. Examples of pagan practices outlawed by the Maccabees as part of their campaign against foreign ways would have been the "Knockers" and "Awakeners" in the Temple, *mMaaser Sheni* 5:15, as analyzed by S. Lieberman, *Hellenism in Jewish Palestine* (New York, 1962, 2nd edition), 139–143. Perhaps the desire to defend Maccabean policy against the possible charge that the dynasty was becoming "soft" in its opposition to the surrounding nations was behind the role attributed to Nehemiah in the second letter at the beginning of 2 Macc., a work written in support of the Hasmoneans. Nehemiah, the builder of the wall around the Jews, separating them off from the nations was invoked as the initiator of a festival commemorating the continuity of worship in the Temple, which took place at the same time as the Maccabean holiday in honor of their restoration of the Temple. This was an especially sensitive point: establishing a religious holiday in honor of a human victory was imitating the ways of the Greeks (see Bickerman, "Genesis and Character," 120–121), and thus ammunition for those who might charge the Maccabees with having deserted the objectives for which they had originally fought. I cannot believe it accidental that it was precisely on this point that Nehemiah was invoked as precedent, as if to say what we Hasmoneans have done is no different, hence not problematic, but fully legitimate. According to the letter at the beginning of 2 Macc., Nehemiah supposedly established a library, as Judah had, a library which was a source of authoritative texts, on which the recipients of the letter in 2 Macc. can draw, when and as needed. The sense in which this aspect of Judah's imitation of Nehemiah was defensive is not yet clear to me.

high priesthood from the hands of Alexander Balas. It was expressed in the decree confirming Simon's rule, quoted above, which praised him for his actions against the gentiles, but which was formulated in Greek style, and was based on the political ideology and practice of Greek democracy.[22] The double names, Hebrew and Greek, of the rulers of the Maccabean dynasty, from the generation of John Hyrcanus down, as well as the nickname adopted by Judah Aristobulus I – *philhellēn*, "lover of Greeks" – are further evidence of the forces pulling in the direction of accommodation with the outside world. Maccabean success was thus to undermine the walls protecting the Jews at least as much as the confrontation with Hellenism.

Comparing expectation and claim with reality reveals the disappointment provoked by the new dynasty. The trauma, I suggest, was greater than it had been at the time of any of the prior attacks on the external border – whether by the old hierarchy or royal decree – hence the consequences more far-reaching. Now the rulers who had just won a revolt and restored traditional rule were being inconsistent in their attitude towards the surrounding cultures. I propose that it was in response to this sense of disillusionment, *of a mixture of blessings and curses*,[23] that sectarianism became fully mature. With the old national perimeter facing a new sort of danger, as a result of an outcome of which Jews might have only dared dream, but possessed of a cultural bias in favor of a situation in which they found themselves protected against the outside world by a perimeter, sects flourished which established new voluntary boundaries of their own against other Jews.

Up until Maccabean times, there had been some boundary marking against Jews not considered faithful to the laws which divided between Israel and the nations. Nevertheless, as emerged from the discussion above, that boundary marking was neither that extensive nor that stringent. Thus, for example, the author of the visions in Daniel 7–12 distinguished between faithful and unfaithful Jews. Jubilees punished those Jews who did not adhere to the requirements of separation from the nations. Nevertheless, in neither of these nor in any other pre-Maccabean source have the faithful organized into some form of socially significant movement.

---

[22] Bickerman, "Genesis and Character," 157–158.

[23] I would stress that the conclusion that sectarians saw their time as a mixture of blessings and curses for Israel is not a figment of my imagination. Note the proof that theirs was the time of the end of days in 4QMMT C:20–21.

This situation was not to endure in the era when the blessings of independence were felt to have become curses, as described towards the end of the ideological section of CD (viii, 3–21b).[24] The princes of Judah hope for healing, but they are really rebels. In fact, they have not forsaken the ways of the faithless, having defiled themselves. Quoting the verse in Dt. 32:33, "their wine is the venom of serpents and the cruel head of asps," the author of CD explained that the serpents were the kings of the nations, and wine their ways (i.e. the ways of the gentile kings, adopted by the Jewish rulers), while the head of the asps was the chief of the kings of the Greeks, who will wreak vengeance upon the Jewish rulers.[25] That is, the Jewish rulers will pay the appropriate price for their sins: those foreign kings whose ways they aped will be the source of their destruction (cf. 2 Macc. 4:16).

All this does not fit the circumstances at the time of the decrees of Antiochus IV, as the hope for healing and the charge that their repentance is false make little sense in connection with the high priests of that era, prior to the victory over Antiochus IV. On the other hand, these hopes and accusations make excellent sense in the aftermath of Maccabean victory, when seen in the light of Maccabean propaganda. At that time, there was a hope for healing, which the author of this section of CD shared. That hope, however, has been disappointed, hence this section of CD holds out the threat of retribution at the hands of a great Greek king, the perfect punishment to fit the crime of the Jewish rulers in a world run according to the principle of measure for measure.

Perhaps this passage in CD alludes to Jonathan's death in 152 BCE (1 Macc. 13:23), at the hands of Tryphon (an ironic but possible

---

[24] My interpretation of this text takes its point of departure from that suggested by J. Murphy-O'Connor, "The Critique of the Princes of Judah (CD VIII, 3–19)," *Revue Biblique* 79 (1972), 200–216. Note that I only use passages from the A text, on the possibility that he is correct in his argument that the A text was directed against the new ruling family, and that this denunciation was then re-worked as ammunition against internal apostates in the B text. On the various suggestions for understanding this text see further Davies, *Damascus Covenant*, 156–172. Against Murphy-O'Connor, see esp. S.A. White, "A Comparison of the 'A' and 'B' Manuscripts of the Damascus Document," *Revue de Qumran* 48 (1987), 537–553; Collins, *Scepter and Star*, 80–82.

[25] Note that at this stage of the argument in CD viii, those who suffered punishment at the hands of the Greek king were the princes of Judah, as they have been the subject throughout the preceding section, and the "builders of the wall" have not yet been mentioned. Cf. B. Nitzan, *Pesher Habakkuk* (Jerusalem, 1986), 137 [in Hebrew].

candidate for the role of "great Greek king").[26] If so, the chronological framework for the maturity of sectarianism according to CD would accord well with the information derived from Josephus, analyzed in the Introduction: Josephus mentioned Pharisees, Sadducees and Essenes for the first time in a remark concerning the reign of Jonathan. On this interpretation, Maccabean victory, coupled with Jonathan's acceptance of the high priesthood from the Seleucid pretender Alexander Balas, was the first step in a series of accomodations with the foreign culture which was to provoke the flourishing of ancient Jewish sectarianism.[27]

Other groups existed, such as "those that built the wall and daubed it with plaster," who offered their own version of boundary marking (if their code name is any indication), as their solutions to the dilemma.[28] Yet these rival answers were inadequate and judged wanting by God, as suggested by the allusion to Ezek. 13:10: according to CD viii, their wall was only "daubed with plaster," as opposed to the "real" fortress erected by the Qumran community (see below). In light of these circumstances, the best/only thing to do while waiting for the divinely ordained denouement, the author of CD viii concluded, was to join the New Covenant in the Land of Damascus and to remain scrupulously faithful to its precepts.[29]

The need for such voluntary boundaries against fellow Jews, at a time when the old institutions had been shaken, was given explicit

---

[26] Jonathan is a leading candidate for the (dubious) distinction of being the figure hiding behind the Qumran code name of "wicked priest." As a member of the family that brought victory to the nation against the decrees of Antiochus IV, he would have been called in the name of truth at the outset (1QpHab viii, 8–9). On the other hand, he died at the hands of the "violent of the nations," that is he was executed by a Greek king, as stated in 4QpPs[a] iv, 10. On the difficulties in identifying the "wicked priest" see above, Introduction, n. 103.

Note that implicit in my interpretation of CD viii above is accepting a shift in focus from a consistent discussion of the sins and punishment of the rulers of Judah (שרי יהודה, in the plural) to understanding the reality behind these statements as being the execution of single high priest.

[27] If my interpretation of CD is accepted, Jonathan's death might have been seen as a divine warning by the Qumran community. Nevertheless, future rulers from his house continued in his erroneous ways, and the inconsistent policy towards foreign culture remained in place under his successors, as outlined above. Sectarianism therefore did not become irrelevant in the generations which followed Jonathan.

[28] The code-name is sufficiently vague that the identity of this group can only be a subject of speculation.

[29] This is not so simple a task as it may seem. Many have been unable to maintain this discipline, and have forsaken the well of living water. They will have no share in the house of the law.

voice of a different sort in 1QH vi, 25–27. A sectarian portrayed himself as someone who:

> shall be as one who enters a fortified city, as one who seeks refuge behind a high wall until deliverance [comes]; I will [lean on] Thy truth, O my God. For Thou wilt set the foundation on rock, and the framework by the measuring cord of justice; and the tried stones [Thou wilt lay] by the plumb-line [of truth], to [build] a mighty wall which shall not sway; and no man entering there shall stagger. *For no stranger* (זר) *shall ever enter it, since its doors shall be doors of protection.*[30]

With old foundations crumbling, a new fortified city was necessary. The excluded stranger who mattered most was now not a non-Jew, but a fellow Jew inadequately faithful to God's truth, whose way of life did not pass when examined by the measuring cord of divine justice. A life of purity now needed to be protected from that "outsider's" defiling presence. Sectarianism now became fully mature.

The new restrictions which sects imposed on their members, in order to achieve these objectives found expression in a number of realms of life: food, dress, marriage, commerce and worship. That identity was voluntary and could be discarded as easily as it had been acccepted, hence it needed to be guarded vigilantly, against the temptations of laxness. It was therefore reinforced by an atmosphere of constant rebuke and admonition. Not all groups legislated in each of these domains, or were equally harsh in creating an environment of permanent and institutionalized reprimand. In general, only the more introversionist insisted on boundary marking in all the aspects of life listed above, or instituted a psychological reign of terror against their members to keep them in line. The regulations of each group, in each of these spheres, will be presented and analyzed in the pages that follow.

FOOD

Food of the gentiles had been an especially sensitive matter in the era leading up to Maccabean victory. The author of Jubilees castigated Jews who ate gentile food, while Antiochus's decrees had attempted

---

[30] I have modified Vermes's translation in rendering זר as "stranger," rather than his "enemy." In support of my understanding see the comments of J. Licht, *The Thanksgiving Scroll* (Jerusalem, 1957), 117 [in Hebrew].

to prevent Jews from living according to their food laws, forcing them to violate these laws by sacrificing and eating pork (1 Macc. 1:47; 2 Macc. 6:18–7:42). The permissible sources of food, not defiled by the gentiles, were severely limited at the time of the persecutions, according to 2 Macc. 5:27. It is therefore no surprise to note the importance placed on food by the different sects.

On a more general level, according to Josephus, *Ag. Ap.* 2.173–174, food is the point of departure of the law and connects directly to social relations. As anthropologists explain it, this is for two reasons: food is essential to the most basic body functions, while processed food, handled by various people of differing status, is imprinted with the social order. A person or group expresses crucial aspects of their identity and of their relationship to other components of society through the regulations which govern their behavior in accepting processed food from others.[31] Commensality is the other side of the same coin: eating is a potentially dangerous activity, which deflects attention away from the world and its hazards. Those with whom one eats are friends of a special sort, and those with whom one refuses to eat marked as foes.[32] When the sectarian is the host, who is permitted to share the food, and under what conditions? For all these reasons, regulations concerning food were therefore a boundary enforced by virtually all ancient Jewish groups.[33]

As the passage from 2 Macc. 5:27 quoted above indicates, wild food was the only alternative to that *defiled by gentiles* at the time of rebellion. When the new rulers disappointed and did not sufficiently reinstate the old borders, under the new purity distinctions of the sects – treating insufficiently observant Jews as outsiders of a new sort – wild food was the only alternative to food *defiled by other Jews*, when food prepared under the auspices of the sect was unavailable.[34]

---

[31] See e.g. M. Douglas, *Purity and Danger* (London/New York, 1984); Dumont, *Homo Hierarchicus*; J. Goody, *Cooking, Cuisine and Class – A Study in Comparative Sociology* (Cambridge, 1982).

[32] See W. Burkert, "Oriental Symposia: Contrasts and Parallels," in W. Slater (Ed.), *Dining in a Classical Context* (Ann Arbor, 1991), 7; H. Hazan, "Holding Time Still with Cups of Tea," in M. Douglas (Ed.), *Constructive Drinking* (Cambridge, 1987), 205–219.

[33] This conclusion was stated already by Smith, "Dead Sea Sect," 352.

[34] For a discussion of the place of food regulations in the medieval period see R. Meens, "Pollution in the Early Middle Ages: The Case of the Food Regulations in Penitentials," *Early Medieval Europe* 4 (1995), 3–19. In the case of modern Jewish fundamentalist groups, analyzed as enclaves by E. Sivan, "Enclave Culture," in

Josephus was an extremely astute observer of the behavior of Jewish groups of his day on these matters. Thus he reported that his ex-master Bannus, whom he followed for three years, ate only such things as grew of themselves. Bannus extended the concern with the purity of processed products to his clothing, wearing only such clothing as trees provided (*Life* 11). John the Baptist, according to the gospels, ate locusts and wild honey. His clothing consisted of a garment of camel's hair and a leather girdle (Mt. 3:4 and parallels). By the standards set by Bannus, John the Baptist was equally careful concerning his sources of food, but much less so concerning his clothing. Nevertheless, John's refusal to eat bread and drink wine (two processed foods which occupied central roles in the diet of Jews of his era)[35] made ordinary people think he was possessed (Lk. 7:33). This comment is an explicit indication of the high significance of John's eating patterns in the eyes of his contemporaries, confirming the sensitivity to crucial matters displayed by Josephus in his comments concerning Bannus.[36] In the cases of both Bannus and John the Baptist their diet is a critical indication of a high degree of tension between themselves and the rest of Jewish society of their day.

Essenes

Josephus's comments on the Essenes were no less perceptive. An expelled Essene could not eat food processed by others, hence he was limited to mere "grasses," which grew of themselves:

M. Marty (Ed.), *Fundamentalism Comprehended* (Chicago, 1995), 11–68 = *Alpayim* 4 (5752), 45–98 [in Hebrew], these concerns find expression in their insistence on specific *kashrut* supervision, with the only acceptable supervision virtually unique to each group.

[35] See Broshi, "Diet of Palestine," 41–56.

[36] Josephus, one assumes, was not Bannus's only disciple, while John had numerous followers. Neither Josephus nor the gospels specified whether this same level of observance was required of the followers of these leaders. Perhaps the followers were less restricted in their eating (and clothing). In any case, in Josephus's account of John the Baptist, *Ant.* 18.116–119, he did not mention John's restricted diet. This may indicate that John's special practice did not continue down to the generation of his disciples whom Josephus might have known. For Christians, however, John was conceived as a forerunner. Perhaps this would have led them to preserve more detailed knowledge of his unusual practices.

Compare my analysis to that of J. Taylor, "John the Baptist and the Essenes," *Journal of Jewish Studies* 47 (1996), 265–271, who after a lengthy and heavily theological discussion of John's asceticism, notes the verse in 2 Macc. 5:27 and comments that "perhaps" there was "an issue of purity involved in the wilderness life-style of John and Bannus."

> Those who are convicted of serious crimes they expel from the order;
> and the ejected individual often comes to a most miserable end. For
> being bound by their oaths and usages, he is not at liberty to partake
> of other men's food, and so falls to eating grass and wastes away and
> dies of starvation (*War* 2.143).

Essene preparation for a meal, and their behavior at meals and after-
wards, invested these events with the aura of the sacrificial cult:

> After this purification, they assemble in a private apartment which none
> of the uninitiated is permitted to enter; pure now themselves, they repair
> to the refectory as to some sacred shrine. . . . When breakfast is ended . . .
> laying aside their raiment as holy vestments, they again betake them-
> selves to their labors (*War* 2.130–132).

As in the Temple of old, access to the meal was limited to those
fully members of the group, but now the distinction was not between
Jew and non-Jew but between those Jews who were Essenes, and
those who were not.

The procedure by which one entered the Essene order was organized around these food regulations. Only after three years of preparation and testing could the postulant participate in the common
food (*War* 2.139). Being accepted into the common meal was thus
the culmination of the process, indicating full fledged membership,
together with acceptance of the attendant obligations and restrictions.
When the new Essene was allowed to eat the common food, he could
no longer eat other people's food, marking off his new identity in
the clearest manner.[37]

The food which Essenes did eat had one further characteristic. It
was simple (Philo, *Hyp.* 11.11), frugal (Josephus, *War* 2.133), eaten in
one plate (Josephus, *War* 2.130), and hence likely archaic. If so, this
was a protest against the "new-fangled" tastes in eating that had
become popular from the Ptolemaic era onwards.[38] This suggests that

---

[37] That new Essene could now enjoy fully the privileges of Essene hospitality
when traveling (Philo, *Omnis Probus* 85; Josephus, *War* 2.124–126), another marker
of his new identity. When he was received as a fellow Essene by his hosts, allowed
to participate in their meal as one of the initiated, and when he permitted himself
to eat their food, mutual recognition of a common identity had taken place.

The comments of Taylor, "John the Baptist and the Essenes," 271, "the Essenes
had no known dietary restrictions beyond those which were defined in the Torah
and did not in general exhibit quite such a degree of exemplary faithfulness" pass
belief. One wonders what Essenes she has in mind. Certainly not those described by
Josephus.

[38] See Bickerman, *Jews in the Greek Age*, 75–77; Hengel, *Judaism and Hellenism*, 1.54.

the Essenes adopted old-fashioned ways as yet another part of establishing their identity, as against a "modern" world with which they found themselves in conflict. This observation will find reinforcement when the discussion turns to Essene dress and occupations below. Nevertheless, we should be careful not to turn the Essenes into ascetic vegetarians: their diet included meat and wine (Josephus, *War* 2.133), appropriate to a movement whose members were drawn from the better off classes, as discussed above, Chapter One, at n. 81.

Dead Sea Sect

Much the same analysis can be offered for the rules of the Qumran group. There too food regulations were employed as a means of sharply marking off their sect from others. The Qumran group was characterized as a place where people ate together, prayed together and decided together (1QS vi, 3). Accordingly, someone outside that community could not participate in the common meal, because he and his food were impure. For that same reason his food was prohibited to members. Thus, when describing those who refused to accept the discipline of the community in 1QS v, 13–16, they may not "partake of the pure meal of the Saints." No member of the community may "eat or drink anything of theirs." In Qumran too, the new member went through a process of acceptance which culminated in his being allowed to participate in the pure meal, signifying his status (1QS vi, 17–23).

One of the means of control extensively employed in 1QS was reducing the food allowance of members as punishment for infractions. This system was effective because members were forbidden to eat food not prepared under community auspices,[39] hence when a member's food allowance was cut that member had that much less to eat and went hungry for the period of his punishment. The expelled Qumran member was in an even worse position: he was assumed to

---

[39] The remote location of the Qumran site may have also contributed to the effectiveness of this means of discipline. Alternate sources of food may have been hard to obtain on the shores of the Dead Sea.

The extreme nature of Qumran purity regulations and the differences they reinforce make it very difficult for me to conceive of the Qumran group as anything but an introversionist sect of the most severe sort. For this reason, among others, I cannot accept the reinterpretation of the Dead Sea Scroll group's history recently offered by H. Stegemann, discussed at length in the Introduction, n. 31.

still be bound by his oaths to eat only food prepared by the community, but was now denied all access to those meals. Thus he was perceived as remaining in the vicinity, and as asking friends, still members of the community, to supply him with food. Current members were therefore warned not to comply with such requests, lest they also be expelled (1QS vii, 22–25).[40]

The havurah

The Essenes and the Qumran sect were not the only groups to operate along these lines. The *havurah*, of which we learn from Rabbinic sources, esp. *tDemai* 2:2 (Lieberman, 68), organized its life in a similar fashion. Here too there was a process of acceptance, which entailed increasingly stringent observance of purity regulations which restricted the member's ability to eat the food of other people.[41] Here too these rules restricted the possibility of interaction between the member and other Jews. Here too a divide existed, in this case between the *haver* and the *am ha'aretz*, which was reinforced by these observances.[42] The *am ha'aretz* was considered a potential source of impurity, from which the *haver* was required to guard himself by means of these regulations.

Pharisees

Whatever may have been the relationship between Pharisees and *haverim*, the Mishnah informs us that Pharisees situated themselves in a clear hierarchy of those observing purity rules, thus separating themselves off from those below them in that hierarchy, and being differentiated from those above them:

---

[40] One is entitled to wonder whether a Qumran member could give his food, as a gift, to a needy outsider. Perhaps this would have been considered desecration of holy food and thus been forbidden. Our sources do not allow a definite answer. Contrast Josephus's remarks on the Essenes, *War* 2.134, according to which Essenes were free to offer food to the needy, as they saw fit.

[41] At the initial level, that of being considered "trustworthy," one was required to tithe all produce one bought or sold, and not to eat in the home of an *am ha'aretz*. A *haver*, at the higher level, took three additional obligations upon himself: (1) not to give heave offerings or tithes to an *am ha'aretz*, (2) not to prepare sacred offerings in the presence of such a person, and (3) to eat ordinary food in a state of purity. On the meaning of these regulations see Lieberman's comments *ad loc*.

[42] The basic study remains that of Lieberman, "Discipline," 199–206. On the vexed question of the relationship of the *haverim* to the Pharisees see E.P. Sanders, *Jewish Law From Jesus to the Mishnah* (London, 1990), 131–254.

> For Pharisees the clothes of an *am-haaretz* count as suffering *midras* uncleanness;[43] for them that eat heave offering the clothes of Pharisees count as suffering *midras* uncleanness (*mHag* 2:7).

The Pharisees were in the reformist category of sect, much less at odds with the mainstream institutions of their society, in fact sometimes controlling them, hence their restrictions on food consumption were less stringent than those of Bannus, John the Baptist, Qumran or the Essenes we have seen above. Nevertheless, Pharisaic practice concerning the consumption of food confirmed the boundaries they drew around themselves, separating themselves off from the rest of Jewish society.[44]

Rabbinic texts on the *havurah* teach little definite about these matters, as doubts concerning the identification of *haverim* and Pharisees bedevil the effort to reach firm conclusions. Nor do the Rabbinic House of Hillel and House of Shammai passages on food consumption help much, as they focus on purity necessary for food to be eaten by priests, and not on that fit for Pharisees.[45] I therefore turn to Mk. 7:4, a verse which has received surprisingly little attention in studies of the Pharisees, but which directly relates to Pharisaic eating practices. Mk. 7:3 tells us that:

> Pharisees and all the Jews do not eat unless they wash their hands, observing the tradition of the elders.

Mk. 7:4 continues:

> when they come from the marketplace, they do not eat unless they purify (*rantisontai*; some mss. read *baptisontai* = immerse) themselves.[46]

"Purifying themselves" of the latter verse is explicitly different from the washing of hands prior to eating, mentioned in 7:3: at the most

---

[43] As defined by H. Danby, *The Mishnah* (Oxford, 1933), 795, this is the degree of uncleanness suffered by an object which any of those enumerated in Lev. 12:2, 15:2, 25 sits, lies, or rides upon or leans against. Any object which is fit to sit, lie or ride upon, or which is usually sat, lain or ridden upon is deemed to be susceptible to *midras* uncleanness.

[44] For this reason, among others, the Pharisees may have called themselves "separatists," as I have argued in A.I. Baumgarten, "The Name of the Pharisees," *Journal of Biblical Literature* 102 (1983), 411–428.

[45] See Sanders, *Practice and Belief*, 431–437.

[46] I understand the verb, in middle plural, as referring to the Pharisees immersing themselves, rather than some objects. This understanding of *ean mē ran/baptisontai* is natural when following *ean mē . . . nipsontai*. Cf. the discussion and literature cited in R. Guelich, *Word Bible Commentary Mark 1:8–26* (Dallas, 1989), 365.

obvious level, purifying themselves when they come from the market-
place involves a purification of the whole body, not just the hands.
Furthermore, as one does not go to the market prior to every meal,
handwashing would be necessary for all meals, while purifying the
entire body would be required only after a visit to the market. Both
purifying themselves on returning from the market and hand washing prior to eating likely go back to the *paradosis* of the Pharisees (the
collection of laws not mentioned in the Bible observed by the Pharisees, under attack in Mk. 7).[47]

Such immersion by the Pharisees prior to eating is not explicitly
mentioned in any Rabbinic, apocryphal, or pseudepigraphic source.[48]
The practice does appear, however, in one other place in the New
Testament, in Lk. 11:38.[49] A Pharisee, apparently thinking that Jesus
belonged to his group, or was at least willing to conform to the host's
demands,[50] invited him to dinner. When Jesus "did not first immerse
himself (*ebaptisthē*) before dinner,"[51] his host was shocked. As the story
is told from the perspective of the followers of Jesus, it ends with
Jesus rebuking his host. Had it been told from the point of view of
the Pharisees it might have ended with Jesus being disinvited.

---

[47] On these laws in general see Baumgarten, "Pharisaic *Paradosis*," 63–77. Immersion
of the self prior to eating has no Biblical source, and as such is an ideal candidate
for inclusion in the *paradosis* of the Pharisees.

[48] See further H. Strack and P. Billerbeck, *Kommentar zum neuen Testament aus Talmud
und Midrasch* (Munich, 1922–61), 2.14, where no parallels are listed. In the elaborate
description of a Jewish meal based on Rabbinic sources, *ibid.*, 4b.611–639 there is
also no mention of purification prior to eating. According to Strack and Billerbeck,
this Pharisaic practice is mentioned in no Rabbinic, apocryphal, or pseudepigraphic
source. This is not quite the case: Is it an accident that Judith, who had been living
in the camp of the gentiles on her own food, bathed, stayed in her tent all day and
then ate (Judith 12:9)? Even if absolutely completely unknown outside the New Testament, this is inadequate reason to reject the historicity of the account of Pharisaic
practice in Luke. The nature of our evidence on Jewish sects, as has recently been
stressed by Goodman, "Note on the Qumran Sectarians," 162, is such that there is
relatively little overlap between the information provided by various authors. We
should therefore not expect them to regularly confirm each other.

[49] It is therefore wrong to assert, as does Guelich, *Word Bible Commentary Mark*,
365 that there is no evidence for this practice in Jewish sources.

[50] Only understanding the invitation as having been extended under a misapprehen-
sion will explain the astonishment of the host at Jesus's behavior, which will follow.

[51] Some translations, e.g. Delitsch's into Hebrew, render this passage as if Jesus
had failed to wash his hands, notwithstanding the explicit use of *ebaptisthē*, and the
omission of all mention of hands in the Greek. See also J. Fitzmyer, *The Gospel
According to Luke (X–XXIV)* (New York, 1985), 947 who struggles to make this passage
refer to washing hands only, against its explicit meaning. I take this testimony of the
gospels to reflect Pharisaic practice in the first century, whether or not it is explicit
evidence for incidents in the life of the historical Jesus.

The reasons Pharisees immersed themselves on returning from the market, before eating, are not specified in these passages, hence we can only speculate. I think it fair, however, to conclude that such immersion was deemed necessary because Pharisees believed that they had contracted impurity while in the market, from "bumping into" people of indeterminate status, Jewish and/or non-Jewish. Eating could only take place after the elimination of this impurity,[52] and in the company of others who were also pure (lest an impure person present reintroduce the impurity which had just been removed by immersion, which would then start the cycle going again, and prevent the Pharisee from eating).[53] Perhaps Pharisees behaved this way because, as has been argued often by others, they were raising the level of holiness in their lives by behaving as if they were priests, treating their ordinary food as if it were subject to some of the restrictions on sacred food consumed by priests.[54]

The purity boundary maintained by the Pharisees, as it emerges from these New Testament passages, was less extreme than that of the Essenes or the Dead Sea Scrolls. A member of the former had been in the market (see also Mt. 23:7), presumably buying his food there, while the latter was restricted to food prepared under the auspices of his group. The Essene or Qumran sectarian had no home other than the sect, while the Pharisee could apparently invite Jesus to his home (*par' autōi*). Unlike the Essene or Dead Sea Sect meal, exclusively communal, the Pharisee and Jesus seem to have been eating alone. Whether Jesus was a Pharisee or not, he could meet

---

[52] This suggestion was already made by Strack and Billerbeck, *Kommentar*, 2.14. It does not seem that this immersion was done as preparatory to entering a higher degree of sanctity, such as the immersion of already pure priests before beginning service in the Temple, or of Essenes before their meal. The passage in Mk. seems to specify that this immersion was necessary because the Pharisee was returning *from the market* to eat. Had he not been in the market the immersion might not have been necessary. Note, that even according to Sanders, *Practice and Belief*, 437, Pharisees "preferred not to dine with people who routinely had *midras* impurity."

[53] I have discussed a possible Rabbinic background to this practice in "Greco-Roman Voluntary Associations," forthcoming.

[54] The Pharisees, as priests *manqués*, has been one of the ongoing themes in the writing of Neusner on the topic. See e.g. J. Neusner, *Rabbinic Traditions about the Pharisees Before 70* (Leiden, 1971), 3.288. See further H. Harrington, "Did the Pharisees Eat Ordinary Food in a State of Ritual Purity?" *Journal for the Study of Judaism in the Persian, Hellenistic and Roman Period* 26 (1995), 42–54; M. Hengel & R. Deines, "E.P. Sanders' 'Common Judaism', Jesus and the Pharisees. A Review Article," *Journal of Theological Studies* 46 (1995), 41–51. Against these views see the position of Sanders, *Jewish Law*, 131–254; *Practice and Belief*, 431–440.

their standards and join a Pharisee at dinner by immersion, unlike
the requirements of Qumran or the Essenes, where a long period of
preparation was required before a potential member was eligible to
share in the food of the order. The moderate nature of Pharisaic
food regulations would help explain how they could participate in
the life of the court over many years of the Second Temple period,
at times even banqueting with the King, as in the story in Josephus,
Ant. 13.289 and *bQidd.* 66a (note that according to Josephus, Hyrcanus
was their disciple when he invited them to feast with him, hence he
would have met their requirements for commensality at that time).
Nevertheless, Pharisees demanded a degree of stringency concerning
those with whom they ate, as a matter of purity. If the conjectures
above are correct, Pharisees could only eat with other Pharisees, or
with those who maintained their standards (perhaps only temporarily).
The Pharisees thus supply an example of a sect erecting purity barriers concerning food, albeit more modest ones, as appropriate for a
reformist group, differentiating between its members and other Jews.[55]

Dress

Dress is another aspect of personality through which identity is expressed; it too can be a statement of how a person regards the society
all round, and what barriers if any exist between that person and
the larger society. New fashions in dress were also part of the changes
instigated by Jason, associated with the encounter with Hellenism:
young men exercising nude in the gymnasium (which, in turn, according to 1 Macc. 1:14–15, followed by Josephus, *Ant.* 12.241, led these
men to give up circumcision, so that they might look fully Greek
when exercising). This consequence seemed especially horrific to the
author of Jubilees, as going counter to the practice of Adam and
Eve on expulsion from Eden, who covered their genitals, and did

---

[55] The purity barriers were not to return to the national perimeter until the eve
of the Great Revolt, when according to the view of many scholars, the eighteen
decrees separating between Jews and non-Jews were enacted. On the eighteen decrees
see I. Ben Shalom, *The School of Shammai and the Zealots' Struggle Against Rome* (Jerusalem, 1993), 252–272 [in Hebrew]. I know of no comprehensive work on the role of
purity rules in the Rabbinic period, after the destruction of the Temple. For the
Talmudic period, J. Neusner, *The Idea of Purity in Ancient Judaism* (Leiden, 1973), 72–
107 abandoned the focus on practical purity rules which had characterized previous
chapters of his study and concentrated on ideology and theology. See the critique
of Neusner's procedure by Douglas, "Afterword," 142.

not uncover themselves as the gentiles did (Jub. 3:31). New fashions included wearing a Greek hat, which symbolized the extreme height of hellenism, according to 2 Macc. 4:12. For these actions Jason earned the role of one of the primary villains of the account in 2 Macc., denounced as ungodly and denied the right to the title of High Priest in 2 Macc. 4:13. Accordingly, adoption of particular forms of dress was a means of expressing opposition to contemporary practices. Note, for example, Bannus's refusal to wear "normal" clothes and his insistence on wearing only things as grew of themselves. This was a piece of the same whole as his diet, as discussed above.

Essenes

Our sources are most explicit on Essene dress. They wore standard clothes, as children under strict discipline (*War* 2.126) – that is, similar to the members of the ephebate, who wore a standard uniform.[56] Even their leader wore the same standard dress, and had no distinctive marks of his office (*War* 2.140). The sense of equality of members of the group, already in place as a consequence of a common purse and common meals, was thus reinforced.[57]

Philo is less specific. He reports that the Essenes not only have a common table but also common clothing, (*Omnis Probus* 86; *Hyp.* 11.12).[58] He adds that for winter wear they "have a stock of stout coats ready and in summer cheap vests (*Hyp.* 11.12)." These comments do not necessarily imply a fixed common dress, but they also do not exclude such a conclusion. In any case, Philo teaches us that Essene dress was distinctive for its simplicity, for its being plain clothes. Clothes and food were corollaries of each other for Bannus and John the Baptist: so too for the Essenes. Their clothes and food were all plain, and I would argue old-fashioned. Openly disdaining interest in modern tastes in food and dress, the Essenes proclaimed thereby their devotion to a higher way of life (compare *Ep. Arist.* 140–141).

---

[56] On the ephebate in the Hellenistic world see H. Marrou, *A History of Education in Antiquity* (New York, 1956), 147–157, esp. 151.

[57] I overlook for the moment the internal divisions among the Essenes noted by Josephus, *War* 2.150. As Josephus states explicitly in the passage quoted above from *War* 2.140, even those in charge of the Essene order did not have outward marks of superiority in dress: the four grades of Essenes did *not* find expression in their clothing. One wonders in what way, if at all, these differences were articulated outwardly.

[58] In context in Philo this seems to mean a common store of clothing from which all took as needed, but could it also mean a common dress worn by all and indicative of membership? See further below.

Pharisees

The Essenes were not the only group recognizable by their dress.
Mt. 23:5 informs us of the distinctive dress of Pharisees, who are
denounced for doing things only to be seen, for making "their phylacteries broad and their fringes long." These dress patterns were
distinctive enough to be meaningful charges against behavior characteristically Pharisaic. Note, however, that the reformist nature of the
Pharisees is forcefully confirmed by this passage, and by comparison
of Pharisaic dress with that of the Essenes. Pharisees wore the same
clothes as everyone else, with only the minor statement of special
identity expressed through *broad* phylacteries and *long* fringes. Contrast the special dress of the Essenes, which was old-fashioned, as I
have argued above.

MARRIAGE

Those whom one considers permissible to marry are marked in a
crucial way, as on the other side of the coin are those whom one
may not marry, marked explicitly as outsiders. The place of marriage
patterns as part of the boundary defining mechanisms of Second
Temple groups is not well known. According to Philo and Pliny the
Essenes were celibate. Josephus reports that some Essenes were celibate, but others married, and that those who did checked to make
certain their brides were fertile. Josephus does not mention other
Essene criteria for accepting or rejecting potential spouses (*War* 2.161).
There is an ongoing debate concerning the degree of celibacy which
prevailed at Qumran. Those who believe that some married couples
lived there are tempted to see in 4Q340 a list of those with whom
marriage was prohibited, but this text is so fragmentary that it allows
no conclusions concerning the reasons marriage with these people
was forbidden.[59] Perhaps it had something to do with women who
had been sexually active in impermissible ways (See CD D^c Fragment
1, i, 11–15).

Nevertheless, there is at least one indication of special sectarian
criteria for marriage in 11QT. If a man seduced a virgin who was
not betrothed he was required to marry her (Exod. 22:16). 11QT 66:9

---

[59] See Broshi and Yardeni, "On Nethinim and False Prophets," 45–50.

adds that this requirement was to be enforced only when the girl was eligible to marry her seducer according to the law. Only if the seducer and the seduced virgin met the special sectarian criteria for marriage was the regulation in Exod. 22:15 to be enforced. 11QT 66:9 still does not transmit the content of these special sectarian criteria, but it is likely evidence for their existence.

The Mishnah reports an interesting tradition concerning the houses of Hillel and Shammai: in spite of their disagreements they did not refrain from marrying each other (mYeb. 1:8). Whether this idyllic picture is wholly accurate or not is beyond the frame of reference here. Whatever the case, this text teaches us the normal expectations, which reinforce the interpretation of 4Q340 and 11QT 66:9 offered above: like the Hillelites and Shammaites of the Mishnah, sects had their own marriage regulations. These differences of interpretation concerning laws of marriage usually led members of groups to refuse to marry each other, treating each other as if they were outsiders with whom marriage was prohibited.[60]

If the arguments above are accepted there were special sectarian criteria for marriage, above and beyond the general obligations in the Torah, but the nature of these criteria is unknown. One possible example of a special sectarian criterion of the sort I have in mind in this sub-section is suggested by CD v, 8–11. That text is explicit in its denunciation of uncle-niece marriages, which other Jews of the Second Temple era (especially those of means?)[61] considered as permissible, nay even desirable and laudable, according to Rabbinic

---

[60] This understanding of the comments on marriage in mYeb. 1:8, as indicating that sectarians normally refrained from marrying those who were the products of unions they considered illegal, is strengthened by reflection on the comments on purity laws in that same passage. According to mYeb. 1:8, in spite of their different interpretations of purity rules, Hillelites and Shammaites accepted each other's food as pure. That not all groups were so accommodating (again, I leave aside whether Hillelites and Shammaites were, in fact, so cooperative) is now clear from the ideological summary of 4QMMT in which the author explained that on account of differences in purity rules he and his followers could not accept as pure foods prepared under other standards. Thus when mYeb. 1:8 asserts that Hillelites and Shammaites did not draw certain conclusions as a result of their different interpretations we should understand this as an unusual consequence: most "normal" groups would have behaved differently, and not married each other or accepted each other's food as pure.

[61] Uncle-niece marriages preserve the property of one brother, inherited by his daughter, in the family, in the control of the other brother, her husband. Hence they are usually favored by aristocrats and others of means, who have property interests to protect.

sources.[62] There should have been a reasonable number of such unions and a fair supply of offspring of these matches. If Qumran members married, one may wonder whether they would have taken a spouse who was the product of an uncle-niece marriage. One may also wonder whether someone who came to join the Qumran community, who was descended from an uncle-niece marriage, would have been accepted.

COMMERCE

Essenes

Essenes, according to Josephus, did not buy and sell among each other, but gave each other freely whatever they needed (*War* 2.127). This was but one aspect of Essene egalitarianism (already encountered in their common meal and dress),[63] meant to insure the total devotion of a member to the group. According to Philo (*Hyp.* 11.17), this egalitarianism culminated in the celibacy of members of the order: a man with a wife and children makes them his first care, ceases to be the same to others (that is to be devoted wholly to the community of which he was a member), and has passed from freedom into slavery.[64] Exclusive commitment to the community was to reach a point where a member was allowed to donate freely to help those in need, but presents to relatives required the approval of the leadership (*War* 2.134), as such presents were an expression of individuality, hence needed to be controlled.

More important from the perspective of boundary definition under discussion here was the Essene restriction of their commercial activity to agriculture. This fact is obscure in Philo and in Josephus's excursus in *War* 2, but is made explicit in *Ant.* 18.19: the Essenes devote themselves solely to agriculture. The concentration of activity is significant in context of the old-fashioned dress and diet of the

---

[62] On this point see further M. Broshi, "Anti-Qumranic Polemics in the Talmud," *Madrid Qumran Congress* 2.596.

[63] On Qumran as a "greedy institution," in terms of the perspective suggested by L. Coser see Introduction, at n. 32. Much the same is true of the Essenes, as outlined below.

[64] On the changes which took place among Protestant clergy, when they were permitted to marry and raise a family, see the incisive discussion in Collinson, *Religion of Protestants*, 1–188.

Essenes, discussed in previous sections of this chapter. Most inhabitants of the ancient world had no choice but to live a life of subsistence agriculture. The somewhat better off members of ancient Jewish sects, Essenes included, were not in that position. They could engage in various commercial or intellectual activities. If Ben Sira's comments on the virtues of the sage are any indication (38:24–34), I would venture the guess that most better off members of ancient society saw their freedom from subsistence agriculture as one the great blessings of their higher status. For the Essenes to choose egalitarian agriculture was thus a step consistent with their other old-fashioned ways. It was a statement of protest against commercial life as it was now being lived. In this sense, Essenes hoped to live like the honest rustic, hero of T. Issachar, who worked the land, spoke the truth and was wholly righteous, all in contrast to others at the time of the author and readers of the work.[65] Significantly, as part of this archaic lifestyle, Issachar of T. Issachar also wore simple clothing and ate a plain diet (T. Iss. 4:2).

Dead Sea Sect

As indicated by our sources, only the most introversionist of the groups applied the principle of exclusion from the impurity of other Jews to their commercial activities. Qumran members, as a consequence of their version of egalitarianism,[66] did not engage in business activities with each other (CD xiii, 14–15).[67] As many other Jews, they could

---

[65] The date of the Testaments of the Twelve Patriarchs has been much debated. See the summary of positions in H.C. Kee, "Testament of the Twelve Patriarchs," in Charlesworth, *Old Testament Pseudepigrapha* 1.775–781. I agree with Kee concerning the second century BCE date for the work, but disagree concerning the provenance. Kee rules out Palestine, while I would argue that the increasingly extensive similarities between the Testaments and materials to be found at Qumran makes Palestine a likely place of origin.

On the archaic nature of the appreciation of agriculture see also Hengel, *Judaism and Hellenism*, 1.54; Bickerman, *Jews in the Greek Age*, 208–209.

[66] What to make of the differences between Qumran egalitarianism and that reported of the Essenes by Philo and Josephus has been the focus of much scholarly discussion. See my treatment of this matter, at an earlier stage of my research, in "Rule of the Martian," 134.

[67] See especially the interpretation of this text proposed by J. Baumgarten, "The 'Sons of Dawn' in Damascus Document = CD 13:14–15 and the Ban on Commerce among the Essenes," *Israel Exploration Journal* 33 (1983), 81–85. According to the interpretation proposed by J. Baumgarten, one wonders about the meaning of the continuation of the text in CD xiii, 15–16, requiring a written agreement for a partnership, and the approval of the leadership. Does this also concern *internal* arrangements

not buy and sell freely with non-Jews (CD xii, 6–11).[68] The rules
affecting their commercial relations with other Jews, however, deserve
particular mention in the context of the discussion of this chapter,
especially as they do not seem to have merited sufficient attention in
other treatments of Qumran purity rules.[69]

A Qumran member could not work with an outsider, nor could
he be involved in a business venture with such a person:

> Likewise no man shall consort with him (a non-member) with regard
> to his work or property lest he (the member) be burdened with the
> guilt of his (the non-member's) sin. He shall keep away from him in all
> things. . . . No member of the community shall . . . take anything from
> them, except for a price. . . . For all those not reckoned in His cov-
> enant are to be set apart, together with all that is theirs. . . . All their
> deeds (those of the non-member) are defilement before Him, and all
> their possessions unclean (1QS v, 14–20).[70]

Virtually all economic contacts, other than cash purchases, were
forbidden. Only in a cash purchase was sufficient distance to avoid
defilement maintained between the two parties: sales for credit, joint
ventures, or employment of one by the other involved the two parties too intimately.[71] All economic connection other than cash sales

---

between members, or have we turned to relationships with outsiders? If the former,
what is the purpose of a written partnership agreement between two people who
are already supposed to be sharing everything with each other? What is there for
the leadership to approve or disapprove (cf. the approval of the leadership required
for Josephus's Essene to give gifts to his relatives, *War* 2.134)? In spite of these
difficulties J. Baumgarten prefers this possibility, and argues that the scope of private economic activity permitted according to the CD was sufficiently wide to give
meaning to the regulation in xiii, 15–16. See *ibid.*, 84. If the latter, partnership with
outsiders would seem to be forbidden according to texts from 1QS quoted below.
Is the passage from CD xiii, 15–16 then an indication of the gap between the two
texts, with the 1QS forbidding all partnership, but CD permitting it with certain
limitations? Or is CD xiii, 15–16 to be understood as restricting the ability of a
member to buy or sell from/to outsiders except by written agreement and with the
approval of the leadership (with the requirement that such transactions be for cash
taken as obvious)? In that case, the requirements of this passage would seem to be
even stricter than those of 1QS.

[68] On this passage see L. Schiffman, "Legislation Concerning Relations with non-
Jews in the Zadokite Fragments and in Tannaitic Literature," *Revue de Qumran* 11 (1983),
379–389. Note that the restrictions on trade with gentiles in CD are less stringent
than those on trade with other Jews according to 1QS, as will be set out below.

[69] Cf. Schiffman, *Law, Custom*, 248–252.

[70] It seems too obvious to require explicit mention that one was not allowed to
work with an ex-member, or join property with his (CD xx, 7).

[71] The Essenes of Philo and Josephus seem to have worked for outsiders for pay.
See esp. Philo's comment, *Omnis Probus* 76, that the Essenes practiced crafts and in

or purchases were prohibited, because they implicated the member, inevitably, in the impurity of the non-member.[72] The same attitude was exhibited in 1QS ix, 8:

> As for the property of the men of holiness who walk in perfection, it shall not be merged with that of the men of falsehood who have not purified their life by separating themselves from iniquity and walking in the way of perfection.

In both these texts, the mechanisms of purity and impurity were explicitly employed to separate between insiders and outsiders.

Due to the purity barriers existing between members and outsiders, the property of postulants could not be merged with that of the community. Only when a postulant became a full-fledged member, could his property be mingled with that of the other members. Only then did his property not convey impurity to theirs, and thus to the community itself. Thus, at a stage prior to full membership his property was registered, but only on completion of the process was it merged into the community fund.[73] Similar rules governed the new member's work. In accord with the logic of the system, once someone became a full-fledged member the restriction that he not work outside the sect applied to him (1QS vi, 20–22).

Worship

Those with whom one refuses to worship God (by sacrifice or prayer) are identified as outsiders. For that reason, non-Jews were excluded from the Temple in Jerusalem. The sects, especially the more extreme introversionist ones, employed this boundary defining mechanism fairly freely, while the little known of Pharisaic worship practices confirms their reformist nature, much as the analysis of their eating regulations or their dress, above. As part of the denunciation of the Pharisees in Mt. 23, Jesus accused them of loving the best seats in the

---

this way were useful to their neighbors. Might this be another difference between the Essenes of classical authors and the Qumran community?

[72] Were cash purchases of food permissible at all stages of food preparation or only at some preliminary point(s)?

[73] Perhaps there were other, practical, reasons for deferring the transfer of property to the community until the end of the period of novitiate. Until both sides were certain that they had chosen each other, it would have been premature to require the transfer of property. Our sources, however, present the issue in purity terms.

synagogue (Mt. 23:6). This is socially significant. The Pharisees demanded recognition of their stature, yet could be found in the synagogue along with everyone else.

Essenes

Essene practice at their meals has been noted in the passage from
Josephus, *War* 2.130–132, cited above. They behaved as if their
meal were a ceremony taking place at the Temple, from which non-
members were excluded. The Essenes wore special garments at these
meals, which they took off when their meal was completed, as the
priests did not wear priestly garments outside the sanctuary (based
on Ezek. 44:19), lest they communicate sanctity outside the area where
it was supposed to be confined.[74] The Essenes were behaving as if
they were priests, taking upon themselves some of the restrictions of
serving priests (cf. the Nazirite, who also raised the sanctity of his life
by taking on some of the obligations of serving priests;[75] cf. also the
discussion of the Pharisees above). While priests, however, separated
themselves off from other Jews as an expression of the holiness they
kept on behalf of the entire community, and with its approval, Essenes
acted as if they were priests as a protest against the main-line institutions of the society. There could be no more explicit indication of
the boundary Essenes erected between themselves and other Jews.[76]

In the case of the Essenes, their rules of purity guaranteed a mutual
delegitimation between themselves and the main institutions of organized Jewish life, which was expressed in the realm of worship. If as
Josephus reports (*Ant.* 18.19) Essenes performed purity rites of their
own (offered red heifers of their own, in my view), for which they

---

[74] See the discussion of this text and its consequences in A.I. Baumgarten, "The
Paradox of the Red Heifer", *Vetus Testamentum* 43 (1993), 448–449. Note the provi-
sion in Euhemerus's utopia, according to which priests who set foot outside the
sacred area may be killed by anyone who comes upon them, *FGrH* 63 F 3.46.4.

[75] For this interpretation of the Nazirite see further A.I. Baumgarten, *"Hatta't*
Sacrifices," *Revue Biblique*, 103 (1996), 341. The idea that the level of sanctity in one's
life can be raised by taking on all or part of the life style of those in a higher place
in the hierarchy has its equivalents in a number of other traditions. See Dumont,
Homo Hierarchicus, 192.

[76] An analogous pattern of thought may have led Karaites to exclude those not
members of their group from their services. See H. Ben-Shammai, "Between Ananites
and Karaites: Observations on Early Medieval Jewish Sectarianism," *Studies in Muslim-
Jewish Relations* 1 (1992), 19–29. I would like to thank Prof. Ben-Shammai for calling
his article to my attention.

were excluded from the Temple,[77] Essenes could only have seen other Jews, purified by standards/means they believed improper hence ineffective, as unfit to worship in purity with them. The Temple authorities, as just noted above, returned the compliment, excluding Essenes from the Temple.[78]

Dead Sea Sect

The community at Qumran also had its own version of purity ritual, which it believed solely effective.[79] This may have included offering their own red heifers.[80]

Even more significant were the effects of the Qumran calendar. Whether calendar disputes have a quality which makes compromise particularly difficult is not so obvious a conclusion as widely thought.[81] Whatever the circumstances, Qumran denunciations of those who did not follow their calendar were harsh. They were people walking in error, with whom one is to have no connection, the new sort of outsiders at the heart of the definition of sectarianism proposed at the outset of this study.

Around this calendar and purity rules the Qumran community organized itself as a replacement for the Jerusalem Temple. This attitude culminated in the decision (reinforced by the policy of the authorities?) to withdraw to the desert, and to prepare the way for the Lord there (1QS viii, 13–16). By this action the extreme introversionist nature of the group was underlined.

---

[77] I have discussed this evidence at length in "Josephus on Essene Sacrifice," 169–183.

[78] Perhaps as I suggested in A.I. Baumgarten, "He Knew that He Knew that He Knew that He was an Essene," *Journal of Jewish Studies*, 48 (1997), 56–57, this task was made feasible for the Temple police by the distinctive dress of the Essenes, discussed above.

[79] J. Baumgarten, "The Purification Rituals in DJD 7," in Dimant and Rappaport, *The Dead Sea Scrolls*, 199–209.

[80] J. Bowman, "Did the Qumran Sect Burn the Red Heifer?" *Revue de Qumran* 1 (1958), 73–81.

[81] See above, Introduction, n. 116 and Chapter One at n. 130. Furthermore, there are textual grounds for wondering whether 4QMMT began with the Qumran calendar. Only one of two MSS. that has the beginning of the B section has the A section before it (4Q394). In the other MS. (4Q395), there is ample room for text prior to the B section, but it is blank. See further J. Strugnell, "MMT Second Thoughts on a Forthcoming Edition," in E. Ulrich and J. VanderKam (Eds.), *The Community of the Renewed Covenant – The Notre Dame Symposium on the Dead Sea Scrolls* (Notre Dame, 1994), 61–62. See also L. Schiffman, "The Place of 4QMMT in the Corpus of Qumran MSS," in J. Kampen and M. Bernstein (Eds.), *Reading 4QMMT – New Perspectives on Qumran Law and History* (Atlanta, 1996), 82–86.

ADMONITION

Sects presented themselves as havens of harmony in a troubled world. Those at Qumran saw saw the divisiveness of their age as one of its curses. As these texts – 4Q390 2 i 6 in particular, as analyzed by Dimant,[82] make clear – the Qumran sectarians and authors of allied works saw their common life, and its attendant accord, as one of their distinguishing characteristics: outside the sect all was dissension, inside there was equity and peace.[83] According to Josephus, the Essenes were distinguished among the Jewish groups for their devotion to each other (*War* 2.119). The Book of Acts described the primitive Christian community as living in similar circumstances: "all who believed were together and had all things in common (Acts 2:44)." In a similar vein we are told:

> Now the company of those who believed were of one heart and soul, and no one said that any of the things which he possessed was his own, but they had everything in common (Acts 4:32).

Reality, however, was different: harmony was achieved with difficulty, and required paying a high price. In a voluntary association, lacking means of enforcement such as are available to an established hierarchy (note the powers granted Ezra by the Persian king, Ez. 7:26), the methods employed to achieve this goal could verge on a psychological reign of terror. Furthermore, particularly in communities where goods and life were shared, such as the Essenes and Qumran, the sin of any one member implicated all others. Constant admonition of every member by every other one was essential to preserve the status of each member, as well as of the community as a whole.

Josephus reports that an Essene was expected to expose liars, and to conceal nothing from members of the sect (*War* 2.141). In effect,

---

[82] See D. Dimant, "New Light from Qumran on the Jewish Pseudepigrapha – 4Q390," *Madrid Qumran Congress* 2.428, 437–441.

[83] See 4Q183 ii, 2–4 (*DJD* V, 183) and the comments of M. Kister, "Marginalia Qumranica," *Tarbiz* 57 (5748) 317 [in Hebrew]. Iambulus's "Children of the Sun" also lived in perfect harmony: their settlements on seven islands all followed the same customs and laws (D.S. 2.58.7).

Dissent inside the sect posed an embarrassment to its members, as it might indicate that the sect's teachings were not true. The Qumran covenanters dealt with this by arguing that God had chosen to make truth and error contemporary, hence the "responsibility" was His. See 1QS iv, 17–18. Essenes were required to transmit teachings as received (*War* 2.142), a regulation likely intended to minimize dissent and prevent factionalism. On other ways in which groups dealt with such dilemmas see Cohen, "Virgin Defiled," 1–11.

an Essene was to be a permanent spy on the activities of fellow members, and I suppose that the information provided by Essenes about each other was used by the leadership to control the lives of members. According to Josephus, serious crimes were punished by expulsion (*War* 2.143), but we never learn how the group dealt with less serious offenses. In light of the other examples accumulated below, rebuke likely played a part.

The role of admonition is explicit in 4Q477, recently published by E. Eshel.[84] Qumran members were rebuked there for specific offences, such as doing evil, being short-tempered, haughty, or too devoted to their relatives. 4Q477 thus offers us an inside look at the way members of the Qumran community were chastised for inappropriate behavior, inconsistent with the norms of the sect.

Chastisement was not, however, limited to the Essenes or Qumran. In Josephus's version of the banquet hosted by a Hasmonean ruler, John Hyrcanus in this case, the ruler was presented as a loyal disciple of the Pharisees who implored his guests, "if they observed him doing anything wrong or straying from the right path, to lead him back to it and correct him (*Ant.* 13.290). As a good Pharisee, Hyrcanus was inviting rebuke, hoping (one imagines) that it would be mild and trivial at best.[85] To his dismay, according to the story, it touched a crucial aspect of his reign. As a group that employed admonition in this way, the Pharisees were as much sectarians as the Essenes or Qumran.[86]

---

[84] E. Eshel, "4Q477," 118–121. In this way, the obligation of rebuke in CD vii, 2 was fulfilled. For my purposes, the discussion whether these were the rebukes of the overseer or of some other official or group, is besides the point. See S.A. Reed, "Genre, Setting and Title of 4Q477," *Journal of Jewish Studies* 47 (1996), 146–147.

[85] More is at stake here than merely the mutual frankness characteristic of the atmosphere at a Greek symposium, as I suggested earlier in Baumgarten, "Rabbinic Literature," 44, n. 107.

[86] Note also the role of rebuke among the Epicureans, considered a sect by J. Rist, *Epicurus: An Introduction* (Cambridge, 1972), 12. Membership in the Epicurean order was voluntary, hence discipline in that group was maintained by means of rebuke. Epicureans swore an oath on entry to be faithful to the way of life taught by Epicurus (Philodemus, *Peri Parresias*, 45, 8–11): "We will be obedient to Epicurus, *according to whom we have made it our choice to live.*" As Seneca, *Epist.* 25.5, put it: "*Sic fac omnia tamquam spectet Epicurus.*"

The members of this school believed that true security was possible only in a community of friends, safe from its neighbors (D.L. 10.154). Only there could physical and mental serenity be achieved. Within the confines of this community they taught new members, who were organized in various orders of seniority, rebuking them as necessary. Slyness and secretiveness were considered the worst offenses against

Rebuke also had its place among early Christians, according to
Mt. 18:15–17. The process described began in private, as a personal
matter ("If your brother sins against you"), but culminated in rebuke
in church. The brother who refused to listen, even after having been
rebuked before the community, was to be considered "as a gentile
and tax collector." That is, he was to be ranked as an outsider. In
the early Christian case the circumstances leading to rebuke began
as a private affair. This was not an organized chastisement in the
name of the community, as at Qumran, perhaps the Essenes, or among
the Pharisees. In this way, the institution of admonishment was taken
over but re-shaped by the early Christians.[87] Nevertheless, enough of
the old framework remained: those who did not comply with rebuke
were deemed outsiders.

CLOSING THE CIRCLE

This chapter began with the assertion that disappointment at the
attitude of the new dynasty played a crucial role in the maturity of
sectarianism. It began with a cause and then went on to describe the
effects in boundary marking in various realms of life as a result of

---

the friendship they were trying to establish (Philodemus, 41, 1–4). Reporting of
misdemeanors committed by fellow-students was approved as an act of genuine friendship and failure to report such a person stamped a man as "an evil friend and a
friend to evil (Philodemus, 50)." The environment was such that even seniors had
to accept constructive criticism when it came from their inferiors (D.L. 10.120;
Philodemus X[a], 1–5 and X[b], 11–13). See the discussion in N. De Witt, "Organization and Procedure in Epicurean Groups," *Classical Philology* 31 (1936), 206–207.

Epicureans lived lives of much less devotion and intensity, with far less restriction
or boundary marking than Pharisees, Essenes or Qumran sectarians. Nevertheless,
as a consequence of their being a voluntary organization, rebuke played an equally
important role as a means of discipline.

Rebuke was equally important among the Rabbis, heirs of the Pharisees. See e.g.
SifreD 1 (Finkelstein, 3–4). Sages of the era after Yavneh lament the fact that theirs
is not a time when people know how to rebuke or be rebuked effectively. As if to
contradict that impression, the text continues with a story of how R. Akiba was
admonished by R. Yohanan b. Nuri, and how R. Akiba responded by loving his
rebuker even more, in accordance with the verse in Prov. 9:8, "reprove a wise man,
and he will love you." According to the Rabbis, rebuke brings satisfaction, goodness
and blessing to the world (*bTam.* 28a). One of the reasons for the destruction of the
Second Temple was that Jews of the time did not rebuke each other for their sins,
and thus shared in the evil deeds of their fellows (*bShab.* 119b).

[87] The transformation of rebuke should have some connection with the distinct
nature of Christian sectarianism, and the sense in which it did not fit into the pattern of other Jewish groups, a conclusion suggested a number of times in this book.

that sense of failure and disillusion. The most appropriate conclusion for the chapter is to recall the old-fashioned ways of the Essenes, noted in passing, in the realm of food, dress and commercial activity. These are results which testify to a world jigged out of place, which the Essenes would have liked to avoid, jumping back to more tranquil days before the transformation, and marking themselves off from those who accepted the changes of which they disapproved. The dialectic can begin with the cause and then work its way to a greater understanding of the results, or it can begin with the effects and reflect back to shed additional light on the causes. In whatever direction attempted, or in both simultaneously, the changes which culminated in the mid second century BCE and the flourishing of ancient Jewish sectarianism help elucidate each other.

Radical reform imposed by royal fiat, such as at the time of Antiochus IV affected all levels of Jewish society, and led to an armed revolution. The issues under consideration in this chapter were of a different and more nuanced sort. With the victory of the Maccabees extreme Hellenism was discredited (and Jewish sensibilities on this matter were to be respected even by later rulers such as Herod the Great), but the disappointment at the blessings of victory become a curse were a different matter. They would have been of greatest concern to the Jerusalem elites, who were most directly involved in the realization of these blessings, hence most frustrated at their unsatisfying conclusion. This situation, I propose, provoked some of the Jerusalem elites to turn inwards, separating themselves off from a society which they felt had gone astray, and thus leading to the flourishing of the sects who are the subject of this book.

Finally, the analysis of boundary marking mechanisms employed by ancient Jewish sects in different realms of life confirms other conclusions argued for above (Chapter One, at nn. 60–66). Thus, the basic similarity of the rules of the various sects is now explicit, what I called there the sense of their being variations on the same theme. At the same time, the difference in extent and comprehensiveness between the regulations of reformist groups and those of the introversionist sort is now sharper. The introversionist movements, as anticipated in the brief presentation in the Introduction, made much more extensive demands on the total loyalty of their members. They were egalitarian, and their voluntary boundary markers were higher, less permeable, more strictly guarded, and applied in many more realms of life than those of reformist groups.

CHAPTER THREE

LITERACY AND ITS IMPLICATIONS

SECTARIAN FERMENT

Periods of intense sectarian activity are often times of sectarian conflict, with the polemic between groups extreme.[1] The ancient Jewish cases under investigation in this book were no exception. In considering the similarities between the groups in Chapter One, at nn. 60–66, their clashing claims to key favorable attributes, such as accuracy in observing the Law, was noted. Qumran attacks against other groups, such as those called by the code names of Menasseh, Ephraim,[2] or the Seekers after Smooth Things,[3] also deserve mention. Another set of opponents, perhaps originally of internal descent, were the House of Absalom and the House of Peleg.[4] According to ARNA 5 (Schechter, 26), Sadducees denounced Pharisees for their belief in a reward in the afterlife, while Josephus noted that Pharisees and Sadducees had extensive debates concerning the status of the Pharisaic *paradosis* (*Ant.* 13.298). In (the imagination of the author of?) Acts, all Paul needed do when tried before the Sanhedrin was mention that he was a Pharisee, charged with believing in the resurrection of the dead, and this caused Pharisees and Sadducees to fight each other so intensely that Paul and his case were nearly forgotten (Acts 23:6–10).

What might have yielded this intense sectarian ferment, this inability to agree on basic practices and beliefs? At one level, the nature of the Bible as a gapped text, requiring interpretation and specification if one is to live by its laws, was responsible. As Origen noted, as stressed by Cohen, "the variety of the interpretations of the writings of Moses and the sayings of the prophets" was one of the major

---

[1] Note, for example the comment of W. Haller, *The Rise of Puritanism* (New York, 1947, 2nd edition), 179: "The history of the dissenters is occupied almost as much with the strife of sects with one another as with the attacks of the sects upon the main body of the orthodox from which all had sprung."

[2] E.g., in 4QpNah ii, 4–9.

[3] E.g., CD i, 18.

[4] House of Absalom: 1QpHab v, 9–12; House of Peleg: CD xx, 22.

factors that caused Jewish sects to come into existence.[5] Each of the
sects was filling in the gaps in Biblical law in its own way, but in
spite of Origen, explaining the causes of sectarian ferment by appeal
to the gapped nature of the Bible is an inadequate answer, as the
sects of the Maccabean era were not the first to discover the gaps in
the Bible. Attempts to close these gaps can already be seen in the
books of Chronicles, and traditional interpretation existed as well to
cope with these difficulties.[6] Thus, to mention one example, the
"morrow of the Sabbath," when the sheaf of the wave offering is to
be brought, and which is to serve as a point of departure for count-
ing seven weeks until the next holiday, is not further specified in
Lev. 23:11, 15. Nevertheless, traditional interpretation as preserved
in the Septuagint translation of the verse, and as confirmed by the
comments of Philo (*Spec. Leg.* 2.162, 176) and Josephus (*Ant.* 3.250,
252), indicates that the "morrow of the Sabbath" was understood as
being the day after the first day of Passover. What was wrong with
this interpretation that it became unacceptable to those at Qumran,
who built their calendar around the interpretation that the "morrow
of the Sabbath" was a Sunday? Given the potential role of calendar
controversies in establishing sectarian identity, as discussed above,
Chapter Two, at n. 81, what led the Qumran group to insist on their
interpretation of the verse, and thus drive a wedge between itself
and Jews loyal to the Temple and its calendar? What causes might
have led to this devotion to particular interpretations, with their attendant consequences? That is, in light of the discussion in the Introduction, at nn. 68–71, of the need for people to see the utility of ideas
before they pursue them, what circumstances brought about the situation in which commitment to specific understandings of the Bible –
especially interpretations which differed from those accepted by the established
authorities – became actual?[7]

In more specific terms, the discussion below will focus on a question
made acute by full knowledge of 4QMMT. That text represented an

---

[5] Origen, *Contra Celsum* 3.12, as cited by Cohen, *Maccabees to the Mishnah*, 134.

[6] Cf. J. Blenkinsopp, "Interpretation and the Tendency to Sectarianism: An Aspect
of Second Temple History," in E.P. Sanders (Ed.), *Jewish and Christian Self Definition*
Volume Two: Aspects of Judaism in the Graeco-Roman Period (London, 1981), 1–26.

[7] In this sense as well, see Introduction, at nn. 49–50, Nehemiah was a forerunner
of more full blown Jewish sectarianism, opposing his layman's understanding of the
requirements of the law to that of the priestly establishment. See esp. Smith, "Dead
Sea Sect," 353.

agenda for radical change in the way Jewish life was being run, with
appeal repeatedly made there to what is written in the Bible as the
basis for the plea to uphold the proper way of fulfilling the law: in
the text of 4QMMT as reconstructed by Qimron, appeal was made
to what is written in the Bible at least eleven times, six in the halachic
section (B 27, 38, 66, 70, 76, 77) and five in the ideological (C 6, 11,
12, 12, 21).[8] What conditions promoted the formation of such agendas,
particularly those which disagreed with practice in force in the Temple?
The answer to this question will yield a further level of understanding of the processes which resulted in the flourishing of ancient Jewish sectarianism. It will require a survey of the history of education
and the spread of literacy, as well as consideration of the implications of literacy.

EDUCATION AND LITERACY

Prior to the destruction of the first Temple, education was in the
hands of the parents, particularly the father. Many verses repeat the
idea that the father is to teach his children (e.g., Dt. 6:7), or that
children are to ask their fathers and other elders if they have questions
(Exod. 13:14; Dt. 32:7). All this transfer of information is explicitly
oral. From another point of view, God dictates a poem to Moses
which he is to write down and then teach the people. They, in turn,
are to know and remember this poem in the future, when punished
for their misdeeds (Dt. 31:19). One should note, however, that the
Israelites of the future are expected to know the poem by heart,
rather than its written version, or the written text of the Pentateuch
as a whole. Furthermore, the information the Israelites at large are
expected to have is contained in a poem, a virtually certain indication that this knowledge is to be preserved orally.[9] The practical
implications of these considerations are straightforward. In an educational context such as this, the knowledge of the father usually served
as a limit on the learning of his children: normally, they did not

---

[8] See further M. Bernstein, "The Employment and Interpretation of Scripture in
4QMMT: Preliminary Observations," in J. Kampen and M. Bernstein (Eds.), *Reading 4QMMT – New Perspectives on Qumran Law and History* (Atlanta, 1996), 29–52, esp.
38–52.
[9] On the fundamental link between poetry and oral culture see e.g. E. Havelock,
Preface to Plato (Cambridge, 1963).

know more than he did. In particular, when he did not know how
to read neither did they; when his culture was oral so was theirs.
There were exceptions, of course, but they should not have been
numerous.[10] Extensive knowledge of the law would have been restricted
to the priests and other temple personnel, who "teach the law to
Jacob (Dt. 33:10)." This same perspective can also be found, at least
in part, in Dt. 24:8 where one learns that the priests possess special
instruction on the disease of leprosy which has been commanded by
God *to them* (note the third person plural suffix). This information is
not available to the commoner, who can only go to the priest and
learn from him what God has taught the latter.

During the Persian and Hellenistic period the law continued to be
the domain of the priest. The ordinary Jew, according to Mal. 2:7
receives knowledge of God from the lips of a priest, who is the
messenger of the Lord of Hosts. Instruction for the ordinary Jew is
still explicitly oral: he and the priest do not look up the relevant
sources, rather instruction comes from the lips of the priest. This
perspective can be found echoed in Hecataeus of Abdera, at the
beginning of the Hellenistic era, according to whom the Jews are
ruled by priests and have always been ruled by priests. The High
Priest is the messenger of God's will (compare Mal. 2:7 above), who
announces the word of God to the people, who bow down in obei-
sance.[11] In Ben Sira 45:17 (roughly a hundred years after Hecataeus,
at the time of the Seleucid conquest) it is Aaron who is given authority in God's statutes and judgments, and whose task is "to teach
Jacob the testimonies and enlighten Israel with his law." This is also
the case in the book of Jubilees, where it is the role of the priest to
teach the law (31:15–17). It is Levi, according to Jubilees, who inherits
the family library of Jacob to study it and pass it on to his descendants forever (45:15). In a similar vein, the author of the Testament
of the Twelve Patriarchs has Levi advising his descendants to learn
to read and write so they can fulfill their duties, while he does not
place similar recommendations in the mouths of the other sons of
Jacob: "Teach your children letters also, so that they might have

---

[10] Those who joined Wisdom schools would be an important group of exceptions. On the other hand, even there the convention was that the teacher addressed
his pupils as a father to his sons. One may well wonder how much of this was pure
literary form.

[11] See Stern, *Greek and Latin Authors*, #11, 5–6.

understanding throughout their lives as they ceaselessly read the law
of God (T. Levi 13:2–3)." It is worth noting, according to T. Levi,
that reading is important not for writing or receiving love letters, nor
even to enable government to function; its purpose is to facilitate a
knowledge of the law, a necessity for the sons of Levi. As one indication of the "realization" of these arrangements, the library inherited
by Levi was passed down to members of later generations of the
family, according to 4QTQahat, so that it could serve as a warning
to his descendants.

There was also a countervailing tendency. While Dt. 24:8 acknowledges the special teachings on leprosy in the possession of priests, the
book of Deuteronomy itself is meant to be read by a lay person,
who is advised to seek the expertise of a priest in case of suspected
leprosy. In the mid third century BCE the Pentateuch was translated
into Greek, an act which brought it to the possible attention of a
wide circle of readers, far exceeding even the limits of the Jewish
world. As part of this process, perhaps the circle of the literate was
expanding throughout the Biblical period.[12]

In spite of this tendency towards more widespread knowledge of
the Bible, it seems fair to conclude that in reality the Bible remained
principally in the hands of priests during the Persian and Hellenistic
eras. Its accessibility must often have been more theoretical than
practical. This would have been particularly true if literacy was as
restricted as discussed above, and concentrated in priestly families as
the Testament of Levi implies.

The status of the Bible began to change with the Seleucid conquest. The first sign can be seen in Ben Sira, here pointing more
forwards than to the past. Identifying the Bible with the Wisdom by
which the world was created and which all seek (Ch. 24), Ben Sira
insisted that this international wisdom dwelt in Jacob and was identical to the Torah. The Bible was thus removed from its parochial
Jewish context and given a universal role. To put this conclusion in
other terms, as suggested by Bickerman, the Bible was now the foundation of Jewish education, much as Homer was the basis of Greek

---

[12] See further A. Demsky, "Writing in Ancient Israel and Early Judaism," in
J. Mulder (Ed.), *Miqra, Compendia Rerum Iudaicarum ad Novum Testamentum, Part II* (Philadelphia, 1988), 10–11. Nevertheless, we should be careful not to overstate the speed
with which this skill spread among the population. See further N. Na'aman, "Historiography, the Fashioning of the Collective Memory, and the Establishment of Historical
Consciousness in Israel in the Late Monarchical Period," *Zion* 60 (5755), 453–460
[in Hebrew].

education.[13] The Jews will therefore know the Bible, quote it when relevant (and when not), and draw conclusions for the present based on it, much as the Greeks did with Homer. This text was moving from being effectively restricted to the circle of the priests to being more widely known by members of the nation.

The next step is attested in the second of the two letters prefaced to 2 Macc. Written in Palestine (in Jerusalem, I would argue) early in the reign of Alexander Jannaeus,[14] this letter – addressed to the Egyptian Jewish community – is a strong assertion of the prerogatives of Jerusalem as the place chosen by God, as confirmed by miracles which took place after the return from the Babylonian exile. Nehemiah, according to this source, founded a library and "collected the books about the kings and prophets, and the writings of David, and letters of kings about votive offerings (2 Macc. 2:13)." Continuing and expanding on Nehemiah's activities, Judah Maccabee:

> also collected all the books which had been lost on account of the war which had come upon us, and they are in our possession. So if you have need of them send people to get them for you (2 Macc. 2:14–15).

Nehemiah supposedly established a library, which Judah restored after the upheavals of the persecution and the rebellion.[15] This library,

---

[13] Bickerman, *Jews in the Greek Age*, 169–171. Bickerman sees this as Ben Sira's innovative contribution to Jewish culture. This conclusion is attractive but is not obligatory, hence I have formulated the matter in less definite terms.

[14] This conclusion is very controversial. I follow the opinion of J. Goldstein concerning the date of this letter at the time of Alexander Jannaeus, but have reservations concerning Goldstein's suggestion of an Alexandrian provenance. Goldstein offers little proof for this assertion, while conceding the repeated emphasis in the letter on the centrality and holiness of Jerusalem, and on the achievement of the Hasmoneans. In his view, this letter was written by a supporter of the Maccabean house who probably was in Egypt at the time he forged it. Is this degree of complication necessary? See further Goldstein's extended discussion of the letter in J. Goldstein, *II Maccabees* (Garden City, 1983), 157–167 and in J. Goldstein, "How the Authors of 1 and 2 Maccabees Treated the 'Messianic' Promises," in J. Neusner, W. Green & E. Frerichs (Eds.), *Judaisms and their Messiahs* (Cambridge, 1987), 81–85. For a sympathetic discussion of Goldstein's conclusions concerning the letter at the head of 2 Macc. see J. Collins, "Messianism in the Maccabean Period," *Judaisms and their Messiahs*, 104. On the authenticity of the second letter at the head of 2 Macc. compare B. Wacholder, "The Letter from Judah Maccabee to Aristobulus: Is 2 Maccabees 1:10b–2:18 Authentic?" *Hebrew Union College Annual* 49 (1978), 89–133.

[15] As should be clear from the formulation, I am inclined to treat the claims concerning Judah's activities as more likely historical than the claims about Nehemiah's deeds. Furthermore, even if Judah himself did not do these things, I am certain they were being done during the reign of Alexander Jannaeus when the letter was written, as argued in the previous note. On this text see further S. Leiman, *The Canonization of Hebrew Scripture: The Talmudic and Midrashic Evidence* (Hamden, 1976), 29–30.

however, now seems to serve a new role. If Egyptian Jews have need of books they can now turn to the library for authorized copies. Egyptian Jews need no longer wait to apply, as imagined by the author of the letter of Aristeas, rather the Jews of Jerusalem initiate that offer. The Bible has thus taken one more step out, towards being the possession of the nation as a whole, as preserved and propagated by the Temple in Jerusalem, and its Hasmonean priests.

The nature of the Pharisaic chain of tradition as preserved in *mAbot* 1 is the next indication. As has been recognized by scholars since Finkelstein, one characteristic of that list is its total omission of priests. Even if some of the members of the chain are priests, that fact is not given prominence.[16] Nevertheless, these are the men who received the Torah as it was handed down from Moses at Sinai. Why are the priests missing? The omission cannot be accidental, but can only be explained as part of an anti-priestly orientation, as an assertion against what others might believe, as a claim that the Torah is the patrimony of all and not restricted to the priests.[17]

Consistent with these data is the tradition preserved in Rabbinic sources of the establishment of a system of public education at the time of Simon b. Shetah.[18] According to this source Simon introduced three reforms, one in the realm of marriage, a second concerning the purity of vessels, and the third that children be taught. The main focus of the passage is the reform concerning marriage, hence the change in education is not elaborated. It is therefore difficult to know the exact import of this tradition, and to judge its historicity. If the source has any value,[19] I would propose that its meaning is that it preserves some memory of steps taken to expand knowledge of the law at about this time. Education was no longer in the hands of the father and his knowledge no longer served as a limit on that of his children.

Testimony to the end of this process comes from both Philo and Josephus. Philo asserts that all Jews had expert knowledge of their laws, acquired as a result of Sabbath assemblies where a priest or

---

[16] M. Herr, "Continuum in the Chain of Torah Transmission," *Zion* 44 (5739), 43–56 [in Hebrew].

[17] See further Sussmann, "Research," 70–71.

[18] *yKet.* 8.11.32c.

[19] See the analysis by D. Goodblatt, of a parallel tradition concerning Joshua b. Gamla, "The Talmudic Sources on the Origins of Organized Jewish Education," *Studies in the History of the Jewish People and the Land of Israel* 5 (1980), 83–108 [in Hebrew].

one of the elders read the law and expounded it to the group (*Hyp.* 7.12–14). Josephus in *Against Apion*, perhaps drawing on Philo, perhaps on some mutual source, writes in much the same vein:

> For ignorance our lawgiver left no pretext. He appointed . . . that every week men should desert their other occupations and assemble to listen to the law and to obtain a thorough and accurate knowledge of it (2.175). . . . Should anyone of our nation be questioned about the laws he would repeat them all more readily than his own name (2.178).

The claims for profound mastery of the law to be found in these passages, as I have discussed elsewhere, may well be exaggerated.[20] Nevertheless, Josephus and Philo are both stating an ideal, one which has the power to shape reality in its image even if that reality is not completely coherent with the ideal.[21]

The discussion above has not been specifically formulated in terms of literacy.[22] When put in those terms, however, the conclusions are equally evident. When one of the characters of the long-ago past in the book of Jubilees is mentioned as having been literate, such as Cainan (Jub. 8:2) or Abraham (11:16), it is explicitly reported that he possessed this skill because he had been taught by his father. Jacob, the scholar and heir to the promises of the covenant, knew how to write, but Esau the hunter and warrior was illiterate (19:14). Levi, as noted above, was the only one of the sons of Jacob to order his sons to learn to read and write according to the Testament of the Twelve Patriarchs. It was he who inherited the family library in Jubilees. This situation should be contrasted with the comments of Josephus writing at the end of the first century CE. He writes that: "The Law orders that children shall be taught to read and shall learn both the laws and the deeds of their forefathers (*Ag. Ap.* 2.204)." The context in *Against Apion* is one in which the law is assumed to be the absolute standard by which all Jews live, hence if the law orders, that is what all Jews supposedly do. Here too, as above, Josephus is certainly exaggerating: Josephus himself, to note the most obvious point, described the weekly reading of the law (*Ag. Ap.* 2.175–178, cited above) as an event in which most participants *listened.* One person at a time,

---

[20] A.I. Baumgarten, "The Torah as a Public Document in Judaism," *Studies in Religion* 14 (1985), 19.

[21] See further *ibid.*

[22] In general, my assessment of the extent of literacy follows the revisionist and minimizing views of Harris, *Ancient Literacy.* See further above, Chapter One, n. 36.

as noted above, read the law according to Philo. Nevertheless, Josephus's testimony is an indication of a change which has taken place: literacy in Josephus's day and in his circles was more widespread than it had been several centuries earlier, sufficiently more extensive to allow Josephus to write as he did. Without seeking to quantify that change, there had been a significant rise in those able to read, of the sort which took place at a number of other key moments in the history of the West (see further below). Specifically, while there are many passages in the Bible in which parents are ordered to educate their children (see several of these noted above) there is no explicit verse commanding parents to teach their children how to *read*. Nevertheless, for Josephus, reading is so self-evidently the essence of education that he understands the verses ordering education of all as commandments to teach all children to read.

What circumstances fostered this change?[23] Here much can be learned from the studies of the phenomenon of the spread of literacy in general, chief among which is the seminal article of Lawrence Stone.[24] Stone suggests that a number of factors have combined over the past few centuries to produce a significant increase in the number of those able to read. While unwilling to assign a relative ranking to these factors, he notes that social stratification, job opportunities, Protestantism, sectarian competition, demography, economics and politics all played a part. A major driving force over the past two centuries has also been the direct intervention of the state, providing tax supported free schools.[25] The Maccabean example fits well into Stone's paradigm. It presents us with a case of sectarian competition much like that of Puritan Britain. The Jews of the period were becoming independent, requiring them to acquire the skills to run their new mini-empire, one of which is literacy.[26] Finally, there are the

---

[23] What might have been the role of the "scribes" known from Rabbinic literature and the New Testament in this process? As our information on the scribes is itself quite problematic, and the literature on the topic extensive, I omit a consideration of their possible role in the discussion below.

[24] L. Stone, "Literacy and Education in England 1640–1900," *Past and Present* 42 (1969), 69–139.

[25] *Ibid.*, 96–97.

[26] On literacy as a means of social control and repression see further Harris, *Ancient Literacy*, 332–333. The need for a literate corps of officials to run a state might have been particularly evident to a group that had lived for a little more than a century under the rule of the Ptolemies. On the place of a literate bureaucracy in the Ptolemaic empire see Harris, *ibid.*, 121–122.

Talmudic traditions noted above of the creation of some sort of system of public education. Obviously, literacy rates among Palestinian Jews in the Maccabean era did not even approach those of recent times. Nevertheless, it does seem reasonable to invoke Stone's analysis as explanation of the reasons for the jump in the number of those able to read, which did take place.

CULTURAL IMPLICATIONS OF LITERACY

The impact of learning to read is a phenomenon which has received extensive attention in scholarship of the past generation. Cultures are transformed profoundly as a result of this change, ostensibly merely technical in nature.[27] For example, oral cultures, where explicit comparison of statements in different contexts against each other is impossible, readily tolerate contradictions. Written culture is fundamentally different. Thus, only in a written culture could a concept such as verbatim memorization emerge.[28] There backwards scanning and careful contrasts are possible. As Ong writes:

> A sound dominated verbal economy is consonant with aggregative (harmonizing) tendencies rather than with analytic, dissecting tendencies (which would come with the inscribed, visualized word).[29]

Written cultures invest their members with new discriminatory powers. A feel for precision and for analytic exactitude is created and interiorized.[30]

---

[27] I have learned much from Havelock, *Preface to Plato*, as well as from W. Ong, *Orality and Literacy: The Technologizing of the Word* (London/New York, 1982). One of the earliest discussions of these issues is by J. Goody and I. Watt, "The Consequences of Literacy," *Comparative Studies in Society and History* 5 (1962/3), 304–345. Goody has returned to these themes a number of times in his career. See further J. Goody, *The Domestication of the Savage Mind* (Cambridge, 1977); *Logic; The Interface between the Written and the Oral* (Cambridge, 1987). Goody deals with a number of objections raised against his hypotheses in essays in the latter work.

[28] See further Goody, *Interface*, 188. Verbatim memorization is (was) regularly a characteristic of the curriculum of schools, while schools and their standardized order of study are unthinkable in anything other than a literate culture, *ibid.*, 234–241. In oral cultures there is great variety between versions of the same story as retold by the same individual at different times or different individuals, hence the notion of verbatim memorization is impossible without a standard written text to serve as the archetype.

[29] Ong, *Orality and Literacy*, 73–74.

[30] *Ibid.*, 104–105.

The intellectual context in which this new passion for precision will be expressed will vary from one culture to another. Thus in Greece, according to Havelock, the drive for exactness was a primary force in the intellectual drama which will lead to the birth of the Platonic theory of ideas.[31] In the Near East, this same impulse will lead to the rise of Babylonian and Egyptian science, based on recorded (i.e. written) observation.[32] In a Jewish cultural setting the results should be different. Reading and writing for ancient Jews, as confirmed explicitly by T. Levi 13:2–3, are intended to enable the reader to know and study God's law. If more widespread literacy in the ancient Jewish case produces results similar to those studied by anthropologists in other cultures, and yields a passion for precision, that desire for exactness among ancient Jews should find its expression in a commitment to studying the law, interpreting its provisions, and living by those interpretations as accurately as possible.

New readers have come to the Bible, interpreted it and become committed to living by it a number of times in the history of the Biblical tradition. Experience indicates that these were periods of considerable dissent, much like the Maccabean examples which are our focus here. This facet of the impact of the Bible on Puritans has been well recognized by Haller, who comments:

> The fact was, as experience was to demonstrate, that scripture, which had more poetry in its pages than law, worked upon men of uncritical minds, lively imaginations, differing temperaments and conflicting interests not as a unifying but as a divisive force.[33]

Compare also the remarks of C. Hill:

> The Bible is a large book, in which men find different things in different ages and different circumstances. In the sixteenth century newly literate people were reading it for the first time, with no historical sense and believing all its texts to be divinely inspired.[34]

---

[31] Havelock, *Preface to Plato*, esp. 194–233, 254–275.

[32] See further Goody, *Interface*, 73–75. Note that this effect results in spite of the difficulty of learning the writing system. In the Jewish case, to be argued below, written texts still required the supplement of an oral reading tradition (to supplement the purely consonantal written version, which did not always include a mark for division between words) to be meaningful. Nevertheless, by comparison to Babylonian examples, these facts did not deter me from concluding that literacy among Jews had the effects I am ascribing to it.

[33] Haller, *Rise of Puritanism*, 14.

[34] Hill, *Society and Puritanism*, 146.

Virtually inevitably, when people are inspired to live by the Bible they must adapt it in one way or another, and they draw very different conclusions from the book. This, as Ankori suggests, was the fate of Karaite pluralism, which fell a victim to the tendency of splinter groups to form around their particular version of "Biblical Truth," as can be learned from Qirqasani.[35]

True to the perspective proposed above, the reasons these results ensued must be elaborated. Granted that the encounter with the Bible on the part of the newly literate encourages them to determine to regulate their lives by this book and to be passionately devoted to its interpretation, but why are the interpretations favored by these new players in the game often ones which go counter to those promulgated by the existing mainline institutions? Why aren't the understandings of the Bible current at the time always sufficient for these new arrivals, why must they usually find their own? In other terms, why the need for such strong spiritual sustenance, which may lead members to find themselves outside the circle of most believers, who are satisfied with weaker stuff?

Perhaps the first point to remember, in answering this question, is that times when new readers come to the Bible, like the second century BCE under consideration in this study, were often eras of radical change, in which old interpretations lost at least some of their relevance. New readers of the Bible, not bound by tradition or habit to the old answers, might be best placed to recognize the need for new ways of understanding the text, which would meet the requirements of the new era. As it is never easy to convince people to change their minds, particularly about fundamental issues in which they may have a vested interest, the foundation for a conflict between the old leadership and the newly literate was well laid.

Furthermore, much depends on the attitudes of the old establishment and the new players towards each other. To begin from the vantage point of the establishment, at least two viewpoints are possible, represented by the responses of Joshua and Moses to the outpouring of Divine spirit in Num. 11:28–29: Joshua wanted the new prophets arrested, while Moses wished that all of God's people would become prophets. On the basis of his own experience, the reader of the Bible was supposed to understand how unusual Moses (the most

---

[35] Ankori, *Karaites in Byzantium*, 219–220.

humble man on earth, as the reader of Numbers will learn a few verses later, 12:3) was in his generosity. The old leadership was thus likely to be reluctant to allow the newly literate to take a place befitting their new status, to share the power which flows from control of the sources.[36] The foundations were being laid in yet one more sense for tension between the two groups. If the newly literate made themselves obnoxious to the establishment in the way they stated their claims or by means of the criticism they directed against the ways life was being run by those in power, the likelihood is even greater that circumstances will become such that the interpretations of the Bible discovered by the newly literate will regularly disagree with those held by the established authorities, the exegetical situation and social circumstances being mirror images of each other.

These processes, I suggest will explain the ferment surrounding Biblical interpretation of the Maccabean era. In particular, they will help clarify how movements composed of the better sort of people, the natural allies of the ruling elite, as shown in Chapter One, also came to disagree violently with the way religious life in the Temple and State was being run, appealing against those perversions of the truth to their understanding of what was written in the Bible.[37]

HISTORICAL ANALOGIES

The thesis for which I am arguing does not stand in splendid isolation, but (as alluded above) has a number of parallels in western historical experience. Three of the most important will be discussed in detail in this section.[38]

In the eleventh century European Christendom experienced a significant jump in the number of those able to read and write, as well as fairly wide scale outbreaks of heresy. Analyzing these movements, Brian Stock discusses at length the various attempts to understand the context responsible for the surge of heretical movements,

---

[36] On this aspect of the consequences of literacy see Stone, "Literacy," 71–73.

[37] Compare the conclusion above with Cohen, *Maccabees to the Mishnah*, 172.

[38] Goody's position on this point, in the essays collected in *Interface*, is not consistent. At some points he comments that written religion prevents sectarianism, and that education sometimes tended to eradicate heresy by introducing standardization, *ibid.*, 133, 242. At other places he notes the ways in which preserving the word of God in written form encourages innovation, or that the experience of education makes people argumentative, *ibid.*, 161, 242.

focusing on the difficulties involved in each of the major approaches.[39] As an alternative to these scholarly strategies Stock suggests that we focus on these heresies as textual communities, as groups which arose around specific sources mastered by the group's leader (at the very least). That leader, appropriately, usually came from the better educated strata of society.[40] The texts around which the community was drawn then served as points of departure, employed as the basis for a program of reform of social and religious institutions. Appeals for support were then made to the unlettered who, it was hoped, would share in advocating the reforms championed. This process was only possible because of expanding literacy and favorable valuation of the written word in the eleventh and twelfth centuries.[41] The path from increased literacy to formation of groups postulated by Stock is virtually identical to the one I propose for Second Temple Judaism. Two significant differences are (1) that in the Ancient Jewish case less is known about appeals for support to those outside the sectarian circle; the dominant tone in the evidence at hand seems to be one of disdain towards the "people of the land," or the "sons of darkness." At best they fall into the category of misguided innocents (see above Chapter One, at n. 43). (2) In the ancient Jewish examples leaders and their followers came from the better off strata.

The second instance consists in Puritan analogies.[42] At least part of the inspiration for the Puritan revolution was provided by the

---

[39] Stock, *Literacy*, 92–99.

[40] *Ibid.*, 90. One imagines that there must have been exceptions to this pattern in the Middle Ages, as there were in antiquity. Note, for example, the disciples of Jesus forming a group around a rustic, whose level of learning according to the standards of the "professionals" was regularly called into question. Was this really a textual community? As noted several times in this book, Introduction, n. 53, Chapter One, n. 19, Chapter Four, n. 35, and Chapter Six, n. 10, this is yet another sense in which the movement around Jesus represents an exception to the rule of ancient Jewish sectarianism.

Nevertheless, sometimes an unlearned person became the focus of a textual community. See, for example, Chiesa and Lockwood, *al-Qirqasani on Jewish Sects and Christianity*, 103 on Obadiah, also known as Abu-Isa-al-Isfahani, who although he was an ignorant tailor who had never been taught and could neither read nor write, produced books and pamphlets which his followers regarded as miraculous.

[41] See Stock's summaries, *ibid.*, 128 & 150.

[42] In candor, an important difference between the Puritan case and any ancient analogy must be conceded at the outset. Thanks to the widespread diffusion of printed books, it is estimated that there was one Bible for every fifteen people in the years from 1550 on. See Reay, "Popular Religion," in B. Reay (Ed.), *Popular Culture in Seventeenth Century England* (London, 1985), 105. The Biblical text – in any form – cannot possibly have been so widespread in ancient Judaism.

Protestant Reformation and its taking the Bible out of Latin and out of the exclusive domain of the clergy and tradition, placing it in the vernacular, in the hands of a much wider circle of readers. Confronting the Biblical text, with all its difficulties outlined above, the Puritans too found it a source of inspiration and power. The desire to know the Bible and live by it was whetted by the appetite for sermons, which was "stimulated by, as well as stimulating, the protestant emphasis on 'the priesthood of all believers,' on the importance of each individual striving to understand the Bible for himself."[43] This interest in sermons displayed itself and its consequences in many aspects of life, from the architecture of Puritan churches,[44] to the choice of careers,[45] to the nature of Puritan worship services.[46] A fairly direct line, in the opinion of contemporaries, led from sermons to sedition. Hill summarizes the situation as follows:

> Gilbert Ironside was more explicit than most about the reasons for distrusting preaching. Adulation of sermons made every youth straight down from the university insist on becoming a preacher as soon as he was ordained. So, "partly through ignorance, partly through impudence, faction is fomented, the people humored and misled."[47]

Sermons, in the opinion of another, have led people to be "possessed with strange errors in religion, and hurried by a spirit of giddiness of faction, of rebellion."[48] The Duke of Newcastle was equally explicit: "There should be more praying and less preaching, for much preaching breeds faction, but much praying causes devotion."[49] As Hunt notes, "many loyal members of the Church of England found the emphasis on preaching and Biblical exegesis both arid and *divisive*."[50] Finally, sermons could serve as a stimulus to political activity, even of the most extreme sort:

---

[43] Hill, *Society and Puritanism*, 80. See also Hunt, *Puritan Moment*, 94. Note the paradoxical circularity in Hill's remarks. The Protestant Reformation was one of the causes of a process of which it was a result. Perhaps some of that same paradoxical circularity existed in the relationship between sectarianism and literacy in Maccabean Judaism. Sectarianism may have lead to an increase in literacy, yet that same increase in literacy will intensify tendencies towards sectarianism.

[44] See C. Hill, *The Century of Revolution* (New York, 1961), 82

[45] See Hill, *Society and Puritanism*, 65.

[46] *Ibid.*, 71.

[47] *Ibid.*, 65.

[48] W. Nicholson, *ap.* Hill, *Society and Puritanism*, 71. On the connection between preaching and discord see also Hunt, *Puritan Moment*, 93.

[49] *Ap.* C. Hill, *Puritanism and Revolution* (New York, 1964), 284.

[50] Hunt, *Puritan Moment*, 148. The emphasis is mine.

Colonel Axtell, we are assured, was literally preached in to taking up arms for Parliament, since he and others like him "verily believed that they should be accursed of God forever if they had not acted their part."[51]

All this activity with its consequences is explicable as part of the response to the new contact with the Bible.

A third instance, albeit secular and not religious, which conforms well to the pattern which I am attempting to reveal and understand is that of the *obreros conscientes* in twentieth century Andalusia, as analyzed by Hobsbawm. Male illiteracy in that part of Spain in the early 1900s ranged from 50 to 65%, while hardly any women could read.[52] The *obreros conscientes* who formed the vanguard of the village anarchist movement which broke out were those who had learned to read, who read and educated themselves with a passionate enthusiasm typical of the newly literate. The lasting impression they made on their admirers were of people who were *"always reading, always arguing* (emphasis mine),"[53] glorying in the wonders of the modern scientific understanding they had acquired and were passing on. Those who first brought the good news of modern knowledge to their fellows, perhaps by reading newspapers to the illiterate, came to enjoy the almost blind trust of the villagers, particularly so when devotion of their lives to the cause reinforced this conclusion.[54] Admittedly, there is no evidence for the proliferation of rival groups in Andalusia as a result of these processes. Nevertheless, the links between literacy and the emergence of a loyal group devoted to a leader and his agenda are particularly clear in this example.

ANCIENT JEWISH EVIDENCE

The thesis argued above rests primarily on the logic of the case, on the overlap between the pool of the literate and of those attracted to sectarianism noted in the previous chapter, and on a number of historical analogies. It is speculative in the sense that while I can point to evidence for an expansion of the circle of the literate and

---

[51] Hill, *Society and Puritanism*, 77.
[52] Hobsbawm, *Primitive Rebels*, 75.
[53] *Ibid.*, 85. According to Wilson, one of the four conditions necessary for the emergence of sectarianism in the contemporary world is literacy. See the summary of Wilson's views above, Chapter One, n. 108.
[54] Hobsbawm, *Primitive Rebels*, 86.

for a context in which that development seems plausible in the second
century BCE, I cannot cite an ancient source which explicitly connects those changes with the rise of sectarianism. Origen's testimony
(quoted above, at n. 5), partial at best and not contemporary with
the phenomenon, in any case, is far from equivalent to the evidence
available to Stock, who can cite at least one contemporary witness to
the Milanese Patarene movement he studied, who explicitly connected
the rise of a sect with increased literacy.[55] Nevertheless, lest this book
blast off into the unexplored realms of uncontrolled speculation, it
seems appropriate to note a number of indications in the ancient
sources that the approach taken here is in fact supported.

For example, many years ago M. Greenberg suggested that the
first efforts to establish a stable text of the Hebrew Bible took place
during the Maccabean period.[56] Some would argue that the endeavor
should now be dated later than the Hasmonean era, perhaps during
the first century CE, in the light of what is now known of Qumran
Biblical manuscripts, but this disagreement is less significant than the
common conclusion that Jewish authorities, most likely at the Temple,
were active in establishing a fixed version of the Biblical text.[57] This
action is a first indication of the growing reverence for an authoritative text, crucial to the processes I am invoking in my attempt to
understand the growth of sectarianism.[58]

In addition, pseudepigraphy is conceivable only in a written culture.
Only there will the great works of the past be sufficiently revered so
that others will attempt to pass off their own creations as the work
of honored predecessors. Only in a literate society will the works of
the past be available in written form to serve as models of style and
organization to be imitated by later forgers.[59] Pseudepigraphy becomes

---

[55] Stock, *Literacy*, 166–167.
[56] M. Greenberg, "The Stabilization of the Text of the Hebrew Bible, Reviewed
in the Light of the Biblical Materials from the Judean Desert," *Journal of the American
Oriental Society* 76 (1956), 157–167.
[57] See further E. Tov, *Textual Criticism of the Hebrew Bible* (Minneapolis, 1992), 28.
[58] The nature of the fixed text chosen by the Temple authorities coheres well with
the means of adaptation by interpretation which was to emerge as victorious. The
text designated as authoritative was one in which the difficulties requiring adaptation were as prominent as possible, and all likelihood of interpolative editing was
reduced. It seems as if the editors were applying a version of the principle of *lectio
difficilior*: the most reliably genuine text is the one which presents the greatest challenges of apparent contradictions to those who intend to live by it. Thus the Torah
as we know it teaches us in Dt. 16:3 to eat unleavened bread at Passover time for
seven days, while in Dt. 16:8 unleavened bread is to be eaten then for six days.
[59] Stock, *Literacy*, 59–62.

a means of choice – by which one pays one's loyalty to the authoritative sources of the past, while adapting them as necessary by bringing their heroes back for an encore on the stage of history, in which these protagonists say exactly what need be said in the contemporary context in the opinion of the "real" author of the work.[60] The Second Temple period is not only the great age of Jewish pseudepigraphy, but the connection between those works and sectarian circles was particularly close: a large number of the pseudepigraphic compositions produced in that era were written by sectarians of one sort or other.[61]

In a similar vein, Havelock[62] and Goody[63] have noted that in oral cultures information on various topics is usually stored separately, in the various contexts to which it is attached. Only the mind of the *reader* brings these pieces together into logical order, and creates the context in which organized treatises on different topics are possible. Whether oral or not at some stage in its history, the Torah too is characterized by the fact that laws on various topics are scattered throughout, across various incidents and settings. Indicative of the move to a literate culture is one of the fundamental characteristics of the Temple Scroll: the desire to unite material on each topic in one place, as part of one consistent overall framework.[64] Yet another work in which this literate perspective finds expression is the Mishnah, organized into tractates on different topics, gathered together into orders. Finally, to conclude the discussion of this point, a fascinating indication of the extent to which things were still in flux even at the end of the era in question is provided by Josephus. When introducing his topical summary of Biblical law, he feels the need to explain to the reader:

> All is here written as he (Moses) left it: nothing have we added for the sake of embellishment, nothing which has not been bequeathed by Moses. Our one innovation has been to classify the several subjects;

---

[60] See further E.J. Bickerman, "Faux littéraires dans l'antiquité classique," *Studies in Jewish and Christian History Part Three* (Leiden, 1986), 209–211.

[61] See esp. M. Smith, "Pseudepigraphy in the Israelite Literary Tradition," in K. von Fritz (Ed.), *Pseudepigrapha I, Entretiens sur l'antiquité classique, Tome XVII* (Geneva, 1972), 192–227.

[62] Havelock, *Preface to Plato*, 185–186.

[63] Goody, *Savage Mind*, 68–69.

[64] See Schiffman, *Reclaiming*, 259. Note, in light of the previous discussion, that the Temple Scroll is one of the outstanding attempts at pseudepigraphy. Its style and vocabulary are modeled on that of the Torah.

for he left what he wrote in scattered condition, just as he received
each instruction from God. I thought it necessary to make this preliminary observation lest perchance any of my countrymen who read this
work should reproach me at all for having gone astray (*Ant.* 4.196–97).

Josephus, the sophisticated priest, who had tried out the three major
sectarian groups of his day, preferred the topical organization typical
of a literate mentality. His fellow countrymen, who might reproach
him, had not yet necessarily adopted the new outlook. Nevertheless,
a change incomplete in Josephus's day will soon become dominant:
the topical organization favored by readers will become canonical
with the publication and adoption of the Mishnah.

Yet one more indication of the move to a written culture is the
place of writing in texts such as Jubilees, the Damascus Document
and 1QS. Jubilees emphasized repeatedly the fact that certain laws
were written in heaven on high and hence were eternal (e.g. 6:24,
31). What was written and hence ordained by God was to be distinguished from what might be invented – even by an angel, not to
mention a human being – from his heart (6:35). Enoch was the first
human to discover writing, while both he and Noah wrote books
(4:17, 23; 10:13), books which were later quoted by Abraham in his
parting words to Isaac (21:10). The written library passed down from
Abraham and ultimately deposited with Levi has been noted above.
Finally, the righteous man was written down on high, attesting to his
status (2:20; 30:20–23; 36:10).

A similar situation prevails in CD. In at least three places (iii, 3;
iv, 4–5; xiv, 4) to be written down among the righteous was to attain
the highest rank possible. To be *written* among one's brothers was a
formula for becoming a full member of Qumran community (1QS
vi, 22). Conversely, to be registered on the bad list, or to to be struck
from the list of the righteous was a punishment (CD ix, 18; xiii, 12;
xix, 35).

The outlook in Jubilees, CD or 1QS is similar to that found in
organizations of the newly literate, educated out of subsistence agriculture, studied in Africa by Goody.[65] They too are proud of their

---

[65] Goody, *Interface*, 144–146, 204. For a non-academic, but wonderfully evocative
account of the process, as witnessed by Baroness K. Blixen in her years in Africa,
see I. Dinesen, *Out of Africa* (New York, 1972), Part Two, Chapter 3, 121–124. The
response of Africans to the written word, as she notes, was much the same as what
she had heard from very old people when she was a child concerning the spread of
literacy in Europe a century earlier. It was a chance "to catch the past by its tail,"

mastery of writing and the groups they form while back home during holidays (typically, a Young Men's Association)[66] stress their ability, and their desire to associate with their peers. Typically, these groups have a written constitution, and conduct their business by correspondence, going to all this trouble in spite of the fact that they are active only for short periods of the year. Analogous too are the Hellenistic associations analyzed by Weinfeld. A new member of the Iobacchi applied to join in writing, was registered in the rolls of the group, and received a *written* certificate attesting to his new status.[67] In all these cases, in Africa, CD, 1QS or the Iobacchi, the life of the group of the literate was run on the basis of a written code, setting forth the terms of agreement between members.[68]

Finally, and most important of all, there is the matter of *akribeia*. Fundamental to the argument above was the notion that a culture of readers recognizes and then internalizes the value of accuracy. I hypothesized above that it was this passion for exactness, applied by the Jews to the Torah, that played a key role in the process by which agendas were born. At least part of this argument, however, is more than mere hypothesis. Josephus's statements, which have been summarized elsewhere in this study (Chapter One, at n. 60) explicitly connect the self description of the Pharisees with their claim to *akribeia*, accuracy, precision and excellence in observing the law. The Dead Sea Scroll community also stressed its knowledge of how to live by the exact interpretation of the Torah, perhaps even aiming these claims polemically against other competitors. The passion for accuracy, which played a significant role in my reconstruction above, is thus reflected in the sources, a fact which I take to be a significant confirmation of the plausibility of the scenario which I have suggested.

---

ibid., 121. See in particular the story of the worker who received a letter, read to him by Baroness Blixen, recounting how his correspondent had "cooked a baboon," *ibid.*, 123–124. The context was such that it was clear that the writer's intention was to convey that he had "caught a baboon," yet no amount of reasoning could convince the recipient that the written word was false.

[66] Note the significance of the name chosen for the group. On the role of such groups in promoting national identity see further B. Anderson, *Imagined Communities* (London/New York, 1991, 2nd edition), 119–120.

[67] Weinfeld, *Organizational Pattern*, 22–23.

[68] In this, as in other instances noted in this study, Nehemiah was a forerunner of mature Jewish sectarianism. See the written covenant, sealed by the Princes, Levites and Priests who accepted it, in which he and other Jews joined, Neh. 9:39–10:39. On the significance of this passage see Smith, "Dead Sea Sect," 355.

The Other Side of the Coin

A full explanation of the contingencies which explain the rise of ancient Jewish sectarianism should also include a discussion of the negative case. That is, an adequate attempt to answer our question should also include an explanation of how changed circumstances, later in Jewish history, contributed to the waning of sectarianism. Thus, there is virtually unanimous agreement that in the aftermath of the destruction of the Temple, in the generations between 70 CE and the publication of the Mishnah, Jews learned how to live together without paying the price of sectarian divisiveness. Why was that achievement possible for Jews of that era, when it eluded their predecessors?

One piece of the answer to this latter question may be connected with the partial return to orality in the era of the Mishnah. The basis of the latter work was the oral discussion of the rabbinic academies, and in the view of many scholars the Mishnah itself was published and transmitted orally.[69] The very term "oral law," was coined and promulgated at Yavneh.[70] This, however, is a *secondary orality*, one which arises after a literate culture with its outlook has already been established.[71] Thus the Mishnah was organized topically, as was noted above. Furthermore, it was based on careful comparison of Biblical verses and a desire to draw out their halachic implications as carefully as possible. Abstract analysis predominates. All these characteristics arise only in the world of literate culture.[72]

---

[69] See Lieberman, *Hellenism*, 83–99.

[70] See J. Neusner, "Rabbinic Traditions About the Pharisees Before 70: The Problem of Oral Transmission," *Journal of Jewish Studies* 22 (1971), 1–18. See further L. Schiffman, *The Halakhah at Qumran* (Leiden, 1975), 20–21. Perhaps this orality was the contribution of the Pharisees to the Jewish world at Yavneh, according to the view that they had regularly kept their traditions orally, even in the era when the Temple was standing. On this aspect of the Pharisees see further J. Baumgarten, "The Unwritten Law in the Pre-Rabbinic Period," *Journal for the Study of Judaism in the Persian, Hellenistic and Roman Period* 3 (1972), 7–29. Against this conclusion note, however, the list of heads of the Pharisaic school in *mAbot*. List making, as has been discussed at length by Goody (see e.g. *Domestication*, 74–111), is yet one more characteristic of a written culture.

[71] For the term secondary orality and a discussion of some of its consequences see Ong, *Orality and Literacy*, 136–138.

[72] For the impact of literacy on legal systems and thinking see Goody, *Logic*, 127–171. The secondary orality of the Mishnah may be profitably compared to the blind Milton composing *Paradise Lost*. Oral devices such as a cumulative style can be found there, yet the work as a whole is based on extensive knowledge of written sources and a highly literate culture. See further Goody, *Interface*, 91–92.

Secondary orality, as Ong stresses, nevertheless has much in common with primary orality, one aspect of which noted by Stock may be helpful for this stage of our inquiry. Oral cultures, Stock argues, are characteristically small isolated communities, tied together by a strong network of kinship, with high group solidarity, an enhanced level of comradeship. Their reaction to the outside world is frequently one of fear and hostility.[73] Orality, as analyzed by Goody in the case of the Vedas (an instance analogous to the Mishnah in which a writing culture preserves its key sources orally), guarantees internalization, the complete molding of the individual in the image of the authoritative source, who may be required to transmit it orally as proof of mastery.[74] Moreover, the possibility of being autodidact does not exist in oral transmission: one must have a teacher, with whom one develops a personal relationship and ties of loyalty.[75] A cynic might remark that this situation assures the control of the master over his disciples; it guarantees the masters of these sources a standing in society from which they cannot be easily displaced.[76] If such is the nature of oral cultures the ability of the scholars of the mishnaic age to maintain a higher degree of coherence than their predecessors of the Second Temple era can be readily understood. Whether their secondary oral culture was an indication of a concord already existing on other grounds, or whether that oral culture helped create that unity is not particularly relevant. The nature of oral cultures and the coherence they encourage reflects accurately the character of the world of the Rabbis, where disputes exist but in which these disputes never lead to the formation of splinter groups. The return to orality in the Yavnean period, I conclude, is no accident, but inherently connected with the ability of the scholars of that era to agree to disagree.

LITERACY AND SECTARIANISM

Orality and literacy, indeed, have much to do with the process by which groups acquire their agendas, hence arise, as both the positive and the negative examples indicate. The spread of literacy, as one aspect of the rapid changes which took place as a result of the events

---

[73] Stock, *Literacy*, 16.
[74] See further Goody, *Interface*, 112.
[75] *Ibid.*, 114.
[76] *Ibid.*, 118–119.

of the second century BCE, is therefore a likely candidate for an important role in the quest to answer the questions which form the basis of this study. Its effects, when taken together with the nature of the Biblical source, which people studied more carefully than ever as a result of their newly obtained skill, helped create the circumstances under which groups generated the agendas with which they set out to change the religious and social world in which they lived. Some agendas for change were moderate, others radical, and thus some groups were able to maintain better relations with the established structures, while others came into greater conflict. Despite the relatively conservative background of the members of most groups of the time, as discussed in Chapter One, the analysis above helps explain the origins of sectarian radicalism, and specifies one kind of leaven which helped produce the sectarian ferment, whose history is the subject of this book.

CHAPTER FOUR

URBANIZATION AND ITS CONSEQUENCES

URBANIZATION AND LITERACY

The next link in the chain of explanations is a direct continuation of the circumstances discussed in the previous chapter. Literacy often goes hand in hand with urbanization:[1] perhaps those who learn how to read are not satisfied with a life of subsistence agriculture and therefore move to the city, perhaps the dynamic is in the other direction – those who move to the city for any number of reasons need to be able to read to survive there, hence acquire the skill. The reasons these two phenomena are associated with each other matter little, but the consequences can be momentous, leading to dramatic changes in the lives of these emigrants. That pool of newly literate people, experiencing the effects of literacy, as suggested in the previous chapter, are also the newly urban and thus subject to the changes engendered by their move to the city. The cumulative effect of these processes, as I will argue below, contributes to creating the atmosphere of sectarian ferment under investigation here.

REFERENCE GROUPS

One of the key manifestations of the social nature of human life is the need for reference groups, and the role these play as a means of orientation in a confusing world. Reference groups provide a sense of direction and meaning, without which we humans cannot exist.[2] Loss of reference groups, whatever the cause(s) may be, is a painful experience, leading those so afflicted to search to re-establish their relationship to their surroundings, and to discover a new frame of reference.

A move to the city leads to a loss of reference group. The effects of this experience on religious life, however, have rarely been uniform.

---

[1] See Bar Ilan, "Illiteracy," 46–61.

[2] See the classic study by W. Runciman, *Relative Deprivation and Social Justice* (London, 1966).

While migration from small to very large places of life strips some people of traditional beliefs, it causes others to redouble their devotion to tradition, especially to more extreme versions or interpretations of their faith. For the purposes of this chapter, my interest is in the latter group, and in their tendency to join sects.

To specify the process I seek to identify in greater detail, the disrupted and uprooted new urban population seek a master who can guide them in their new and confusing circumstances, thus making them receptive to the attractions of sectarianism. Perhaps their position is such that they see more clearly than others the senses in which the established leadership and its institutions do not meet the needs of the age; perhaps the established leadership is unwilling to allow these new arrivals to enter its ranks. Whatever the case, these new urbanites are especially prone to join sects, which provide them with the master they seek. When this dynamic encouraging the formation of sects is added to the processes at work among the same pool of people as a consequence of their being newly literate, the results are more fully comprehensible.

HISTORICAL ANALOGIES

The place of the city in the Puritan revolution has been well noted by scholars who have written on the subject. Thus Keith Thomas comments:

> The religious groups which came to exist outside the Anglican Church provided the same all-embracing framework. . . . It is not surprising that they were particularly successful in London, where they may well have functioned as a home-from-home for first generation immigrants, just as modern South African separatist churches have helped fill the gap created by decaying tribal loyalties.[3]

Discussing another religious revolution, in a different tradition, time and place Arjomand notes:

> In view of an incontestable historical association between urban strata and congregational religiosity, especially of the ethical type, the contemporary Islamic revival in the wake of rapid urbanization in the Islamic world should not have generated the surprise it has. The connection between congregational religion and urban life is at least as firm if not

---

[3] K. Thomas, *Religion and the Decline of Magic* (New York, 1971), 153. Compare similar remarks made by Hill, *World*, 40–42.

firmer in Islam as in Christianity. . . . Movement from the rural periphery into urban centers has been historically associated with increasing religious orthodoxy and a more rigorous adherence to the legalistic and puritanical central tradition of Islam.[4]

Writing as if by prescription to guide a study such as ours, Arjomand summarizes:

> Urbanization and the expansion of higher education in the fifteen years preceding the [Khomeini] revolution are the two dimensions of rapid social change most relevant to our problem. . . . Thousands of religious associations spontaneously came into being in the cities and in universities and acted as mechanisms of social integration for a significant proportion of the migrants into the cities and of the first generation university students. . . . There is nothing new about dislocated, uprooted men and women finding new moorings in religious associations, sects and revivalist movements.[5]

As Kupferschmidt has observed, contemporary urban Egypt has witnessed an upsurge in Islamic fundamentalism, as part of which:

> The number of new private mosques skyrocketed to 40,000, and numerous Islamic *gama'at* (societies) were established all over the country.[6]

To conclude this part of the discussion with an example from yet another corner of the contemporary world, researchers have noted that people of village origins who now live in the big cities are likelier than others to join the Moonies.[7]

The search for a master, noted above, can be found across the spectrum of historical analogies just cited. Thus radical Moslems in contemporary Egypt emphasize the duty of every Moslem to find an *amir*, swear allegiance to him (*bay'ah*), and to obey his commands thereafter.[8]

---

[4] S. Arjomand, *The Turban for the Crown – The Islamic Revolution in Iran* (New York, 1988), 91.

[5] *Ibid.*, 199. Arjomand's comments on the role of higher education are especially pertinent in view of the conclusion of the previous chapter. See further Arjomand, "Social Change," 92–101 & 107.

[6] U. Kupferschmidt, "Reformist and Militant Islam in Egypt," *Middle Eastern Studies* 23 (1987), 411. In Egirdir, a provincial town of 9,000–12,000 inhabitants in Turkey, with a strong tradition of toleration, the Tappers found that those few religious extremists in town were largely people of recent village origin. See R. & N. Tapper, "'Thank God We're Secular,' Aspects of Fundamentalism in a Turkish Town," in L. Caplan (Ed.), *Studies in Religious Fundamentalism* (London, 1987), 61.

[7] See Wilson, *Social Dimensions*, 255.

[8] See S. Zubaida, "The Quest for the Islamic State: Islamic Fundamentalism in Egypt and Iran," in L. Caplan (Ed.), *Studies in Religious Fundamentalism* (London, 1987), 41. For one case study of the career of a fundamentalist moslem in contemporary

As such their experience accords well with that of seventeenth century Puritans, who were also searching to find a master in the distressing conditions in which they were living. As Hill has commented:

> Professor Walzer has suggested that Puritan insistence on inner discipline was unthinkable without the experience of masterlessness. Their object was to find a new master in themselves, a rigid self-control shaping a new personality. Conversion, sainthood, repression, collective discipline, were the answer to the unsettled condition of society, the way to create a new order through creating new men.[9]

This was what they hoped to achieve through membership in radical religious groups.

The master and the agenda he and his movement supply fill the void created by the loss of reference group. To create such an agenda the master ought to be learned himself, but neither the possibility of leadership by a charismatic personality full of the spirit of God (as opposed to book knowledge),[10] nor that of sheer charlatanism can be excluded.

Contemporary research clarifies two further points concerning this dynamic. First, those searching are not necessarily satisfied with their first selection, moving from group to group before they settle down (see above, Chapter One, n. 49). Second, not all those afflicted with the ills of being uprooted in the city make the same choices. The latter phenomenon, in particular, is best explained on the basis of interpersonal networks. As Stark and Bainbridge stress, personal loyalty and attachment are much more important than ideological or religious commitment to a way of life at the earliest stages of choice. People join movements because of their friends, well before they fully adopt the life style of the new group, burn their bridges with past identities, or become convinced of the truth of the new ideology. Mormons, as Stark and Bainbridge comment, are explicitly instructed to develop extensive personal relationships with potential converts, long before they ever raise the subject of faith or lifestyle. Only after a strong personal bond has been established are they to attempt to bring their new friends into the faith. Experience has taught the

---

Egypt see J.G. Kennedy, *Struggle for Change in a Nubian Community: An Individual in Society and History* (Palo Alto, 1977), 69–169.

[9] Hill, *World*, 47–48.

[10] This alternative might explain the attraction of the earliest Christian disciples to Jesus, whose mastery of book learning was regularly called into question.

Mormons that this is one of the most effective methods of missioniz-
ing.[11] Each new member thus becomes a recruiter, helping to bring
any friends not yet in the circle into the movement, while the path
of friendship is the surest route to winning the hearts of those uprooted
and adrift, who are the likeliest pool of new members.

THE ANCIENT GRECO-ROMAN EVIDENCE

Non-political private associations flourished in the cities of the Hellenistic world.[12] Such clubs had been few in fourth century Athens, but
they now enjoyed enormous growth. They were primarily social and
religious bodies, who met in a temple or shrine of their own once or
twice a year; in many a founder was revered.[13] Even more pertinent
is the explicit testimony of Posidonius of Apamea (135–51 BCE)
concerning the situation in Syria of his day. Posidonius writes that:

> the people in the cities, at any rate, because of the great plenty which
> their land afforded (were relieved) of any distress regarding the neces-
> saries of life; hence they held many gatherings at which they feasted
> continually, using the gymnasia as if they were baths, anointing them-
> selves with expensive oils and perfumes, and living in the *grammateia*
> (local names for clubs, possibly designated by letters)[14] – for so they
> called the commons where diners met – as though they were their
> private houses, and putting in the greater part of the day there in
> filling their bellies – there, in the midst of wines and foods so abun-
> dant that they even carried a great deal home with them besides –
> and in delighting their ears with sounds from a loud-twanging tortoise
> shell, so that the towns rang from end to end with such noises.[15]

Posidonius considers the phenomena he is describing to be thoroughly
deplorable, but when one removes the heavy layer of his criticism he
testifies to urban associations thriving as a regular feature of life in
the prosperous cities of Syria of his day, contemporary with the period
of Jewish sectarianism.

---

[11] Stark & Bainbridge, "Networks of Faith," 1385–1389.

[12] I summarize here ideas discussed at greater length in Baumgarten, "Greco-
Roman Voluntary Associations," forthcoming.

[13] See W.W. Tarn, *Hellenistic Civilization* (New York, 1952, 3rd edition), 93–95. See
further Meeks, *First Urban Christians*, 31–32, 77–80, and Weinfeld, *Organizational Pattern*.

[14] On the explanation of this term see I.G. Kidd, *Posidonius, II. The Commentary: (i) Testimonia and Fragments 1–149* (Cambridge, 1988), 301. Note that Posidonius did not expect
this term to be meaningful to his reader, hence he explained it immediately below.

[15] Frag. 62a, b *ap.* Athenaeus, *Deipn.* 12.527E–F.

The flourishing of these clubs in the Hellenistic cities indicates that they met needs in the lives of their members. What might these needs have been? The Hellenistic era brought a significant new population to the cities, especially to the great centers such as Alexandria created in the wake of the expansion of the Greek world. In these new centers people who had originated in different corners of the world came together. The impact of these encounters can be clearly felt in the literature of the period, as the cultural life in these major urban areas set the tone for the Hellenistic world at large. In this atmosphere, in the aftermath of such extensive change, authors wrote nostalgically of the old ways, and of the "simple" life of the rustic. On the social level, private associations – often of people who had originated from the same place in the "old country" and of their descendants – provided a place of meeting and focus of orientation in the new urban scene. These groups, as assessed by A.D. Nock, were instruments of religious innovation, an opportunity for evolution of new religious ideas, and a place where people who had sensed a problem and discovered a common solution came together.[16]

Life in these clubs is reminiscent of the groups formed in response to urbanization in seventeenth century England or in the contemporary Moslem world discussed above, but there are also significant differences.[17] Thus the Hellenistic clubs were much more a popular phenomenon. They did not require a comprehensive commitment to a way of life according to Scripture (the Greeks had no revealed religious text, equivalent in function to Scripture for Christians or Moslems). The Hellenistic organizations thus occupied a far smaller place in shaping the lives of their members. These Greek associations might have a founder whose memory was revered, but this is quite different from the role of a master in a religious sect. Nevertheless, these Hellenistic clubs were contemporary with the Jewish groups that are my focus. The comparison of the consequences of urbanization across different cultures and periods, taken together with the direct evidence for the Hellenistic world, suggests that it is worth inquiring

---

[16] A.D. Nock, "On the Historical Importance of Cult Associations," *Classical Review* 38 (1924), 105. Note that according to the ideal description of Jerusalem and Judea in *Ep. Arist.* 107–111 the population drain to major cities, characteristic of Alexandria, with all its deleterious effects, had *not* taken place in Judea, perhaps on account of the prudent planning of the founders of Jewish life in the area.

[17] For a discussion of the similarities and differences between Greco-Roman private associations and the Pauline Christian communities, see Meeks, *First Urban Christians*, 78–79.

concerning the significance of the impact of urbanization and the role of the city of Jerusalem in the rise of ancient Jewish sectarianism.

The Ancient Jewish Evidence[18]

The sources provide a number of indications that ancient Jerusalem – the only city worthy of the name in Judea[19] – experienced substantial growth. This increase had begun even before the arrival of the Greeks, as is made clear by the comparison between the situation at the time of Nehemiah (when the population was so thin that people of the countryside had to be encouraged to live in Jerusalem), and that at the time of Hecataeus of Abdera.[20] One important cause of growth during this period was the higher birthrate, a direct consequence of prosperity brought by the relative peace under the Persian Empire.[21] Another important reason for the increasing affluence would have been the impact of technological innovations in agriculture.[22] This pattern of economic accomplishment and attendant rise in the birthrate will continue during the two centuries or so between the conquest of Alexander and the establishment of the independent state under the Maccabees. Prosperity due to peace and favorable economic conditions will be particularly prominent during the Ptolemaic era.[23]

The lure of the city, where even more money can be made by trade or other business activity,[24] will be a reason for people to leave

---

[18] I have discussed this issue in a preliminary way in A.I. Baumgarten, "City Lights – Urbanization and Sectarianism in Hasmonean Jerusalem", in M. Porthuis and C. Safrai (Eds.), *The Centrality of Jerusalem: Historical Perspectives* (Kampen, 1996), 50–64.

[19] See the comment attributed to Hecataeus of Abdera, *ap.* Diodorus, 40.3.6 (= Stern, *Greek and Latin Authors*, #11, 3; 1.28), that Moses founded many cities, including the one that is the most renowned of all, Jerusalem. In a similar vein, Josephus (*Ag. Ap.* 1.197 = Stern, *Greek and Latin Authors*, #12, 197; 1.39) quotes Hecataeus as writing: "The Jews have many fortresses and villages in different parts of the country, but only one fortified city." The authenticity of the citations of Hecataeus in Josephus' *Ag. Ap.* has been a subject of discussion since ancient times. See the comments and bibliography in Stern, *Greek and Latin Authors*, 1.23–25. See now also B. Bar Kochva, *"Pseudo-Hecataeus" on the Jews: Legitimizing the Jewish Diaspora* (Berkeley, 1996).

[20] Tcherikover, *Hellenistic Civilization*, 123.

[21] See Bickerman, *Jews in the Greek Age*, 70, 152. As Bar Ilan, "Illiteracy," 50–52 notes, prosperity and urbanization regularly go hand in hand.

[22] See S. Applebaum, "Jewish Urban Communities and Greek Influences," *Scripta Classica Israelica* 5 (1979/80), 160, n. 10.

[23] Bickerman, *Jews in the Greek Age*, 151.

[24] The acquisitive nature of Hellenistic civilization is well known. See for example, Applebaum, "Jewish Urban Communities," 159–160.

the farm for Jerusalem. Ben Sira, representing the conservative point of view he regularly embodies, laments the situation in his day in which farm work is despised. "Do not hate toilsome labor, or farm work, which were created by the Most High (7:15)," he warns his reader, thus indicating the status of farm work in the eyes of many.[25] As the life of the city is much more attractive, Ben Sira will remark a few verses later: "Do you have cattle? Look after them; if they are profitable to you, keep them (7:22)." Ben Sira thus agrees with Mattathias and his followers, who lived a generation or so after he wrote, who took not only their wives and children but also their cattle with them when they fled to the hills at the beginning of the revolt against the decrees of Antiochus IV (1 Macc. 2:30). Mattathias and his followers, however, represented the most traditional strata of Jewish society of their day in all respects (not merely religious). People who were more "up to date" might not have had such a high regard for cattle, or been so dependent on them.

Ben Sira was living at a time of change, when the old and new were coexisting. He therefore plays a Janus-like role, sometimes looking backwards wistfully to the past, at other times looking forward to the future. In the case of the city, he fills both parts simultaneously. Thus, while Ben Sira has just been seen reacting unfavorably to the increasing importance of city life, another set of verses in his work testifies to the opposite conclusion. In 38:25–39:11 the author reviews various ways of earning a livelihood, contrasting them with the life of the scribe/sage, and utilizing that contrast to praise the scribe. Farmers and different types of artisans are all considered, but only the sage attains wisdom and the respect it commands. In all this, the city is assumed to be the highest form of human organization:

> all these (farmers and artisans) rely upon their hands, and each is skil-
> ful in his own work. *Without them a city cannot be established*, and men can
> neither sojourn nor live there (38:31–2).

The route which brought Ben Sira to this conclusion may have been the following: since he identified himself with the scribe/sage, and since the latter finds his truest and highest place in the city to which he gives wise advice (see 38:33–34; 39:4–11), the city must be the supreme form of human association.

---

[25] This interpretation of Ben Sira 7:15 is supported by the comments of Di Lella-Skehan, *Wisdom*, 201.

One possible explanation for the favorable comments on the city is to be rejected: The sole reason Ben Sira reached these conclusions *was not* because of the process of hellenization which was taking place in his time. Views of the city, according to which it represents the pinnacle of human existence, can be found as far back as the Epic of Gilgamesh. The wild man Enkidu, brought into the city because of the harlot, learns how to be civilized there. When he is dying he curses the harlot and is then rebuked as follows (VII.iii. 35–39):

> Why, O Enkidu, cursest thou the harlot lass,
> Who made thee eat food fit for divinity,
> Who gave thee to drink wine fit for royalty,
> Who clothed thee with noble garments,
> Who made thee have fair Gilgamesh for a comrade?

All these were benefits of city life, which Enkidu had not known before he came to the city, and which he enjoyed only as a result of the actions of the harlot. Whatever the route might have been, Ben Sira's comments on the city, both those favorable and unfavorable, teach us about the increasingly large role it was filling in the lives of Jews of his day.

Alexandrian authors, nostalgic for the "good old days," as noted above, had created a literary tradition in which the virtues of the rustic life were praised. Something similar was taking place in Jerusalem by the second century BCE when the author of the Testament of Issachar[26] composed his portrait of Issachar as the simple, honest, farmer. Jews of that era were experiencing similar feelings to those of Greeks in Alexandria, hence this sort of composition was meaningful to them.[27] The position of Jerusalem as the city of the Jews may have been enhanced by its acquisition of *polis* status as part of the complex process connected with the decrees of Antiochus IV. However these events be understood, Jerusalem's place as the center of Jewish life was reinforced when Judah and Simon transferred Jews from Galilee and Arbatta to live there (1 Macc. 5:23).[28]

Jerusalem was therefore becoming a big city in local terms, far

---

[26] On the date and provenance of T. Issachar see above, Chapter Two, n. 65.

[27] On this aspect of T. Issachar see Bickerman, *Jews in the Greek Age*, 208–209.

[28] On population transfers, in the aftermath of military upheavals as causing an explosion in the population of Jerusalem at an earlier point in its history see M. Broshi, "The Expansion of Jerusalem in the Reigns of Hezekiah and Manasseh," *Israel Exploration Journal* 24 (1974), 21–26.

bigger than any Jewish settlement known in its vicinity. This conclusion, based on literary texts, can also be confirmed by archeological
evidence.[29] Jews were leaving farms to move there, and the feeling of
nostalgia for less complicated rural life was present. To the extent
that Hellenization was a factor in Jewish life of the pre-Maccabean
era, a most controversial question,[30] it should have been most advanced
in Jerusalem. It is therefore plausible to expect that urbanization
affected ancient Jews in ways similar to its effect on inhabitants of
seventeenth century London, or contemporary Cairo: the loss of reference group yielding a context in which groups formed around masters and their agendas, who provided a new sense of meaning to
rootless men. This, I propose, is what was taking place in Maccabean
Jerusalem.

URBANIZATION AND ANCIENT JEWISH SECTARIANISM

Fortunately, this suggestion about the role of urbanization in promoting
ancient Jewish sectarianism is not purely hypothetical. In considering
the provenance of those who joined Jewish sects in antiquity in Chapter
One, at nn. 20–24, I noted the special place of Jerusalem and other
townspeople. Even more important is the prominence of those who
were not born in Jerusalem among the first generations of leaders of
the Pharisees. Thus this group was apparently founded by the two
Yose's,[31] one of whom was from Jerusalem, the other from *Zeredah*
(north and slightly to the west of Jerusalem in Samaria). In the second generation, Joshua b. Perahya and Nittai of *Arbel* (in the lower
Galilee) were the chief Pharisees.

In addition to this direct evidence, ancient sources provide other

---

[29] See e.g. Josephus's description of the need to expand the defenses of Jerusalem,
War 5.142–155, reflected in the remains of the ever-increasing set of walls around
the city, as now better known from excavation. See e.g. S. Ben-Arieh, "The 'Third
Wall' of Jerusalem," in Y. Yadin (Ed.), *Jerusalem Revealed-Archaeology in the Holy City
1968–1974* (New Haven/London, 1976), 60–62. The growth of the city is revealed
also in the enlarged water supply, as well as the expanding necropolis. See further
G. Barkai, "Jerusalem of the Hasmonean Era," in H. Eshel and D. Amit (Eds.), *The
History of the Hasmonean House*, (Jerusalem, 1995), 234 [in Hebrew]; N. Avigad, *Discovering Jerusalem* (Jerusalem, 1980), 72–74. Admittedly, the greatest growth of the city
took place after the Hasmonean era, during the reign of Herod, *ibid.*, 81–83.

[30] See above Introduction, n. 121.

[31] For a discussion of the chronological implications of the list in *mAbot* 1, above,
Introduction, n. 59.

indications in support of the case being argued. First, one may note the term of disdain employed in Rabbinic sources to contrast between *haverim* (whoever these may have been) and non-members: "the people of the land (*am haaretz*)." The defining characteristic of these "people of the land" is their lack of interest in learning the Torah, and inadequately stringent observance of various aspects of Biblical law.[32] This term expresses perfectly the contemptuous attitude of the literate urbanite, who has been educated out of subsistence agriculture, and who now has higher aspirations and standards. Such perspectives are widespread among the ranks of the newly schooled in Africa, studied by Goody.[33] Those who employed this term of scorn for those "down on the farm," who did not meet rigorous standards of observance, were themselves likely to be among the newly urban.

Next, I propose to turn to the first chapter of *mAbot*. This choice is prompted by several considerations. First, as has just been noted, several of the key figures contained in the chain of Pharisaic tradition in *mAbot* were identified as coming from places other than Jerusalem, hence they indicate that the pattern of first generation migrants to the big city may have had an important place in the history of the leaders of the group who appear on the list. Next, while the list has undergone at least some revision over the generations – the most obvious example being the insertion of R. Judah I and his family – nevertheless, it still contains valuable information from periods well before the formation of the Mishnah. What will be discovered in looking at these passages is a new way of seeing familiar material, which looks different in the light of the discussion of the consequences of urbanization above. A number of expressions, consistent with my hypotheses recur. I cannot believe this to be mere chance.

Two themes appear repeatedly in *mAbot* 1, occupying a very considerable part of the whole. The first motif is that of the search for a master, whose importance in the lives of new arrivals in the city

---

[32] The term *am haaretz* has a long history, from the Biblical period into the era of the Mishnah and Talmud. Compare S. Zeitlin, "The Am Haarez," *Jewish Quarterly Review* 23 (1932/3), 45–61 and A. Oppenheimer, *The Am Ha-aretz – A Study in the Social History of the Jewish People in the Hellenistic-Roman Period* (Leiden, 1977), 1–22. Oppenheimer stresses correctly, in my opinion, that the *am haaretz* as the Rabbis knew him had no necessary connection with farm life and regularly lived side by side with the *haver*. On the other hand, Zeitlin correctly noted the origin of the use of the term in its meaning of "ignoramus," or "insufficiently scrupulous in observing the law" in its rural context.

[33] See Goody, *Interface*, 141–147.

was discussed at length above. This theme appears first in *mAbot* 1 in the maxim attributed to Yose b. Yoezer of Zeredah, the first of our non-Jerusalemites. He said: "Let thy house be a meeting-house for the Sages and sit amid the dust of their feet and drink in their words with thirst (*mAbot* 1:5)." This passion is equally explicit in another statement, attributed to Joshua b. Perahya, one of the authorities of the next generation: "Provide thyself with a teacher and get thee a fellow disciple (*mAbot* 1:6)." The term *rav*, which had been employed in the context of the relationship between masters and slaves by Antigonus of Socho (*mAbot* 1:3), has come to denote the leader or teacher of an association of free men who sets the course for them to follow. Unlike the master to whom a slave is sold, and who imposes his authority by constraint, if necessary, this new master is one a free man provides for himself (עשה לך רב): the subjugation of this disciple to the new type of master is voluntary. In the service of such a master one will also acquire a fellow disciple. Like the master, this fellow disciple will also be *created* by voluntary explicit choice ("create" being one of the meanings of Hebrew קנה, as in Gen. 14:19, 22). Thus, having found a master and a fellow disciple, a full reference group will be reconstructed, and meaning to life restored. The importance of a master, who will be a reliable guide to the proper way of observance is also stressed by R. Gamaliel: "Provide thyself with a teacher and remove thyself from doubt, and tithe not overmuch by guesswork (*mAbot* 1:16)."[34] The quest for fellow members and for a master, in other words for a reference group and for an authority who can provide it with direction and precise teaching on the way to observe the commandments, is explicitly expressed in these sources.[35]

---

[34] The desire to find a reliable guide to observing the commandments is also explicit in the description of those who volunteer to join the Qumran community in 1QS v, 7–13. The new member accepts the priests sons of Sadoq, keepers of the covenants and seekers of God's will, as his absolute masters, committing himself to live according to all that will be revealed to them. Effectively, the new member is accepting their authority not only for points of law already known but is also obligating himself to follow their rulings concerning points which will only become known in the future.

[35] In early Christianity, a movement whose patterns of attaining holiness were very different than those of the Jewish sects under consideration here, Jesus charged his disciples not to be called rabbi, father or master, as they were all brethren, and had only one Father in God, and one master in Christ (Mt. 23:8–10). A similar notion was expressed in Jas. 3:1. These were titles of honor in other movements, which Christians were to eschew.

Again, as in the previous chapter, I cannot believe these expressions, so consistent with my hypotheses, to be mere chance.

The second theme concerns the methods of recruitment on the basis of social networks, stressed by Stark and Bainbridge on the basis of Mormon strategy. Friendship is a means to conviction, and regularly precedes conviction. This idea is implicit in the tradition attributed to Yose b. Yohanan in *mAbot* 1:5: "Let thy house be opened wide and let the needy be members of thy household."[36] It appears again implicitly, in slightly different form, in the remarks of Shammai (*mAbot* 1:15), who advises "to receive all men with cheerful countenance." Friends and neighbors, good and bad, are the theme of the comments of Nittai the Arbelite (*mAbot* 1:7). Explicitly in line with the discussion above is the statement attributed to Hillel: "Be of the disciples of Aaron, loving peace and pursuing peace, loving mankind and bringing them nigh to the Law (*mAbot* 1:12)." By loving peace and pursuing peace, by *loving mankind*, one can *bring people near to the Torah*. Hillel too, I suggest, understood the importance of interpersonal networks as a means of recruitment, and advised his followers to utilize these means.

The significance of leaders and their followers, and of the reference group they assist in providing, can help explain one further aspect of the phenomenon under investigation here. Agendas, particularly halachic ones, are not that unique to individual groups, considerable overlap between the positions of different groups being common (see Chapter One, at nn. 126–136). If the only basis for sectarianism were the process which led to the rise of agendas, as discussed in the previous chapter, it would be hard to understand how and why so many groups arose?[37] Can these agendas be so decisive a force in the emergence of sects if that of one group is so similar to that of others? The paths which led to coalescing of groups around leaders, however, help fill the void. Halachic positions may be very few, hence agendas overlap, but the number of leaders is far

---

[36] Yose b. Yohanan, in *mAbot* 1:5, also expresses himself in a particularly harsh way against women. This suggests that the role of women had changed, as part of the overall upheaval that had passed over the Jewish people, and that women therefore needed to be warned to continue to play the roles tradition had assigned to them. See further H. Lazarus-Yafeh, "Contemporary Fundamentalism – Judaism, Christianity, Islam," *The Jerusalem Quarterly* 47 (1988), 37.

[37] On the large number of sectarian groups in the Second Temple period see Lieberman's comments summarized above Chapter One, n. 8.

less restricted. In fact, a cynic might maintain that the only limit on
the number of groups is the number of potential leaders present at
one time and place. The role of loss of reference group and of finding
a new frame of reference in membership in a sectarian movement
and in loyalty to its leader thus helps explain the multiplicity of groups,
a phenomenon which scholars might otherwise be hard pressed to
understand.

The Other Side of the Coin

As in the previous chapter, a consideration of circumstances in the
years after 70, when sectarianism waned, reinforces the plausibility
of the case argued here. Jewish life in the era after the destruction of
the Temple had urban concentrations in Judea and the Galilee, but
none on the scale of Jerusalem in pre-70 days. The typical Jewish
social context in the Mishnah was that of a small farm. The effects
of urbanization which helped contribute to sectarian ferment were
therefore less intense, which found expression in the decline in the
tendency of Jews to split into sects.

"Going Critical"

One consequence of the processes I have been considering must be
noted before passing to the next chapter. Once movements have
coalesced around a leader, an agenda and their supplement to the
Torah, they can then proceed to strengthen their identities. One set
of means to achieve this goal were the boundaries which were the
focus of Chapter Two, but additional methods of reinforcing identity included rituals, procedures to accept, punish or expel members,
and a regular ceremony of renewal of membership. As in the case
of boundary drawing discussed in Chapter Two, not every sect will
strengthen its identity in all of the ways listed above, with only the
most introversionist ones utilizing all the means just listed. As they
make the most extreme demands, but which are ultimately voluntary
in nature, it is no surprise that introversionist groups need a full
array of ways to bolster the identity of their members. Furthermore,
to the extent that a chasm exists between a sect and the main institutions of its society (the extent of this gulf will be different for a
reformist movement than for an introversionist one) an ideology can

now be elaborated to justify that division, as known most explicitly from the case of Qumran.[38]

The circumstances are now ripe and the raw material is now available to permit the creation of the practical and ideological aspects of sectarianism, as necessary in each specific case. Sectarian self definition, in the slang of another era, has the imminent potential of going critical. All it may require to take those final steps is some sort of push. Two factors which each in their own way likely supplied that impulse, will be the subjects of the next two chapters.

---

[38] See Watson, *Paul, Judaism and the Gentiles*, 40. In more extreme cases of schism, according to Watson, that ideology will be based on the techniques of denunciation, antithesis and reinterpretation. That is, opponents will be denounced as not meeting proper standards of behavior; sharp distinctions drawn between those "in" and those "out;" and the common tradition reinterpreted in such a way as to lay exclusive claim to its blessings for the schismatic movement.

For a brief discussion of the ways Watson sees these techniques employed by the Qumran community see *Paul, Judaism and the Gentiles*, 41–43. In the body of his book, in discussions of Paul, Watson sometimes writes as if these tactics had a life of their own, independently dictating the course of events, rather than viewing them as means employed by groups of people to help achieve ideological ends made necessary by their situation vis à vis other groups in the social or religious context.

CHAPTER FIVE

THE PURSUIT OF THE MILLENNIUM

ESCHATOLOGY AND SECTARIANISM

As was noted at the beginning of this study, sectarianism of the type under investigation here is endemic among Jews. Nevertheless, this ever-present potential is not always realized at heightened levels: sectarianism overflows in surges of intense activity, when it shapes whole societies or eras, separated by many years, often centuries, of relative calm when it may be present, but on a far lesser scale. As such, sectarianism is similar to eschatological hopes, also a constant in Jewish life as a result of the Biblical heritage, but also breaking out in waves of intensity and imminent expectation. Since the pattern of the two phenomena – sectarianism and expectations of redemption – is similar, I would like to ask whether the pattern traced by the wave of one overlaps with that traced by the other and particularly if so and if the overlap is frequent, whether there might be an inherent connection between these two waves. Some encouragement that this might be the case is provided by the fact that both sorts of movements flourish to an unusual extent at times of rapid change. This connection is acknowledged by Ankori, writing about the period which saw the emergence of Karaism:

> Indeed, messianism and sectarianism during the early Muslim era march inseparably hand in hand in an endeavor to remold the fate of the Jewish people and the heart of that people as well.[1]

As much as possible therefore needs to be learned concerning the pursuit of the millennium, as it has been experienced by Jews and others, in the hope that it will illuminate the context in which ancient Jewish sectarianism dominated the lives of Jews of the Second Temple era.

---

[1] Ankori, *Karaites in Byzantium*, 10.

THE TERMS OF THE DISCUSSION

Before beginning discussion of the subject, digressions on the use of the terms eschatology, messiah, millennium, apocalypse and their cognates are necessary.[2] The first three – eschatology, messiah and millennium, as these terms will be defined below – were items of faith which had the potential for assuming a definitive role in constructing movements, organized around these beliefs. Not all eschatological or messianic beliefs had such social consequences. Thus, if the end was taken to be far off or the messiah absolutely unknown, these tenets had little practical impact. Given the nature of millennial hopes, however, as will be defined below, they were regularly of great practical effect for those who held them. The last of these terms, apocalypse, is of a different nature. It is not an item of faith, but a literary genre. To dub movements "apocalyptic" may confuse more than clarify (see below, n. 11).

Let me begin with eschatology. I take this to be the term of widest reference, describing the belief in the coming of the final, irrevocable redemption of the world at the end of times, from which there will be no return to the bad old days. Visions of what these glorious new times would be like varied enormously.[3]

Some Jewish eschatological systems were messianic, others not. That is, some connected the eschaton with a specific human redeemer figure, dubbed the messiah, who would play a crucial role in the realization of these hopes. Accordingly, in the discussion below, the term messianic will be restricted to belief systems and movements in which a messiah had a role in the eschatological scenario. This concentration of the term messiah on one specific type of "anointed one" goes contrary to the Biblical evidence, according to which "anointed ones," were many, and some had nothing whatsoever to

---

[2] In the discussion below, I will use these terms in ways which adhere as closely as possible to the definitions proposed. Inevitably, however, when summarizing or quoting others, these terms may be employed with somewhat different meanings, which do not conform with my definitions. For another set of definitions of these terms compare R. Landes, "Lest the Millennium be Fulfilled: Apocalyptic Expectations and the Pattern of Western Chronography," in W. Verbeke, D. Verhelst and A. Welkenhuysen (Eds.), *The Use and Abuse of Eschatology in the Middle Ages* (Leuven, 1988), 205–208.

[3] See especially the seminal study of Smith, "Variety of Messiah Figures," 66–72. As was often the case in his career, Smith here had the distinction of asking the crucial question on which so much of later scholarship would revolve. See also above, Introduction, n. 1.

do with the redemption of the world. Nevertheless, this restricted usage seems so widespread as to require no further justification.[4]

As for millennium, technically, the term refers to a belief in the coming of a thousand year period somehow connected with (usually inaugurating) the ultimate cosmic redemption. Another sense, although etymologically incorrect, has, however, become widespread and is adopted here: millennial expectations are a sub-group of eschatological ones. They set forth the belief in the *imminent* commencing of the eschatological era, leading to ultimate collective salvation.[5] As such, millennial expectations share the beliefs in national and/or cosmic redemption based on the Biblical tradition; what makes them special is their conviction that these events are to occur in the *immediate* future.[6] Since the scenario of salvation will begin to unfold imminently, these beliefs regularly call forth movements, with agendas for action in the last days of the old world, and plans for the new one, soon to be born.

This definition of millennialism leaves two points deliberately vague. First, it does not specify a particular notion of how the world will be organized in those great days as a necessary feature of millennialism. That is, for example, I would not require that a system assert that all will be equal at that time in order to be considered millennial. Furthermore, this definition does not limit millennialism to beliefs or movements which prescribe some specific way of behavior in the here and now, in anticipation of imminent salvation. In contrast to others who have studied these issues,[7] I believe that the phenomenon can be fully understood only when the focus includes a wide variety

---

[4] This is one of the most persistent themes of the collections of essays published as J. Neusner, W. Green & E. Frerichs (Eds.), *Judaisms and their Messiahs* (Cambridge, 1987) and J. Charlesworth (Ed.), *The Messiah – Developments in Earliest Judaism and Christianity* (Minneapolis, 1992). Cf. Collins, *Scepter and Star*, 11–14, 31–34.

[5] This definition is largely inspired by Y. Talmon, "Millenarian Movements," *Archives Européennes de Sociologie* 7 (1966), 159.

[6] See further S.R. Isenberg, "Millenarism in Greco-Roman Palestine," *Religion* 4 (1974), 35, 44, n. 25.

[7] See e.g. S. Rayner, "The Perception of Time and Space in Egalitarian Sects: A Millenarian Cosmology," in M. Douglas (Ed.), *Essays in the Sociology of Perception* (London, 1982), 248. Rayner defines millenarianism by three characteristics: (1) the conviction that the present age is to be ending shortly; (2) the conviction that the new epoch will be established by the external intervention of some powerful agency; (3) the conviction that all men ought to be recognized as moral equals. In insisting on the third point as essential to millenarianism, Rayner and others, in my view, have had their field of vision overly and unnecessarily narrowed by studies such as N. Cohn, *The Pursuit of the Millennium* (London, 1957).

of visions of the glorious end and a broad range of prescriptions for behavior in the last days of the unredeemed world. This flexibility in definition will permit recognition of the full extent to which people of differing social and economic background, or varying religious outlook, have been swept up in enthusiastic anticipation of an imminent grand finale. It will also allow seeing that more than one type of answer has been offered over the ages to the question of how people ought to behave on the eve of salvation.[8]

As defined above, millennial and messianic often overlap; many messianic movements may also be millenarian. As implied in the discussion above, however, such an overlap is neither pervasive nor self-evident enough to permit collapsing the two categories into one.

When millennialism is defined as proposed above, it shares much with apocalyptic texts and the circles which produced the latter. Apocalypses are revelations concerned with two principal issues: (1) the removal of evil from man and the world, and (2) the achievement of the ideal humanity.[9] All this is usually expected to occur in the immediate future, hence the content of apocalyptic texts has much in common with millennial beliefs.[10] In apocalypses, however, these expectations are elaborated by means of a vision of the heavens.[11] This interest in heavenly mysteries made apocalypses different: they

---

[8] See e.g. K. Burridge, *New Heaven, New Earth: A Study of Millenarian Activities* (New York, 1969), 167:

> Knox's remarks concerning the alterations of scandal and rigorism characteristic of enthusiastic movements are not simply good history. The two go together, are integral parts of a transition process in which the new rules are still experimental and uncertain. . . . It could be argued that orgies of sexual promiscuity . . . and the high idealism often connoted by the release from all desire are polar opposites. But the fact remains that both meet in precisely the same condition: that of no obligation.

[9] See J. Bloch, *On the Apocalyptic in Judaism* (Philadelphia, 1952), 17.

[10] On the thin boundary which sometimes divides between apocalyptic and millennial hopes, see further A. Segal, "Conversion and Messianism: Outline for a New Approach," in Charlesworth, *The Messiah*, 297.

[11] See K. Koch, "What is Apocalyptic? An Attempt at a Preliminary Definition," in P. Hanson (Ed.), *Visionaries and their Apocalypses* (Philadelphia, 1983), 25: "(Apocalyptic) writings are dominated by an *urgent expectation* of the impending overthrow of all earthly conditions *in the immediate future* (emphasis Koch's)." For a more recent and more elaborate definition, see J.J. Collins, "Early Jewish Apocalypticism," *Anchor Bible Dictionary* (New York, 1992), 1.283:

> apocalypse is a genre of revelatory literature . . . in which a revelation is mediated by an otherworldly being to a human recipient . . . an apocalypse envisages eschatological salvation and involves a supernatural world . . . an apocalypse is intended to interpret present earthly circumstances in the light of the supernatural

had a mystical side, as a result of which they also encompassed speculative material treating heavenly secrets, such as cosmography, ange-
lology and cosmogony, while some apocalyptic texts concentrated on
pietistic, moral preaching, or what M. Hengel has called "higher
wisdom through revelation."[12] Nevertheless, apocalypses are sufficiently
millenarian to enter the discussion below fairly frequently.

Two Types of Millennial Movements

Millennial studies have enjoyed a certain popularity in the past decades, as a result of which these beliefs have lost their association
with the lunatic fringe and are now understood as a serious response
(in part, at the very least) to specific political, religious or social situations.[13] Visions of ultimate salvation have become recognized as a
valuable source of insight, in which the anguish of the authors at
contemporary conditions is being expressed. As such, they can teach
us much about what troubled these authors in their contemporary
world.[14] Research on millennial hopes has, however, regularly stressed
one conclusion. These aspirations, scholars assert, are normally found
among those who are oppressed or disadvantaged in some sense of
those terms. Thus Burridge begins his study with a quote from
Chinnery and Haddon which explains that:

> the weakening or disruption of the old social order may stimulate new and
> often bizarre ideals. . . . Communities *that feel themselves oppressed* anticipate
> the emergence of a hero who will restore their prosperity and prestige.[15]

---

world and of the future, and to influence both the understanding and behavior
of the audience by means of divine authority.

On the apocalyptic genre, in addition to the works cited above see also M. Stone,
"Apocalyptic Literature," in Stone, *Jewish Writings of the Second Temple Period*, 383–
441; Rowland, *Open Heaven*; Collins, *Apocalyptic Imagination*; J.J. Collins and
J. Charlesworth (Eds.), *Mysteries and Revelations – Apocalyptic Studies since the Uppsala Colloquium* (Sheffield, 1991). These authors differ on the extent to which one should be
strict in using apocalyptic as a designation for a genre of literature and nothing else.

[12] Hengel, *Judaism and Hellenism*, 1.210. The quest for wisdom through revelation
in apocalyptic texts is a point stressed from the outset by Rowland, *Open Heaven*, 2.
See also Stone, "Apocalyptic Literature," 383–384.

[13] In general, one should beware of dismissing movements as being part of the
lunatic fringe. See above, Introduction, nn. 47 and 124. In a similar vein see
M. Douglas, *Natural Symbols* (New York, 1982, 2nd edition), xv. See also Y. Talmon,
"Millennial Movements," 192–193.

[14] See Chapter One, n. 104.

[15] E. Chinnery and A. Haddon, "Five New Religious Cults in British New Guinea,"

Burridge will elaborate, specify and qualify the senses in which he understands these ideas throughout his work,[16] but his fundamental commitment to understanding millenarian hopes as a result of oppression is unaffected.

Much the same is true of the view of Tuveson,[17] who sees millennial hopes among Christians as part of their Jewish heritage, especially meaningful in the years of their persecution, and then tapering off when their movement becomes the dominant religion of the Roman world.[18] Millennial thought, according to Tuveson, will be revived at the time of the Protestant Reformation, but that will be as part of an attempt to understand why things had gone so wrong and now needed to be set right, a process which the reformers believed was finally taking place in their time.[19] Tuveson recognizes that there was what he calls an optimistic millennialism in the seventeenth century,[20] but he is little interested in exploring the situations which helped produce those views and focuses instead on the main theme of his book – the connection between millennial thought and the idea of progress.[21] Nowhere in the book, in sum, is there more than a hint that anything but despair can promote millennial hopes.

A similar conclusion can be found in the analysis of Worsley. Confronted by the fact that the leaders of some millenarian groups were of upper class origin, he nevertheless remained "unrepentant" in his conviction that millenarian movements which have been historically important were movements of the disinherited.[22] The same view can be found in the work of John Gager, who, apparently appealing to the research of Aberle on the connection between millenarianism and relative deprivation,[23] concedes that relative deprivation is sufficient to call forth millenarianism.[24]

Y. Talmon's conclusions are no different. She too insists on viewing millennial groups as the result of despair. As she summarizes matters:

The Hibbert Journal 15 (1917), 455, as quoted by Burridge, *New Heaven, New Earth*, 3.

[16] See e.g., his discussion of Jainism, *New Heaven, New Earth*, 86–96.

[17] E.L. Tuveson, *Millennium and the Utopia* (New York, 1964).

[18] *Ibid.*, 14–21.

[19] *Ibid.*, 29–30.

[20] *Ibid.*, 80.

[21] *Ibid.*, 70.

[22] P. Worsley, *The Trumpet Shall Sound: A Study of "Cargo" Cults in Melanesia* (New York, 1968, 2nd edition), xlii.

[23] D. Aberle, "A Note on Relative Deprivation Theory as Applied to Millenarian and other Cult Movements," in S. Thrupp (Ed.), *Millennial Dreams in Action* (The Hague, 1962), 209–214.

[24] Gager, *Kingdom and Community*, 22, 95–96.

"millenarism is born out of great distress coupled with political help-lessness."[25] Y. Talmon is reluctant to reduce millenarism to class inter-est, and she acknowledges the presence of a frustrated secondary elite among the leaders of these movements.[26] She realizes that the Sabbatean example is one in which Jews who lived in comparative peace participated; some who were well off even joined enthusiasti-cally.[27] Nevertheless, when summarizing her position, she continues to write in terms of "precipitating crises."[28]

A final indication of this mindset among scholars is provided by the introduction by S. Thrupp to her collection *Millennial Dreams in Action*. At least one essay in that volume – the study of the Savonarola movement by Weinstein, to be discussed more fully below – does not fit the pattern of millennial hopes flourishing among the oppressed. Nevertheless, the implications of that essay are entirely overlooked by Thrupp when summarizing the results of the papers,[29] and her theory is unaffected by the facts.[30]

From a Jewish perspective these conclusions have much to recom-mend them. As we learn from *mSota* 9:15:

> With the footprints of the Messiah presumption shall increase and dearth reach its height . . . the empire shall fall into heresy and there shall be none to utter reproof. . . . The face of this generation is as the face of a dog and the son will not be put to shame by his father.

Nevertheless, I find this scholarly consensus unsatisfying for two prin-cipal reasons. First, and less important, is the emphasis on relative

---

[25] Y. Talmon, "Millennial Movements," 185.

[26] *Ibid.*, 186–187.

[27] *Ibid.*, 190–191.

[28] *Ibid.*, 192.

[29] See S. Thrupp, "A Report on the Conference Discussion," in S. Thrupp (Ed.), *Millennial Dreams in Action* (The Hague, 1962), 26–27. In commenting on Weinstein's paper, *ibid.*, 21, Thrupp notes the connection between the Savonarola movement and Joachite prophecies, as well as Savonarola's appeal to civic patriotism and naive self-glorification, but does not mention that all this was called forth, according to Weinstein, by very different circumstances than those found in most other millennial movements analyzed in the volume.

[30] On theory dominating facts see T.S. Kuhn, *The Structure of Scientific Revolutions* (Chicago, 1970, 2nd edition), 62–65. See also the now classic discussion of this point in L. Fleck, *Genesis and Development of a Scientific Fact* (Chicago/London, 1979), 27–38. As Fleck and Kuhn make clear, anomaly which the paradigm accepted by the scientific community cannot explain is usually either resisted or overlooked. Fleck, *Genesis and Development*, 30, cites the example of the orbital motion of Mercury as related to Newton's laws: "Experts in the field were aware of it, but it was concealed from the public because it contradicted prevailing views."

deprivation. I find that notion so vague as to be close to useless as an explanation of why millenarian hopes flourish in certain circumstances. Anyone, anywhere, I would maintain, can always feel relatively deprived by comparison to someone else in some other place. If that is the case, however, what use is relative deprivation in explaining why millenarian movements emerge at specific times and places among particular groups? As Harrison has remarked:

> As it is, the theory of relative deprivation (like the theory of stress and strain) is in danger of accounting for everything and nothing. Almost every millenarian, one suspects, might be shown to be relatively deprived in some way. But why should he or she react to deprivation by becoming a millenarian, and not something else remains obscure.[31]

Even more pertinent are the comments of Rayner:

> The net of relative deprivation is being cast so wide as to render it logically vacuous as a general explanation of millenarianism. . . . Relative deprivation does not stand the test of the negative case where it exists without producing millenarian activity. In this case, relative deprivation may produce a variety of non-millenarian responses. . . . On the other hand, relative deprivation may produce no coherent movement at all, whilst some forms of utopian activity may appeal to members of society who cannot be usefully or sympathetically described as relatively deprived in any sense.[32]

More importantly, however, the focus on millenarianism among the dispossessed overlooks an important group of historical examples which

---

[31] Harrison, *The Second Coming*, 222. Harrison's comment is especially significant because of his general allegiance to the notion of relative deprivation and dependence on authors for whom this notion is central, stated at the outset of his work, 11: "Certain socio-economic factors and a situation in which unusual distress, anxiety, and feelings of relative deprivation can develop are also associated with the appearance of prophets and millenarian movements – and may indeed be necessary conditions for its emergence."

For another statement of doubts about the adequacy of explanations based on relative deprivation see also Schwartz, *The French Prophets*, 216: "Whatever alternatives I propose, I am not the hunter of a wounded animal: I have not assumed that millenarian beliefs are the product of spiritual malaise, socioeconomic deprivation or psychological festering."

I can only guess that Schwartz came to this conclusion, at least in part, because of his analysis of the background of the people he studied, on which see his concluding remarks, *ibid.*, 219–233.

[32] Rayner, "Millenarian Cosmology," 251. Rayner's own attempt to understand these movements is based on Douglas's notions of grid and group. As Rayner does not explore the possibility that the impulse to millenarian activity can be provided by a victory his theoretical comments are not particularly helpful for my endeavor.

indicate the existence of a second route leading people to hopes of imminent divine redemption. Weinstein's essay on the Savonarola movement in the Thrupp volume is a convenient place to start. As Weinstein notes, "Here is a case of millenarianism that did not arise out of the protests of the poor and cannot be explained by economic crisis."[33] Instead, Weinstein proposes to understand the results in other terms:

> As Savonarola emerged as a political leader his prophecy and his doctrine underwent fundamental transformations. Right up to the time of the Medici expulsion he had continued to foretell disaster for Florence. ... After the revolt, however, ... [he] became much more optimistic about the future of Florence. ... The events of those crucial days seem to have persuaded him that Florence was chosen to lead the way to reform. ... The French invasion was the opening of the fifth age of the world, the age of Antichrist and of the universal conversion to Christianity. Both his own mission and the Florentine revolt, he now saw, were part of God's plan.[34]

In other words, millenarian hopes – *particularly the belief in imminent salvation* – were encouraged by a *victory which convinced Savonarola and his followers that God's plans for redeeming the world must now be in the final stages.*

I find significant confirmation for my approach in a study of medieval Jewish messianism written a number of years ago by G.D. Cohen.[35] Cohen begins by noting that medieval Sephardi Jews experienced a number of messianic movements, while their Ashkenazi counterparts did not encounter a single case of a messianic movement or pseudo-messiah until the beginning of the sixteenth century.[36] Sephardi messianism, Cohen insists, was not the quirk of a few cranks or crackpots, and must be taken seriously.[37] Ashkenazi Jews, by contrast, were

---

[33] D. Weinstein, "The Savonarola Movement in Florence," in S. Thrupp (Ed.), *Millennial Dreams in Action* (The Hague, 1962), 187.

[34] *Ibid.*, 194. Weinstein elaborates these themes in greater details in his monograph, *Savonarola and Florence* (Princeton, 1970), esp. 114–116. While Weinstein denies the role of economic crisis in producing the results at Florence, he does insist on the effect of a political revolution in understanding the events, *Savonarola*, 33.

[35] G.D. Cohen. "Messianic Postures of Ashkenazim and Sephardim," *Studies of the Leo Baeck Institute* (Ungar, 1967), 117–156. I owe my knowledge of this article to a suggestion of Prof. M. Lockshin of York University, to whom I am most grateful for the reference. On the medieval Christian side see B. McGinn, *Visions of the End: Apocalyptic Traditions in the Middle Ages* (New York, 1979), esp. his introductory remarks, 28–30, of which the rest of the book is an illustration.

[36] Cohen, "Messianic Postures," 122–123.

[37] *Ibid.*, 153.

free of such movements, but did engage in speculation about when the Messiah would come as part of their exegesis of the Bible. Their dates for his arrival, however, were regularly far in the future, well beyond the lifetimes of those proposing these interpretations. Their activities in this vein were therefore the "very antithesis of millenarist excitation."[38] Most important for our purposes are the social conclusions Cohen draws from his data:

> Contrary to popular impression, there is no discernable connection between persecution and messianic movements. Jewish messianic movements were not "the religion of the oppressed".... Active messianism or quiescence must have derived from sources other than political or economic.[39]

Cohen therefore asks: "What in Jewish culture oriented one group to intellectual or physical activism and the other to basic passivity?"[40] His answer is appropriately nuanced, and concentrates on aspects of medieval Jewish life, not particularly relevant to our topic here. One factor which he notes touches directly on the previous discussion: "the political successes of Jews in Spain must have whetted the appetites of the elite for even further conquests."[41] That is, as I have been arguing above, one can enter the palace of millenarian hopes through a door over whose portals the words success or victory are inscribed.

To consider a non-Jewish case, millenarian ideas in seventeenth century Britain, as Lamont has shown, were quite widespread:[42]

> The philosophical assumptions (though not the political conclusions drawn from them) of Fifth Monarchy men were acceptable to the orthodox mainstream of religious thought of the time ... our concern

---

[38] *Ibid.*, 127.

[39] *Ibid.*, 143.

[40] *Ibid.*, 144.

[41] *Ibid.*, 146. Note that Cohen reaches this conclusion in spite of the significance of *mSota* 9:15, quoted above. Compare the hopes for redemption sparked by the Moslem conquests of the Roman empire. While these hopes were ultimately to be dashed, they are another example of expectations of salvation emerging as a result of a victory. See further B. Lewis, "An Apocalyptic Vision of Islamic History," *Bulletin of the British School of Oriental and African Studies* 13 (1950), 308–338, esp. 323. In theological terms, Maimonides' vision of the messianic age is also one in which the messiah proves his right to the title by a series of victories.

[42] I have selected scholars who discuss the prevalence of these ideas before the latter half of the seventeenth century when a sense of failure and bitterness began to prevail, lest these examples be taken as an opportunity for reintroducing the notion of relative deprivation as the cause of millenarian movements.

is with a quieter sort of men; men who were no less millenarian but who did not see why the forthcoming end of the world should mean the forthcoming end of traditional political allegiances. Their millenarian faith was implicit; there was no reason why it should be made explicit. For that reason it is extraordinarily difficult to track down. This study is an attempt to hunt for this subtler form of millenarianism, but the quarry is elusive.[43]

Furthermore, there were certain periods when millenarian aspirations were particularly prominent. As Keith Thomas writes:

> It is hard to say for certain just why this brief but notable shift from passive to active millenarianism should have occurred during the Interregnum. Probably more important than the effects of high prices and other economic hardships . . . was the apocalyptic sense generated by an awareness of living in a time of unprecedented political change. . . . It also accounts for the conviction held by so many of the Civil War sects that the period in which they lived was somehow the climax of human history, the era for which all previous events had been mere preparation. For the Fifth Monarchy men it was above all the execution of King Charles which left the way open for King Jesus.[44]

In a similar vein Christopher Hill notes that:

---

[43] W. Lamont, *Godly Rule: Politics and Religion 1603–60* (London, 1969), 19, who shows at length the ways in which millenarian beliefs in seventeenth century Britain were shared, while being reinterpreted at the same time in varying ways, by members of different strata of society. This aspect of Lamont's work provoked serious criticism. See B.S. Capp, "*Godly Rule* and English Millenarism," *Past and Present* 52 (1971), 106–117, and Lamont's response, "Richard Baxter, The Apocalypse and the Mad Major," *Past and Present* 55 (1972), 68–90. In my opinion, Lamont's response is convincing.

Lamont's thesis is also confirmed by studies of other millenarian movements which show that their supporters and members come from a wider social range than one might expect. See, for example, Harrison's summary, *The Second Coming*, 221; G. Shepperson, "The Comparative Study of Millenarian Movements," in S. Thrupp (Ed.), *Millennial Dreams in Action* (Hague, 1962), 49. Cf. Hobsbawm, *Primitive Rebels*, 57 who argues that members of millenarian groups totally reject the established world as it is known. A situation such as that proposed by Lamont, in which members of the upper classes would share in millenarian beliefs while interpreting them in ways that would not conflict with their positions of power, would therefore be impossible according to Hobsbawm.

[44] Thomas, *Religion and the Decline of Magic*, 143–144. To be fair, the troubles of the Civil War period may have also had a share in awakening these hopes. B.S. Capp, "Extreme Millenarianism," in P. Toon (Ed.), *Puritans, the Millennium and the Future of Israel: Puritan Eschatology 1600 to 1660* (Cambridge/London, 1970), 76 balances the factors as follows: "such dreams were enticing, especially in the civil war period when political, social and economic security was destroyed and yet miraculous hopes of a new order were appearing." Rare, however, are the victories not preceded by some disturbance, thus the two can be seen as sides of the same coin, as argued below.

Emigration to New England ceased, John Winthrop tells us, because the excitement of the revolution made "all men to stay in England in expectation of a new world."[45]

These ideas formed the core of preaching before the Long Parliament, as studied by Wilson.[46] Most pertinent to my perspective are the comments of Liu, who deliberately raises and rejects the interpretation of Puritan millenarianism in terms of movements of the disinherited:

> The millenarian strain in Puritanism has usually been considered in the past as an aberration rather than an essential part of the Puritan mind.... To Haller, [it] represented the hope of the meaner sort of people in the Puritan Revolution. "Out of the desperation of the poor and humble," writes Haller, "arose hope of the millennium."[47]

Liu continues:

> The Puritan vision of a glorious millennium of Christ's kingdom here on earth is no longer regarded merely as the ideology of the reckless Fifth Monarchy men; on the contrary, it is now considered a central theme in Puritanism during the whole course of the Puritan revolution. Historians now understand that millenarianism was *not merely the fantasy of the alienated who had no command of the reality of society but also a dynamic force in the minds of men who were totally involved in the reconstruction of the world* (emphasis mine).[48]

A further instance in which imminent hopes of national redemption are connected with victory is supplied by modern Israel since the 1967 war. As many observers have seen, beliefs that the final drama must be well under way and close to its glorious finale were raised and continue to inspire large groups of Israelis as a result of those events.[49] These convictions have been translated into programs of political and strategic action on a broad scale by well educated, socially advantaged, and highly motivated leaders, not connected in any way with the dispossessed. This conclusion emerges with particularly clarity

---

[45] Hill, *Antichrist*, 100.

[46] Wilson, *Pulpit in Parliament*, 190–195.

[47] T. Liu, *Discord in Zion* (The Hague, 1973), 3.

[48] *Ibid.*, 4.

[49] On the whole, this conclusion has stood the test of the setbacks endured at the beginning of the 1973 war, and the withdrawal from Sinai, which were interpreted in such a way as not to contradict the consequences drawn from the 1967 victories. On these points see further J. Aviad, "The Contemporary Israeli Pursuit of the Millennium," *Religion* 14 (1984), 199–222.

from the study of Habad messianism by Ravitsky.[50] In a word, this is a millenarianism of the victors not the vanquished.

To put this point in other terms let us return to Burridge. Towards the end of his essay he suggests the following:

> The main theme [of millenarian activities] is moral regeneration . . .
> the creation of a new man defined in relation to more highly
> differentiated criteria. The process involves the creation of new unities,
> a new community, a new set of assumptions within terms of which
> men and women may exploit the resources of their environment and
> order their relations with one another.[51]

True to the premises of his study, Burridge continues and restricts these insights to movements of the oppressed and to cases where the old values have been challenged by various crises. I would insist, however, as the examples discussed above show, that the activities Burridge summarizes have sometimes also been responses to victory.

Closest to my position are the comments of Wayne Meeks.[52] Meeks defines millenarianism and discusses its roots in deprived groups in terms derived from the work of Burridge and others. Nevertheless, he recognizes that this theoretical model accords poorly with what is known of the social level of Pauline Christians, and therefore proposes to understand millenarian hopes in terms derived loosely from the work of Leon Festinger, based on the concept of cognitive dissonance.[53] "Apocalyptic movements," Meeks suggests, "provide relief from cognitive dissonance by offering a new or transformed set of fundamental images of the world and of relationships."[54] Meeks continues by speculating that:

> people *who have advanced or declined* (emphasis mine) socially, who find
> themselves in an ambiguous relation to hierarchical structures, might

---

[50] See A. Ravitsky, *Messianism, Zionism and Jewish Religious Radicalism* (Tel Aviv, 1993), 249–276 [in Hebrew]. I would like to thank Prof. Ravitsky for the sharing with me the principal results of his research on this topic prior to his book's appearance in print. For the possible implications of Ravitzky's analysis for understanding ancient Jewish examples see J. Marcus, "Modern and Ancient Jewish Apocalypticism," *Journal of Religion* 76 (1996), 1–27.

[51] Burridge, *New Heaven, New Earth*, 141.

[52] Meeks, *First Urban Christians*, 172–174. See also Rowland, *Open Heaven*, 23–29, who is reluctant to restrict the term apocalyptic to texts or movements with a high eschatological content. As to limiting the term to texts with a pessimistic view of the present, Rowland apparently adopts this position, *ibid.*, 156–160.

[53] As far as I can tell, Festinger himself did not propose understanding millenarian movements in this way; this is Meeks' contribution based on Festinger's insights.

[54] Meeks, *First Urban Christians*, 173–174.

be receptive to symbols of the world as itself out of joint and on the brink of radical transformation. They might be attracted to a group that undertook to model its own life on that new picture of reality.[55]

Fundamental to these comments, from my perspective, is the clear recognition that one can enter the realm of apocalyptic/millenarian hopes as a result of an advance or a decline in status, that the dispossessed as well as the victors may choose to understand their somewhat disconcerting experiences (different as these may be from each other) in terms of a belief that the grand finale of the old world is soon to come. The anguish with the contemporary situation being expressed in the desire for imminent redemption is either the agony of oppression *or of a person who has begun to enjoy God's blessings as a result of victory, but who feels that redemption to be partial and thus longs for its complete fulfillment.*

If my criticisms of those who have ignored the victorious sort of millenarianism are correct, the reason for their error should also be apparent. The source of the error lies in choosing the paradigms of millenarianism too narrowly, in focusing on too small a group of cases as providing the archetype. More specifically, those who have studied the topic have restricted themselves too exclusively to groups whose members were often ignorant and inarticulate, who did not leave behind a satisfactory written account of their movement.[56] This description simply does not fit the ancient Jewish examples, whose members social level was discussed in Chapter One, the Puritans, or modern Habad. Another sort of millennialism – the victorious kind – was possible in the different circumstances in which these groups arose, and in the light of the different social composition of the groups.

To summarize, I have no quarrel with the conclusion that millenarianism is often a phenomenon of the deprived or the "down and outs" of various sorts. I maintain, however, that another type should not be overlooked – the triumphant version which emerges as a result of events which produce the conviction that we humans and God are now marching together towards the most glorious of all possible new worlds. As victories rarely occur without some prior

---

[55] *Ibid.*, 174. Arjomand, *Turban*, 110 & 198, echoing Weber discusses the dislocations caused by crises of prosperity.

[56] See Y. Talmon, "The Pursuit of the Millennium: The Relation Between Religious and Social Change," *Archives Européennes de Sociologie* 3 (1962), 127.

sense of distress the difficulties which precede the triumph may serve
to prepare the ground for the millenarianism of the victors. Nevertheless, what remains crucial about this second sort is the fact that the
impulse for the immediate inspiration is the sense of victory. Social
scientists, I believe, will need to adjust their theory to account for
the full range provided by historical example, while historians of
Judaism and other religions should be prepared to encounter both
varieties in the past.[57] Both routes to millenarianism, I will argue
below, can be found among Jews of the Second Temple period in
general and specifically of the Maccabean era.[58]

---

[57] If my approach is accepted it has several consequences well beyond the evidence available for the Second Temple period, hence far beyond the limits of this
study. Thus, for example, one may want to ask concerning possible correlations
between the two types of conditions which provoke millenarianism and the analyses
of messianism contributed by Scholem, *The Messianic Idea in Judaism*. Scholem suggests that messianic movements can be divided into two sorts, those that stress,
realistic, earthly redemption, expecting relatively small changes in the natural order
(of which the archetype may be Maimonides); and those that emphasize the coming
cosmic or apocalyptic upheaval, hence expecting dramatic changes in the world as
a result of the redemption. Is there any connection between this way of characterizing movements and my distinction between messianism of the victors and of the
vanquished? Are victors more likely to hold stronger visions of earthly redemption,
as opposed to the more cosmic/apocalyptic dreams of the vanquished, or perhaps
vice versa? Perhaps, after all, there is little or no correlation between these different
ways of describing messianic movements. These questions – interesting as they may
be – cannot be answered on the basis of the evidence available for the Second
Temple period, hence as noted above are well beyond the range of this book.

[58] This will be a fundamental difference between my approach and that of Isenberg,
"Millenarism in Greco-Roman Palestine," 26–46. Isenberg is entirely committed to
recognizing only what I have called the first type of millenarianism, that of the
deprived and oppressed. See his remarks *ibid.*, 35–36. The same exclusive emphasis
on the first type of millenarianism can be found in G. Nicklesburg, "Social Aspects
of Palestinian Jewish Apocalyptic," in D. Hellholm (Ed.), *Apocalypticism in the Mediterranean World and the Near East* (Tübingen, 1983), 641–654. See also Segal, "Conversion and Messianism," 297, who understands millennial movements to be a result of
exploitation.
    At least one social scientist has been convinced by the data of another exception
to the usual conception of millenarian movements. Schwartz, *Sect Ideologies*, 108–109
has noted that the Seventh-day Adventists whom he studied definitely hold millenarian
aspirations as an expression of their feeling dispossessed, yet in their case these attitudes are *not connected with revolutionary sentiment*.

THE SECOND TEMPLE ERA EVIDENCE

The existence of what I have called the millenarianism of the dispossessed has been well recognized by scholars who have written on the Second Temple period,[59] while I hope that recognition of the triumphant sort will be my contribution. For that reason, I prefer to concentrate first on the evidence for the victorious variety.

The prophet Haggai wrote at a time of great upheaval, urging the Jews to complete the rebuilding of the Temple after the return from the Babylonian exile.[60] Having succeeded in convincing his contemporaries to commence work, he turned to events for confirmation that these actions were desired by God and asserted that the blessings of the most recent past proved that famine and punishment were over (2:15–19). A second oracle given the same day predicted the imminent shaking of the heavens and overthrowing of kingdoms, all to conclude with the choosing of Zerubbabel as God's signet ring, i.e. messiah (2:20–23). Much the same atmosphere pervades the first eight chapters of Zachariah. In both cases hopes of imminent redemption were being nurtured as a result of a conviction that *the right* actions were now being taken, that the successes of the present were the best indication that God will bring about the grand finale very soon.

The prophecies of Haggai and Zachariah pose a problem to those who insist on seeing apocalyptic eschatology only as a result of oppression. Thus Hanson must contend with the uncomfortable fact that the images and content of these prophecies is completely appropriate to other expressions of apocalyptic eschatology, while he is committed to understanding the latter as a product of specific historical and social circumstances which do not fit the age and outlook of Haggai and Zachariah. It is awkward, from Hanson's perspective, to admit that the idiom of the vision was being applied as legitimation of a pragmatic political program over which the spokesman's group had control, rather than as the dream of a group of down and outs. Rather than redefine the categories in the light of the data, however, Hanson attempts to explain the data away. He therefore argues that:

> the forms and symbols utilized on behalf of the ruling group bear a *prima facie* resemblance to the forms of deprived apocalyptic groups.

---

[59] See for example the discussion of Isenberg, above, n. 58.

[60] See esp. E.J. Bickerman, "En Marge de l'Ecriture," *Studies in Jewish and Christian History Part Three* (Leiden, 1986), 331–336.

But the "use" made of them in one case is that of underpinning existing
structures, in the other case that of undermining those same structures.[61]

As developed at length above, I would prefer to make the categories
fit the data, rather than the reverse and to conclude as discussed
above, that Haggai and Zachariah are two further examples of those
inspired by success to believe that the final redemption of the world
is at hand. In particular, they should be compared with the manifestations of millenarianism among the ruling classes in sixteenth and
seventeenth century Britain analyzed by Lamont.[62]

Turning to the Hellenistic period, Ben Sira supplies a convenient
point of departure.[63] Writing at the beginning of the second century
BCE he was well aware of national hopes for restoration. These
aspirations were given full expression in 36:1–17,[64] where he prayed
for the complete restoration of Zion, and exacting punishment of
foreign nations. He implored that God's anger be roused, and His
wrath poured out to destroy the adversary and wipe out the enemy.
All of this, however, will take place at some unspecified time in the
future, which the author hoped would come quickly (36:8), and over
which God only has control.[65] Of all this, however, Ben Sira had no
immediate expectation.[66] Significantly, from a social perspective, Ben

---

[61] Hanson, *Dawn of Apocalyptic*, 253.

[62] If this argument is accepted, it may not be appropriate to define apocalyptic
movements with P. Hanson, "Jewish Apocalyptic Against its Near Eastern Environment," *Revue Biblique* 78 (1971), 32: as ones which have visions which they "have
ceased to translate into terms of plain history, real politics and human instrumen-
tality because of a pessimistic view of reality growing out of the bleak post-exilic
condition in which the visionary group found itself." Rather, I would argue, most of
those embracing apocalyptic beliefs fit this model, but not necessarily all.

[63] It is, of course, impossible to be certain whether Ben Sira represents attitudes
widely prevalent in his own time, or the views of a more limited circle, possibly
confined to only himself. What little evidence we possess inclines me to the former
possibility. See further A. Caquot, "Ben Sira et le Messianisme," *Semitica* 16 (1966),
44. On Chapter 36 of Ben Sira in general see further Caquot, *ibid.*, 43–68; Marböck,
"Das Gebet," 93–115.

[64] This text is sufficiently different from other passages in Ben Sira that some
scholars have wondered whether it stems from his pen. See the summary and discussion in Marböck, "Das Gebet," 104. See also Mack, *Wisdom and the Hebrew Epic*, 180.

[65] Might the author's prayers have been evoked by the actions of some specific
foreign ruler? For speculation on the various possibilities (Antiochus III, Seleucus IV
or Ptolemy V, for example) see Caquot, "Ben Sira," 48–49; Marböck, "Das Gebet,"
106. Perhaps this hatred of foreign rulers (contradicted by other passages in the
work in which rulers are sent by God e.g. 10:1–8) declined as it became clear that
the new masters of Jerusalem intended to endorse traditional Jewish privileges
(Josephus, *Ant.* 12.138–144), as suggested by Caquot, *ibid.*, 53.

[66] Perhaps, as suggested by Caquot, "Ben Sira," 47 these comments should be understood as criticism of groups in the author's day who expected imminent redemption.

Sira had no imminent expectations of ultimate redemption, and was also perfectly satisfied with the system of priestly government current in his day. He prayed for its eternal continuation (50:24).[67]

A next stage in the progression is supplied by the second half of the Book of Daniel, written at the time of the persecutions of Antiochus IV. In an atmosphere of crisis, the author looked forward to the redemption of the world in the imminent future, a redemption which will be connected with the defeat of Antiochus IV and the eternal justification of the righteous (11:40–12:3). Inspired by this vision, Daniel and his circle re-discovered world history and its meaning, straining to know it as accurately as possible in order to extract its message for the scenario of the redemption of the world.[68] As such Daniel was in a direct line with the Biblical prophets, who also searched events on the world arena of their day, hoping to learn the ways in which they foretold the ultimate redemption.[69]

Daniel's attitude towards the Hasmonean house is ambivalent, at best. Characterizing them as "a little help" at a time when the wise fell by sword, flame, captivity and plunder (11:33–34), and when the ranks of the wise were filled for less than the best motives ("many shall join themselves to them with flattery"), the Hasmoneans have no role whatsoever to play at the glorious time when Michael the Great Prince shall arise (12:1).

In one sense, of course, Daniel is an example of the non-victorious sort of millenarianism, and has been included in this place in the discussion mainly for the sake of chronological coherence. Nevertheless, one aspect of the book remains intriguing from my perspective. Josephus, a well born and educated aristocrat if there ever was one, devoted an extensive section to a summary of Daniel at the end of *Ant.* 10. Among other comments he noted that "the books which he (i.e. Daniel) wrote are still read by us even now." Daniel enjoyed this popularity because he not only prophesied future things, as did the other prophets, but "also fixed the time at which these would come to pass (*Ant.* 10.267)." Moreover, Daniel was a prophet of good tidings, hence he gained credit among the multitude and won their esteem (*Ant.* 10.268).[70] Josephus thus attests to the widespread popularity of

---

[67] See further Caquot, *ibid.*, 63, 68.

[68] See Bickerman, *Jews in the Greek Age*, 122.

[69] See e.g. Joel 2–3, Zeph. 1–2, Hag. 1–2, Zech. 1–9.

[70] On Josephus and Daniel see further S. Mason, "Josephus, Daniel and the Flavian House," in Parente and Sievers, *Josephus and the History of the Greco-Roman Period*, 161–195, esp. 172–177.

Daniel among Jews of varying backgrounds, including his own, during the decades before and after the destruction of the Temple.

Further evidence for this conclusion comes from Rabbinic sources. According to the Rabbis, great efforts were made to prevent the High Priest from falling asleep on the night of Yom Kippur, so that his purity the next morning might be assured. If the High Priest were not learned and could not expound scripture himself, they read to him as part of this effort. Zachariah b. Kabutal testified that "many times I read before him out of Daniel."[71] A High Priest, presumably a member of the highest classes of Jerusalem jewry, would be sufficiently intrigued by Daniel to stay up all night. Thus whatever the circles and the circumstances in which Daniel originated, it spoke to Jews of a much wider range, even to those in the highest possible social and political ranks. Admittedly, all these Jews were members of a subject nation, under Roman rule. Their interest in Daniel may have been a result of their aspirations to end foreign domination. From Daniel they could learn when this blessing would come to pass. Nevertheless, I find the similarity to the millenarianism of the sixteenth and seventeenth century – widespread throughout all levels of society – impressive.[72]

A more markedly pro-Hasmonean atmosphere pervades 1 Enoch 90, written at approximately the same time as Daniel 7–12, during the Maccabean revolt.[73] There too, at a time of trouble and battle, the author looked forward to the glorious redemption, including the rebuilding of the dismal temple erected by the returning Babylonian

---

[71] mYoma 1:6. From our perspective it matters little if this testimony is historical or not. It was composed to be taken as plausible, hence it reflects tastes of the time, whether or not Zachariah b. Kabutal actually read from Daniel to any High Priest. The other books on the list in mYoma 1:6 and parallels would also be of great interest to a High Priest and thus help prevent his falling asleep: Job is an eternal puzzle, while Ezra and Chronicles would be like "studying the tombstones in the family plot," for a High Priest, as suggested to me by Professor Alan Cooper.

[72] One might respond to my analysis of Haggai, Zachariah 1–9 and the popularity of Daniel by defining apocalypses as a sub-group of works produced only by members of oppressed orders. In that way the connection between apocalypse and oppression might not be lost. Such a move, I would argue, would be self-defeating, as it would arbitrarily deny the apocalyptic nature of Haggai and Zachariah 1–9 in spite of their contents and use of specific images, merely because they do not fit our construct of apocalypse. Moreover, a tack such as that would not help explain the popularity of Daniel, even among upper class jews.

[73] See e.g. Collins, Apocalyptic Imagination, 53–56, 90; G. Nicklesburg, "Enoch, First Book of," Anchor Bible Dictionary 2.511; Rowland, Open Heaven, 252.

exiles to its true grand proportions (1 Enoch 90:28–29), one of the standard expressions of eschatological hopes in the Second Temple period (see e.g. Hag. 2:9, Tobit 14:5). Human agency in bringing about these good tidings has a part to play: the great horned ram (Judah Maccabee in the allegory) fights on behalf of the cause of good, 1 Enoch 90:9–12, and a white cow is born later on, as well as a great beast with black horns, 1 Enoch 90:37–39. These passages are therefore somewhat messianic. These animals, however, do nothing to redeem the world. The only one who is active, the ram, needs divine assistance in order to be victorious, and plays no role in the ultimate triumph. Nevertheless, 1 Enoch 90 is pro-Maccabean, and testimony that some saw the successes of the house as leading up to the fulfillment of hopes for the end of days.

When millenarian hopes are next encountered they are found in quite a different social and political environment. The context is no longer that of the pietists who produced Daniel. Neither is it a vaguely pro-Maccabean work, such as 1 Enoch 90, but rather in what seems to be an official Maccabean setting. The second letter at the beginning of 2 Macc. has been discussed above,[74] and its origins as a piece of pro-Hasmonean writing proposed. That letter ends with an expression of hope that

> God . . . will soon have mercy upon us and will gather us from everywhere under heaven into his place, for he has rescued us from great evils and has purified the place (2:18).

The hope for the ingathering of the exiles is one of the classic formulations of expectations for the events of the final redemption (see e.g. Isa. 66:19–20, Ben Sira 36:11, Tobit 14:5). Crucial and specific to our passage in 2 Macc. is the connection made between these hopes and the events of the recent past. The author has special reason to believe that the redemption is to come in the immediate future because of the great victories which have just occurred. As such, I would argue that this passage from 2 Macc. should be classified together

---

[74] See Chapter Three, at n. 14. The principal discussion there is based on Goldstein, "How the Authors of 1 and 2 Maccabees Treated the 'Messianic' Promises," 69–96; Cf. Collins, "Messianism in the Maccabean Period,", 97–110. Cf. also the comment of J. Charlesworth, "From Messianology to Christology: Problems and Prospects," in Charlesworth, *The Messiah*, 24: "The successes of the early Hasmoneans or Maccabees left no vacuum in which to yearn for the coming of the Messiah." See also below nn. 75 and 83.

with the other examples of millenarian hopes raised as a result of success considered in the previous section of this chapter.[75]

Additional evidence for the argument that some interpreted Maccabean victories as signs of imminent redemption of the world is provided by 4Q471ᵃ.[76] Line 3 of that text quotes the opinion of unnamed opponents, likely Sadducees or Maccabees: "You (our opponents) said 'We shall fight His battles, because He redeemed us (נאלנו).'" In fact, however, the results will be very different than hoped or anticipated. 4Q471ᵃ continues, in line 4: "Your [ ] will be brought low, and they (the opponents) did not know that He despised. . . ." The full context of these events is beyond our knowledge due to the fragmentary nature of this brief text. Nevertheless, one conclusion is worth proposing. If one takes נאלנו in its full eschatological sense,[77] 4Q471ᵃ attacks the certainty of rivals that the redemption is under way, and their willingness to draw practical conclusions on the basis of that belief. It thus can testify to the fact that some members of Jewish society of pre-Herodian or Herodian times[78] viewed events of their era as proof positive that the end of times was dawning, and drew pragmatic consequences as a result of this conviction. As in the end these very people were ultimately "brought low," they can be readily identified as among the leaders of Jewish society of their day. 4Q471ᵃ therefore indicates the existence of a triumphant millenarianism, motivating the *higher* groups in the social, political and religious orders of its day. This phenomenon, I conclude, can only be properly understood when the reality of the triumphalist trigger

---

[75] On the explicit hope for imminent eschatological redemption expressed in this passage see D. Arenhoevel, *Die Theokratie nach dem 1. und 2. Makkabäerbuch* (Mainz, 1967), 110.

[76] E. Eshel and M. Kister, "A Polemical Qumran Fragment," *Journal of Jewish Studies*, 43 (1992), 277–281.

[77] The verb גאל, as E. Eshel and Kister, "Polemical Fragment," 279 note, is relatively rare in Qumran texts. It likely has an eschatological meaning in 4Q176, 1–2, ii, 3, where Isa. 43:1–2 is quoted in the context of prophecies of consolation, which open with a vision of God performing wonders for His people, contending with the Kingdoms, and slaying the evil priests in such numbers that there will be none to bury their bodies (4Q176 1–2, i, 1–4). The eschatological sense of the verb is also apparent in 4Q185 1–2, ii, 10, where God will redeem his people, but slay the wicked. A similar connotation is likely in 4Q385 2, 1, an apocalyptic text dubbed Second Ezechiel, on which see J. Strugnell and D. Dimant, "4Q Second Ezechiel," *Revue de Qumran* 13 (1988), 46–47, 55. Nevertheless, just what sort of salvation is being celebrated in 4Q504 5, ii, 5, or in 4Q381 24, 5 is not clear. It may be eschatologically significant, but is not necessarily so.

[78] The letter forms of the extant copy are Herodian.

of millenarian hopes, for whose existence I have been arguing, is acknowledged.

Much the same environment is present in the old story of Yannai's victories related in *bQid.* 66a. The archaic nature of the vocabulary and other forms of expression have been noted by scholars since the end of the previous century.[79] Scholarly attention has been transfixed by the comparison between the Rabbinic story and the parallel in Josephus, *Ant.* 13.288–298.[80] What has been less discussed is the opening of the story. King Yannai won a desert victory in Kohalit.[81] In celebration, he invited the sages to a party at which mallows (a desert food, see Job 30:4) were served on golden tables. This evoked memories of ancestors who also ate mallows, in poverty, when rebuilding the Second Temple on returning from the Babylonian exile. We eat mallows, as they did, but we do so in an atmosphere of triumph. By implication, our era is one of redemption, as was that of the return from Babylonia, but the salvation in our times will be even greater (more complete?), as we now are victorious.[82] All this according to the story in *bQid.* was done by Yannai at the party he held. As such, this story is the first hint that the triumphalist interpretation of Hasmonean victories was sponsored by the royal house itself.[83]

---

[79] See I. Levi, "Les sources talmudiques de l'histoire juive. I. Alexandre Jannée et Simon b. Shetah. II. La rupture de Jannée avec les pharisiens," *Revue des Etudes Juives* 35 (1897), 213–223.

[80] See M. Geller, "Alexander Jannaeus and the Pharisee Rift," *Journal of Jewish Studies* 30 (1979), 202–211, who follows in the footsteps of G. Alon, "The Attitude of the Pharisees to Roman Rule and the House of Herod," *Jews, Judaism and the Classical World: Studies in Jewish History in the Times of the Second Temple and Talmud* (Jerusalem, 1977), 26–28, n. 22. See also Levine "Political Struggle," 61–83; J. Efron, "Simon b. Shatah and Alexander Jannaeus," *Studies in the Hasmonean Period* (Leiden, 1987), 161–190; Schwartz, "Pharisaic Opposition," 48–49; E. Main, "Les Sadducéens vus par Flavius Josephe," *Revue Biblique* 97 (1990), 190–201.

[81] The place is unknown, but it is mentioned in the Copper Scroll.

[82] Note, however, that no practical steps were taken by the Maccabees to remedy the inability of those ancestors to build a proper Temple. Thus while the Hasmoneans had done some wall building, and had connected the Temple Mount to the Upper City they had not rebuilt the sanctuary. Herod reproached the Hasmoneans for this failure, according to Josephus, *Ant.* 15.380–387 and 17.161.

[83] 1 Macc., written by a house historian of the ruling dynasty, is full of an atmosphere of triumph, stressing that the Maccabean family was chosen by God to be the means of salvation of His people, 1 Macc. 5:62. It seems reasonable to surmise that such claims were employed against the envious countrymen, jealous of the good fortune of the members of the Hasmonean house, whose rebellion against their rule had to be put down (Josephus, *War* 1.67; *Ant.* 13.288, 299).

Divine approval of the new high priestly rulers was reiterated in stories such as the gift of prophecy attributed to John Hyrcanus according to Rabbinic sources

Final testimony for the millennialist understanding placed on victory is supplied by 4QMMT, from an early moment in the history of the Qumran community. The halachic section, which has been the focus of attention thus far, is followed by an ideological statement in which the author explained why he and his friends have seceded from the mass of the Jewish people. As part of this statement the author claimed to be quoting (from Deuteronomy) a verse which conflates Deut. 4:30 and 30:1, as we know them. The text which results states that when the *blessings and curses* of the end of days occur you will call them to mind and return to Me (i.e. God), with all your heart and all your soul at the end of times (C15–17). Some of these blessings and curses already came to fruition in the days of Solomon and from the time of Jeroboam until the days of Zedekiah, when Jerusalem went into exile (C18–19).[84] Clearest of all

---

(*tSot.* 13:5, Lieberman, 232 and parallels) and Josephus (*War* 1.69; *Ant.* 13.282–283). Prophecy, as Josephus asserted (*War* 1.69; *Ant.* 13.300), was a sure sign of divine favor, and a gift which Hyrcanus enjoyed on a regular basis, so that he was "never ignorant of the future (*War* 1.69)."

Divine consent for the accession of Alexander Jannaeus was also intimated by the story of Hyrcanus's dream, in which he asked God which son would succeed him and was shown the features of Alexander, much to Hyrcanus's dismay (he loved best his sons Antigonus and Aristobulus). Hyrcanus tried to prevent this result by human means, sending Alexander to be brought up in the Galilee, and never seeing his son for as long as he lived, but all to no avail (Josephus, *Ant.* 13.322–323). After the year-long reign of Aristobulus – during which Antigonus was murdered on royal command (Josephus, *War* 1.72–80; *Ant.* 13.302–313), a plot in which Aristobulus's wife had a hand (Josephus, *War* 1.76), and the other brothers imprisoned (Josephus, *War* 1.71; *Ant.* 13.302, 320) – the monarchy devolved upon Alexander. This result was managed by Aristobulus's widow (Josephus, *War* 1.85; *Ant.* 13.320), whom Alexander later apparently married. On coming to power, Alexander executed another of his brothers as a potential aspirant to the throne (Josephus, *War* 1.85). These must have been particularly delicate matters, suitably reinforced by the story of Hyrcanus's dream.

In none of these texts, however, is this sense of divine endorsement given an explicit eschatological twist. At most, one can argue for a sense of realized eschatology implicit in the triumphalist atmosphere of the description of the blessings brought by the new dynasty. See further Arenhoevel, *Theokratie*, 58–65. In the story in *bQid.*, by contrast, the evocation of the ancestors who rebuilt the Temple and the imitation of their actions suggest more explicit hope of immediate eschatological redemption, as promoted by the royal house.

For eschatological hope sponsored by royal propaganda in the Middle Ages see E. Kantorowicz, *The King's Two Bodies: A Study in Mediaeval Political Theology* (Princeton, 1957), 42–87; P. Szittya, "Domesday Bokes: The Apocalypse in Medieval English Culture," in R.K. Emmerson and B. McGinn (Eds.), *The Apocalypse in the Middle Ages* (Ithaca, 1992), 375–378. I would like to thank Richard Landes for calling these medieval examples of royal millenarianism to my attention.

[84] The exact connection between these blessing and curses at the time of Solomon and Jeroboam and those of the end of days is not clear. Perhaps 4QMMT intended

is the next passage in 4QMMT. The author stated there unequivocally that

> we recognize that some of the *blessings and curses* have come about that are written in the book of Moses. And this is the end of days, when they will return upon Israel forever (C20–22).

The proof that the end of days was underway was a combination of blessings and curses, or in the terms I have suggested, victories and difficulties. This combination is a bit odd at first sight. Perhaps it can be illuminated by modern Jewish parallels, in which the conviction that now is both the best of times (as proven by Israeli successes, such as that in 1967) and the worst of times (as indicated by specific failures, such as the Holocaust, or the blatantly secular nature of the Israeli government) is the most powerful proof that now must be the dawning of the redemption.[85]

The difference between my interpretation of these passages and that proposed by Schiffman must be stressed. According to Schiffman,[86] the blessings refer to those of the end of days, while the curses are the catastrophic period to precede the onset of the end of days.[87] Thus, while the curses are being experienced in the present (according to the view of the author of the document), the blessings are yet to come, and will only be enjoyed on the final day of blessing (cf. 11QT29:9). As Schiffman proposes to understand the text in a subsequent publication, the present – for the author of 4QMMT – is a time *on the verge* of the final redemption of the world.[88] This interpretation of 4QMMT, I would argue, flies in the face of the plain statements

---

to stress that unlike the former, the latter would last forever and would never be cancelled. See further Qimron and Strugnell, *Discoveries in the Judean Desert X*, 60, on line 18. The reference to Solomon and the exile adds further to the ambiguity surrounding the possible meanings of the "end of days" in Qumran sources, on which see further below, n. 88.

[85] For the modern evidence see further Ravitzky, *The Revealed End*, 149. I owe this idea to a suggestion of Joel Marcus.

[86] Schiffman, "New Halakhic Letter," 72, n. 7; cf. Collins, *Scepter and Star*, 104–106.

[87] Schiffman apparently understands the passages in 4QMMT in the light of *mSota* 9:15, and did not consider other possibilities.

[88] Schiffman, *Reclaiming*, 85. This is not to say that Schiffman is wrong in seeing other Qumran texts as believing that parts of the scenario of redemption remained ahead. A process was underway, which would lead to the eschaton. As I argue below, a date for that was set by the Qumran community, and they paid a price when the moment passed and the bad old world remained. See also the detailed discussion in A. Steudel, "'The End of Days' in the Qumran Texts," *Revue de Qumran* 16 (1993), 225–231; F. García Martínez, "4QMMT in a Qumran Context," in Kampen and Bernstein, *Reading 4QMMT*, 20–23.

of its author that he and his circle recognized that some of both the blessings and the curses have already come about, and that these events were proof that the end of days was at hand.

What might these blessings have been? The temptation is great to interpret 4QMMT in the light of 2 Macc. and the other texts considered above. Since the author of 4QMMT and his friends might not have been unequivocal supporters of the Hasmonean dynasty, one should not expect them to formulate their proof that the end of times was at hand exclusively in terms of Maccabean victories.[89] Nevertheless, it is significant that their proof consisted of both blessings and curses. I would suggest that they viewed events from the Seleucid conquest and the abolition of the decrees of Antiochus IV down to the achievement of independence as the blessings which helped convince them that the final act was well under way, and that the grand finale was imminent.

Two conclusions, one immediate the other a bit less so, emerge from this consideration of 4QMMT. First, it is commonly thought that authors of millenarian works live in the conviction that the present is bad, and the immediate future may be worse but that a great turning point is soon at hand.[90] I have argued above that some millenarian texts, such as Haggai and Zachariah 1–8 do not share that view. 4QMMT is further proof that those who believe in the imminent redemption of the world may see their time as one of *blessings and curses*.

Even more important is the significance of 4QMMT for the matter of the relationship between commitment to *halacha* and millennial beliefs. The Qumran evidence available before the publication of 4QMMT should have been sufficient to convince anyone that this group was devoted to a strict observance of the laws of the Torah, also believed actively in the imminent redemption of the world, and did not find any contradiction between these two aspects of their

---

[89] The notion that one of the issues at the root of Qumran separatism might have been the disappointment of Sadoqite priests at their having been supplanted by the Hasmoneans has been discussed above, Introduction, at nn. 94–98. That notion must now be treated with extreme caution, as outlined in the discussion there.

[90] See J. Licht, "The Attitude Towards Events of the Past in the Bible and Apocalyptic Literature," *Tarbiz* 60 (5751), 14 [in Hebrew]. Compare the frequently quoted comment of H.H. Rowley, *The Relevance of Apocalyptic* (London, 1947), 38: "the apocalypticists had little faith in the present to beget the future." See also G. Nicklesburg, "The Apocalyptic Construction of Reality in *1 Enoch*," in Collins and Charlesworth, *Mysteries and Revelations*, 60.

faith. These were not "two opposing tendencies," in their life.[91] As will be discussed in greater detail below, they are one example among many of a millenarian movement that is committed to scrupulous fulfillment of the commandments. Nevertheless, in case anyone still doubted the possibility of such a stance, 4QMMT makes the point explicit. As discussed above, the author and his circle believed that they were living in the end of days, with greater glories yet to come. Accordingly, they exhorted the addressee of their letter to join them in observing the law as they believed it should be practiced

> so that you may rejoice at the end of time as you find that some of our words are true, and it shall be reckoned to you as righteousness when you do what is upright and what is good before Him, for your wellbeing and that of Israel (C32–34).

The contrast on which many scholars have insisted between belief in imminent eschatological redemption and strict observance of *halacha* may well be an illusion.[92] Indeed, as I will argue below, belief in the imminent redemption of the world may be a ground for even stricter insistence on scrupulous fulfillment of the law.

The Next Phases at Qumran

The next stage, at Qumran in particular, is considerably less optimistic.[93] In fact, the atmosphere of hope for change which pervades 4QMMT has been replaced by the despair engendered by several generations during which the community there has rejected the mainstream, but has also been rejected by it.[94] To complicate matters further, millenarian expectations have been cultivated during these

---

[91] See J. Trebolle Barrera, "The Essenes of Qumran: Between Submission to the Law and Apocalyptic Flight," in García Martínez and Trebolle Barrera, *People of the Dead Sea Scrolls*, 67. Cf. Collins, *Apocalyptic Imagination*, 141.

[92] See e.g. Hanson, *Dawn of Apocalyptic*, 281. On this count I have no quarrel with Y. Talmon, "Millennial Movements," 178.

[93] The details of the history of the growth of Qumran messianism, analyzed in detail by Collins, *Scepter and Star*, 77–84 are of less concern here. My focus is more on the practical consequences of belief in imminent cosmic redemption, to be discussed in detail below.

[94] On despair as the context for Qumran messianism see 1QH iii, 7–10. Note that the language and technical terminology of 4QMMT are proto-Mishnaic. Nevertheless, the work itself dates from early in the history of the Qumran community. See Qimron and Strugnell, *Discoveries in the Judean Desert X*, 121. It therefore antedates the *pesharim*.

hard times. A specific date has likely been set for the redemption, but prophecy has seemed to fail. In spite of all their efforts and concentrated hopes, the bad old world has not yet been replaced by the glorious new one in which the covenanters's views will find complete vindication. These circumstances have led to confusion and disappointment on the one hand, and attempts to strengthen the commitment of those remaining loyal on the other, as one might expect.[95]

One example of these processes is provided by the Qumran *pesharim*. In the hazy view of the covenanters as expressed in their *pesharim* it is difficult to be certain of exact events, their sequence and interrelationships. In general, however, those at Qumran believed that the(ir?) priest (= teacher of righteousness) had the knowledge and insight to reveal the secret meaning of all the words of the prophets (1QpHab ii, 7–9). The prophet Habakkuk did not know when the "end of the end", i.e. the ultimate redemption of the world, would take place, but perhaps (by contrast) the teacher of righteousness, who taught "all the secrets of the words of His servants the prophets" by God, did (1QpHab vii, 1–5). This background illuminates the crucial passage, 1QpHab vii, 5–14:

> (2:3a) *For the vision is yet for the appointed time; but at the end it will speak and will not disappoint.* Its secret meaning is that the "last time" will be long in coming, even longer than the prophets predicted, for the mysteries of God are wonderful (i.e. beyond human comprehension). (2:3b) *If it seems slow wait for it; for it will surely come and will not be late.* Its secret meaning concerns the men of truth, the doers of the law, whose arms will not weaken in the service of truth, when the "last time" seems to them to be delayed; for all God's times will come in their measured sequence, just as He decreed for them in the mysteries of His providence.[96]

---

[95] The Qumran case, as will be argued below, was one in which a specific date for the redemption was set. That date passed, and the members of the community had to contend with disconfirmation. It thus should be included among the historical examples of dashed hopes analyzed by L. Festinger, H. Riecken and S. Schachter, *When Prophecy Fails* (New York, 1964, 2nd edition), 3–25. The pattern of defection at the time of disconfirmation combined with a redoubled effort on the part of the group to retain the loyalty of existing members, would also fit the results of the study by Festinger and his colleagues.

[96] Translation of this passage is mine, based principally on the comments of Nitzan, *Pesher Habakkuk*, 172–174. This passage has been understood differently by other scholars. Compare the translation and comments of W. Brownlee, *The Midrash Pesher of Habakkuk* (Missoula, 1979), 107–117; M. Horgan, *Pesharim: Qumran Interpretations of Biblical Books* (Washington, 1979), 38. For an interpretation closer to mine see Steudel, "End of Days," 235–236.

The author explicitly expressed his disappointment that the end of days was so long in coming, and consoled himself that the fact that it was taking "even longer than the prophets predicted" was according to a divine plan beyond his understanding. The doers of the law (in contrast to others) did not allow their commitment to the sect to be weakened by these circumstances. Their faith in the teacher of righteousness will be rewarded appropriately, in accordance with the verse Hab. 2:4b concerning the righteous who live on account of their faith (1QpHab viii, 1–3).

The passage quoted above contains one phrase which requires further attention. What did the author mean when he wrote that the grand finale would take "even longer than the prophets predicted?" Habakkuk, as noted explicitly, did not know when the "end of ends" would take place, but it would seem that the author of 1QpHab believed that he knew when to expect the eschaton (otherwise how could he have known that end was taking *even longer* than the prophets predicted), whether that knowledge was derived from prophets other than Habakkuk or from the secret interpretations of the teacher of righteousness, or both. That is, the expression "even longer than the prophets predicted" reflects a conviction that the author and his audience believed that they knew when the time predicted by the prophets for the redemption was, that this time had already arrived, and that they were living in a period when that event *was delayed* beyond the time which had been set for its realization. Perhaps the members of the Qumran community had even set a specific date by which they believed the eschaton would break forth, and now were living with the consequences of the disconfirmation of these hopes. If this is the case, the praise of those who remained loyal to the predictions of the teacher of righteousness may be doubly significant. Disconfirmation, as experience has shown, can produce a variety of results. Some may renounce their allegiance to the system whose prophecies have failed while others, especially those who have invested much in their dreams, may work even harder to reinterpret events so as to avoid the necessity of giving up the beliefs on which they had pinned their hopes.[97] Those who continued to believe in the

---

[97] The classic study remains Festinger, Riecken & Schachter, *When Prophecy Fails.* For a more recent discussion of the effects of failure of the millennium to materialize see M.J. Penton, *Apocalypse Delayed* (Toronto, 1985). Penton treats at length the effects of the disappointment when the expected redemption predicted by the Jehovah's Witnesses did not ensue in 1975.

teacher of righteousness and his interpretations, in spite of the redemption taking "even longer than the prophets predicted," deserved
encouragement and praise. Disconfirmation has led to dissent within
the original group, and the bitterness felt towards those who have
not remained faithful to the communal dream is apparent.[98]

At the risk of grossly overstating what the evidence will support let
me state my proposed interpretation in its most extreme form. The
teacher of righteousness, relying on his secret understanding of the
words of the prophets had suggested a date for the final redemption.[99] When that date had come and gone a crisis ensued as a result
of which some members of the group defected. 1QpHab vii, 5–14
reassures those who remained loyal that they will reap the fruits of
that fidelity. As a solution to the dilemma of the failure of the prediction they were told that the delay beyond the date predicted by
the prophets was part of God's mysterious plans and hence beyond
their comprehension. The prophecy was not wrong nor was its secret interpretation by the teacher of righteousness (of course!), but
for some reason known to God alone its fulfillment was being delayed. Furthermore, those who remained faithful to the teacher of
righteousness should not feel bad that this secret was beyond our
comprehension, as it was also not revealed to the prophet Habakkuk.

THE PHARISEES IN HEROD'S COURT

One other instance of active messianic hopes requires detailed attention: the court/harem plot fomented by the Pharisees at the time of
Herod, intended to benefit (among others) Herod's brother Pheroras
and his wife, *Ant.* 17.41–44. As I have dealt with this text a number
of times in the past, I will restrict my comments here.[100] The Phari-

---

[98] Recent examples teach us that it is precisely in an atmosphere of rapid change
that competing reinterpretations of the original message abound. The demise of old
ways leads to the formation of new ones.

[99] Perhaps in accordance with Jeremiah and Daniel, that date was 490 years
(seventy weeks of years) after the destruction of the first Temple by the Babylonians.
We cannot know the chronology of the first temple period as reconstructed by the
Qumran sect. Assuming, however, that it was not that different than our system,
490 years after the destruction of the first temple would yield a date around the
beginning of the first century BCE, a time when the community at Qumran would
have been well established.

[100] Most recently in A.I. Baumgarten, "The Legitimacy of Herod and his Sons as
Kings of Israel", in I. Gafni, A. Oppenheimer & M. Stern (Eds.), *Jews and Judaism*

sees, according to this account, suborned various members of court, making outrageous guarantees of favors which the messianic king would soon confer (such as promising the eunuch Bagoas that he would be given the ability to beget children). Ultimately, they were punished for their disloyalty.

Crucial for the investigation in progress are two points which can be learned from this account. First, Pharisees, too, engaged in messianic speculations, proposed dates for redemption, and devised plans for political action based on these predictions. Perhaps, although this cannot be proved, these activities were not mere exploitation, and those Pharisees so engaged believed wholeheartedly in their prophecies. The Qumran sect was thus not alone in experiencing the excitement of imminent hope and the disappointment of the failure of forecasts to materialize. Second, messianic speculation was carried on by Pharisees at Herod's court, and was used as a means of motivating members of that court, from Herod's brother and his wife down to eunuchs and women of the harem. The conclusion for which I have been arguing, based on the work of Lamont in England of the seventeenth century in particular, is thus confirmed for Second Temple Judaism. At certain times, at the very least, imminent hopes of redemption can be found up and down the social and political ladder. These expectations will be interpreted or utilized differently by people or groups at varying points on these ladders, but they are not the exclusive prerogative of specific social, religious or political classes, as some would have us conclude.

Exiting Millenarian Time

Millennial hope was to remain an active force, sometimes perhaps even a driving one in the lives of Jews from the Maccabean era down to the Bar Kochba revolt. As these issues have been discussed in great detail by numerous other scholars I will merely note the background of messianic fervor against which early Christianity should be seen, the messianic nature of movements started by a number of sign prophets, such as Theudas, the Egyptian or John the Baptist, the possible messianic aspects of the Great Revolt, the likely messianic

---

in the Second Temple, Mishna and Talmud Period Studies in Honor of Shmuel Safrai (Jerusalem, 1993), 31–37 [in Hebrew].

character of the revolt in Egypt, Cyprus and Cyrene, and the attribution of messianic status to Bar Kochba on the part of R. Akiba. Imminent expectations of redemption did not really begin to wane until after the failure of the Bar Kochba revolt. Hope, repeatedly deferred or – even worse – dashed, then gave way to despair. Many Jews of the post-revolutionary era would have agreed with a sense of resignation to the despairing remarks of Edmund Hall, commenting on his age's search for the Antichrist:

> Some make Antichrist a state . . . some a particular man, a king, or a general. Others give out that Antichrist is like the philosophers' stone, much talked on but never seen yet or known.[101]

Messianism was thus a persistent constant in the history of Jews in those years.

WAITING FOR THE MILLENNIUM

This brings us to ask what might be the practical consequences of a belief in imminent redemption. How do people who believe that the world is soon to be saved act in what they are convinced will be the waning moments of the unredeemed world? As noted above, at n. 56, I believe that scholarly opinion has been unduly shaped by an unjustifiably narrow set of examples taken as archetypes. We thus expect members of such a group to renounce all forms of morality or restraint, to live in communal anarchy, sharing partners and property. In fact, this return to the state of innocence in the Garden of Eden is only one side of the coin. The other is represented by millenarian movements which insist on the strictest observance of the rules, as preparation for the ultimate judgement soon to be held. Every opportunity to behave properly must be utilized in the final moments before salvation, because the books will soon be closed and we will no longer have an opportunity to rectify our standing before God. Something of this mindset can be seen even in the preaching of St. Paul. Paul, according to Meeks, drew two diametrically opposed conclusions from his belief in the gospel: (1) radical innovation and (2) *restraint and stability*.[102] The latter, in particular, was important as

---

[101] *Ap.* Hill, *Antichrist*, 135. On Jewish responses in a similar vein see further below.
[102] See Phil. 1:10 and 1 Thess. 5:23, and the discussion in Meeks, *First Urban Christians*, 179. How Paul would explain the apparent contradiction between the

it ran counter to popular perception of Paul's message. A much more straightforward emphasis on scrupulous behavior can be found in the Savonarola movement. Moral purification had always been a central aspect of Savonarola's preaching, but this message had a new enthusiasm and success in the aftermath of victory and its millenarian interpretation.[103] The situation was similar in Britain of the seventeenth century. As Capp has written of the Fifth Monarchy men:

> The aim of the Fifth Monarchists was to use power to enforce godly discipline on the masses. Far from withering away in the millennium, the duties of the magistrate would expand into new spheres. . . . The saints were to behave with purity and sobriety, uncorrupted in a sinful world . . . they would be a "pure and chaste people", not defiled by women. . . . Behavior was to be grave.[104]

In a similar vein, Capp also observes:

> The saints often showed more enthusiasm for uprooting Babylon than for planting Jerusalem, and their favorite text was Psalm 149:8, with its promise of binding kings with chains and nobles with fetters of iron.[105]

Virtually the same conclusion has been reached by Arjomand, analyzing the Iranian revolution lead by Khomeini:

> integrative social movements are reactions to social dislocation and normative disorder [which] explains the salience of their search for cultural authenticity and their moral rigorism.[106]

On a more theoretical level, Barry Schwartz has tried to explain the behavior of those who wait for others to serve them (at the doctor's or dentist's, for example, in the modern world).[107] Such people, he contends, usually occupy themselves with three things: (1) busy work; (2) fantasizing; or (3) preparation for service. Millenarians, however, are waiting on the most superior server on whom one can ever wait: God. Furthermore, the millenarian believes that this server's plans are clear and that the desired service will soon be rendered, hence the millenarian attempts to align his or her life with those divine

---

view expressed here and that put forward elsewhere in his correspondence – one of a number of such differences in his letters – is not the concern here.

[103] Weinstein, *Savonarola and Florence*, 155, 171.

[104] B.S. Capp, *The Fifth Monarchy Men* (London, 1972), 140–141.

[105] *Ibid.*, 142.

[106] Arjomand, *Turban*, 202.

[107] B. Schwartz, *Queuing and Waiting: Studies in the Social Organization of Access and Delay* (Chicago, 1975), 169–172.

intentions – a combination of fantasizing and preparation for service. Each millenarian dream of the glorious future, therefore, brings its own prescriptions for the present in its wake, with the two main categories being licentious abandon on the one hand, and strict chastity on the other.

In a similar vein, one should compare the comments of Burridge:

> Knox's remarks concerning the alterations of scandal and rigorism characteristic of enthusiastic movements are not simply good history. The two go together, are integral parts of a transition process in which the new rules are still experimental and uncertain. . . . It could be argued that orgies of sexual promiscuity . . . and the high idealism often connoted by the release from all desire are polar opposites. But the fact remains that both meet in precisely the same condition: that of no obligation.[108]

This part of the discussion can thus be concluded with a high degree of confidence based on examples from the past: millenarian hopes lead not only to moral anarchy as is widely thought, but can also produce the very opposite – an intense commitment to live one's life by the strictest possible interpretation of the law, whatever that law may be.

THE SECOND TEMPLE ERA EVIDENCE

All this would be purely theoretical were it not for an explicit statement from the concluding ideological section of 4QMMT, quoted above, but which should now be repeated for emphasis. The author exhorted his correspondent to take his teachings seriously, to reach the same conclusions he and the members of his circle have drawn:

> so that you may rejoice at the end of time as you find that some of our words are true, and it shall be reckoned to you as righteousness when you do what is upright and what is good before Him, for your wellbeing and that of Israel (C32–34).

A profound belief that redemption was at hand led directly to calls for scrupulous observance in order to enjoy fully the benefits of the future world soon to be upon mankind.

This analysis allows me to conclude the chapter with the insight for which I have been striving, one I first suggested tentatively in the

---

[108] Burridge, *New Heaven, New Earth*, 167.

paper which formed the impetus for this study as a whole on the basis of an analysis of Jubilees 23.[109] In an environment in which redemption is believed to be imminent, in which the blessings to be enjoyed by the righteous at the time of redemption are stressed,[110] at least some will respond to the situation with enhanced demands on themselves and others to fulfil the precepts of the law as strenuously as possible, according to their interpretation of the law. As Y. Talmon comments:

> The millenarian vision instills in the movement a sense of extreme urgency and a dedication to an all-embracing purpose. Every minute and every deed count and everything must be sacrificed to the cause. The followers are driven to stake everything and spare nothing since their aim is no less than the final solution of all human problems.[111]

These people will work to see that their version of the law is adopted by the nation as a whole, joining together to achieve these goals. Some of the groups thus formed may be more willing to compromise if they are not successful, others less so, but the impulse to form groups around interpretations of the law is derived – at least in part – from the belief in the grand finale soon to come on the world. That belief, along with other factors analyzed above or to be discussed below, contributes its share to the narrowing of the limits of tolerance and the flourishing of sects.[112] In that sense, to echo the comment of Ankori's quoted at the outset, messianism and sectarianism marched inexorably hand in hand in the Second Temple period, as well as in the early Muslim era. The groups, outfitted with an agenda and who had coalesced together around that agenda and a leader as argued in the previous chapters, received an extra push, which moved them over the line into full fledged activity (whether of a reformist of introversionist sort) as a result of the conviction that the redemption was dawning.

---

[109] See Baumgarten, "Qumran and Jewish Sectarianism," 149–151.

[110] See 4Q521, Frag. 2, ii, 3–14, and Frag. 7, 4–6 as published by E. Puech, "Une Apocalypse Messianique (4Q521)," *Revue de Qumran* 15 (1992), 485–495, 500–505.

[111] Y. Talmon, "Pursuit of the Millennium," 132.

[112] On the fractious nature of millenarian environments cf. Y. Talmon, "Millennial Movements," 170–171. According to Arjomand, *Turban*, 208 only the strenuous collective efforts of the Shiite clergy prevented the eruption of factionalism in Iran of the sort known from Puritan England.

The Other Side of the Coin

All this sheds light on one further aspect of the puzzle. Scholars have wondered why Jews, who were unable to agree on a common way of life during the Second Temple period, seemed to have been so much more successful in achieving this goal during the Mishnaic period. Aspects of answers to that question have been discussed at the end of preceding chapters.[113] I would like to add one more consideration in light of the discussion just concluded. The intimate connection between millennial hopes and sectarianism in the Second Temple period has now been demonstrated in detail. While the nature of messianic expectations did not change much in the aftermath of the failure of three revolts,[114] there was a marked change in the date at which Jews hoped these dreams would be realized. Messianism in the Rabbinic period was largely of the realistic, pragmatic sort; apocalyptic hopes for cosmic change do not really enter the picture until the middle ages. Nevertheless, hopes for immediate redemption waned.[115] Typical of the new outlook are the comments of R. Nathan in *bSanh.* 97b:

> This verse pierces me and descends to the very abyss: *For the vision is yet for an appointed time, but at the end it shall speak and not lie: though he tarry wait for him; because he will surely come, it will not tarry* (Hab. 2:3). Not as our Masters, who interpreted the verse, *until a time and times and the dividing of time* (Dan. 7:25); nor as R. Simlai who expounded, *Thou feedest them with the bread of tears; and givest them tears to drink a third time* (Ps. 80:6); nor as R. Akiba who expounded, *Yet once, it is a little while and I will shake the heavens and the earth* (Hag. 2:6); but the first dynasty [the Hasmoneans] shall last seventy years, the second [the Herodians] fifty two, and the reign of Bar Koziba two and a half years.

---

[113] See also Introduction, n. 44.

[114] See M.D. Herr, "Political-Realistic Messianism and Cosmic-Eschatological Messianism in the Works of the Sages," *Tarbiz* 54 (5745), 331–346 [in Hebrew]; P. Schäfer, "Die messianischen Hoffnungen des rabbinischen Judentums zwischen Naherwartung und religiösem Pragmatismus," *Studien zur Geschichte und Theologie des rabbinischen Judentums* (Leiden, 1978), 214–243.

[115] Scholars of the past generation have been so intent in discussing the nature of the expectations and in showing that they remain largely of the realistic pragmatic type that they have not paid equal attention to the change in date of expected redemption.

The contrast between R. Nathan[116] and R. Akiba (who expected imminent redemption) is patent. In this new atmosphere one hears explicit criticism of those who predict the end of days:

> R. Samuel b. Nahmani said in the name of R. Jonathan: Blasted be the bones of those who calculate the end. For they would say (i.e. their predictions make people say), since the predetermined time has arrived and yet he has not come he will never come (*bSanh* 97b).

Finally, those who made such predictions were threatened that their lives would be shortened.[117] In a sense, this was the worst of all possible punishments. If their prediction conformed to the normal pattern it was likely to be to a time close to their own era. Now if this prediction turned out wrong they paid for their temerity in misleading people. If it turned out correct, however, the punishment of having their life shortened was even more harsh, as the effect of the punishment may be that they would not live to see their prediction come true.

I find it tempting to include the waning of hope for ultimate salvation in the near future among the reasons for the ability of Jews to agree with each more easily in the years following the Bar Kochba revolt. That is, with the final redemption pushed off into a more distant future, the environment changed so as to favor schism less. With divine judgement further off, the need to be zealously scrupulous in observing the Law only in accordance with one's particular interpretation lessened, and scholars could agree more to disagree.

---

[116] The Palestinian *Amora* of the mid fourth century is the author of this comment.
[117] See the fragment of a midrash published by A. Wertheimer, *Batei Midrashot* (Jerusalem, 5728), 1.252.

CHAPTER SIX

INDEPENDENCE AND ITS CONSEQUENCES

The groups whose flourishing I am trying to understand have acquired their agendas, formed around these platforms and their leaders, and set out to change themselves and/or the world as a result of their millenarian convictions. Embarked on this route they have come into conflict, whether to a greater or lesser extent, with the mainstream institutions of their society. Sometimes they succeeded in changing the practices of the mainstream, sometimes not. More extreme groups may so violently reject that mainstream as to be rejected in turn by it, while less extreme ones manage to maintain some sort of equilibrium, while continuing to press for the changes they advocate. One final factor plays a role in this process, serving in addition to millenarianism as a drive to action. It consists of the consequences of achieving independence, and it is to this factor that this chapter is devoted.

Independence and its effects have played a large part in the argument of preceding chapters of this book, entering the discussion often as a factor among others in the explanations offered. Thus, the response to independence which did not restore the boundaries of the national perimeter as high and as fully as had been hoped was discussed at length in Chapter Two, while the connection between independence and a growth in literacy figured in Chapter Three. The move to Jerusalem examined in Chapter Four was among the consequences of independence, as was the eruption of hopes of imminent eschatological salvation addressed in the previous chapter. The treatment of the ramifications of independence in this chapter, however, will focus on one aspect which has not been considered in previous chapters. As so much of the groundwork for a consideration of this topic has been laid, however, the analysis here will be succinct.

Autonomy and its Implications

One of the most longstanding institutions in Jewish history was the system of Jewish autonomy established by the Persians in the generations after the return from the Babylonian exile. Renewed by successive conquering empires,[1] it was to survive in modified form down to the emancipation of European Jewry in the years following the French Revolution. Under this system, Jewish religious leadership was established by the imperial ruler, and empowered by him to regulate the lives of the Jews on behalf of the ruler, according to Jewish law.[2] These Jewish leaders were recognized as the authoritative interpreters of Jewish law, with their rule backed up by their imperial connection.

A system of any sort, particularly one that endures over many centuries, is bound to favor certain groups. Its continuing existence insures that certain issues remain beneath the surface, rarely if ever emerging to trouble the calm imposed by imperial fiat. When such arrangements, however, are terminated – whatever the reason for the change may be – much that was previously suppressed or repressed comes into the open. That, in fact, was the case in the aftermath of the French Revolution and the enfranchisement of European Jewry. Troubling aspects of the encounter with modernity, of the desire for legitimate change in Judaism, came to disturb Jewish life in a profound way, opening the door to debates which sometimes still rage as much as two centuries later.[3]

One should not be so naive as to believe that the era that preceded the Maccabean rebellion was free of dissent or of competing visions for the future of the Jewish people. The encounter with Hellenism, which has been mentioned often in this book, took place

---

[1] An outstanding example of one such renewal is the Seleucid constitution of Jerusalem preserved by Josephus, as analyzed by Bickerman, "Charte Seleucide." Cf. S. Schwartz, "On the Autonomy of Judaea in the Fourth and Third Centuries BCE," *Journal of Jewish Studies* 45 (1994), 157–168, who argues that there was a break in this continuity during the reign of the Ptolemies, making the Seleucid confirmation of autonomy analyzed by Bickerman an attempt to turn the clock back. Schwartz hints at political and religious changes which he believes ensued, both from the Ptolemaic innovation and the Seleucid restoration. Thus, he suggests that the pace of hellenization of material culture was increased as a result of the empowerment of the rural elites, who behaved as their rulers expected them to behave, building Greek style houses and developing a taste for Greek style luxuries (*ibid.*, 166). As a result of the rise of a new elite ideas were expressed in writing which this class had long held, but had remained silent, as can be seen from the literary remains of the period such as Ecclesiastes and Ben Sira (*ibid.*, 167). Schwartz hints that the Seleucid restoration could only end in civil war (*ibid.*, 168). As his article is conceived as a brief note (*ibid.*, 167), none of these tantalizing ideas is developed in any detail.

[2] See the arrangements made at the very founding of this system in Ezra 7.

[3] At the risk of stating the obvious, my dependence on the publications of Jacob Katz and others for this aspect of the analysis should be beyond question. See further, for example, below n. 5.

then, an encounter which induced at least some members of the established leadership to collaborate (if not worse) with Antiochus IV when he promulgated his decrees. That period was also no stranger to halachic dissent, as the earliest sections of the Enochic literature, expressing ideas which will be developed more fully in Jubilees and the Qumran corpus, such as adherence to a solar calendar, date from those years.[4] Nevertheless, under the auspices of the old order, for reasons to be explored more fully below, these challenges were not nearly as significant as they became later on.[5]

In sum, the processes to be understood are ones which encouraged the stifling of dissent under autonomy, but stimulated its flourishing once independence was a reality. At a superficial level of analysis, one of the reasons for the change which will ensue is connected with the suspension of the suppression of competing ideas, regularly a part of virtually all forms of government, as a result of revolutionary upheaval. As a consequence, dissent, both old and new, has an opportunity to flourish, particularly if a period of uncertainty follows, in which repression is not effectively maintained by the new rulers. The significance of these notions for helping explain the rise of Puritan groups in England of the seventeenth century was noted in Chapter One, n. 108. The potential utility of these ideas for elucidating the questions with which this book is concerned was also recognized in the discussion in Chapter One. The history of the period under consideration contains a number of excellent opportunities for new ideas to flourish and not be repressed, from the time of the rebellion against Antiochus's decrees until the decade between the death of Alcimus and the rise of Jonathan. The early years of inde-

---

[4] See further Beckwith, "Pre-History," 3–4.

[5] Compare the debate concerning the second day of festivals observed by diaspora Jews. The need to keep those days was already questioned in the Talmudic period, but the doubts raised then were quelled. The subject continued as a point in dispute between Rabbinic Jews and Karaites, occupying a place as a mere rhetorical question among those authorities of the Middle Ages who were not in contact with Karaites. The first to raise serious doubts concerning the obligation to observe those days were returning Marranos, who accepted the written Bible as they understood it, and who could find no justification based on the ancient sources for accepting these days as holy. Nevertheless, the views of these new Christians returning to Judaism did not find any resonance in the Jewish world until the social, economic and intellectual circumstances of western European Jewry in the late eighteenth and early nineteenth centuries turned the observance of the second day of festivals in the diaspora into one of the rallying cries of those who would reform Judaism. On these points see J. Katz, *Halacha in Straits – Obstacles to Orthodoxy at its Inception* (Jerusalem, 1992), 74–77 [in Hebrew].

pendence, when the new regime was still fragile and unstable, may have been yet another occasion for such consequences (successful revolts in the modern world are often won by *ad hoc* coalitions, which do not survive their victory, hence help contribute to greater instability and confusion).

More than that, I believe, was at stake in achieving independence under the Maccabees, and it requires recognition. As has just been seen, autonomy under the rule of world empires, like all existing traditional structures, likely repressed alternatives it perceived as challenges to its authority. But, that was not all. Ultimate responsibility in the years preceding Hasmonean independence resided in the imperial ruler. He appointed the High Priest, and his right to do so was not disputed, even by those who did not approve of his choice.[6] With final authority in the hands of the imperial power, Jews who disagreed on some halachic point with the way the Temple was being run had very few options open. They could lobby with the High Priest and his followers, trying to move them to change. Appeal to the king, however, was not likely to be successful, as the king would barely understand – at best – the issues under discussion. From the king's perspective he had chosen his representative to govern Jewish life, and he expected Jews to abide by that choice. Short of rebellion, the course to be taken in response to *extreme* provocation only, such as posed by the decrees of Antiochus IV, little choice was available except for gritting one's teeth, and hoping for better days when the leadership would see the light. Lack of power and the foreign locus of ultimate responsibility, led to impotence to alter affairs. The latter encouraged a certain degree of toleration of the fact that things were not being done as one would like, even if that tolerance was one born out of an inability to change the circumstances.

Once the dam was broken, however, the results were no longer the same. Independence transfered the ultimate locus of power to the hands of the local ruler. Gritting one's teeth, grinning and bearing the fact that the situation was not to one's liking, became far less plausible responses to unacceptable circumstances under conditions of independence. The possibility of change once independence was

---

[6] See the accounts of the appointment of Menelaus and Jason in the sources informing us about events prior to the decrees of Antiochus IV. The king's choice is deplored, and the policies to be followed by his candidate are criticized, yet the king's inherent right to make the appointment is not challenged.

achieved paved the way for greater insistence, for greater intransigence, that things must be done in accordance with the agenda offered by one's group and endorsed by its leaders. In other words, one of the consequences of achieving independence was that it provided one more impulse for groups to attempt to realize their platforms. Millenarian hopes, discussed in the previous chapter, were one such impetus, the effects of independence another.

In Support of this Thesis

The argument above is even more speculative and even more dependent on hypothesis than that of previous chapters. I would like to offer what support can be found in the sources that this logical picture also has some basis in reality. Of particular interest is the tradition concerning the reforms of Yohanan the High Priest, mentioned twice in the Mishnah, which has been the subject of inquiry by Lieberman and others:[7]

> Yohanan the High Priest did away with the declaration concerning the tithe. He also abolished the Awakeners and the Knockers. Until his days the hammer used to smite in Jerusalem (on the intermediate days of Festivals). And in his days none needed to inquire concerning *demai* produce (*mMaaser Sheni* 5:15 = *mSota* 9:10).

This series of reforms, as argued by Lieberman, was put into effect by John Hyrcanus, ruler from 135–104. Each of these reforms, as interpreted by Lieberman, was motivated by a concern for more precise and accurate observance of the law. In each case, a practice of apparent long standing was ended.[8]

Yohanan's reform concerning the declaration about the tithe, as usually understood, was based on the conclusion that the declaration was no longer apt. It called on God to bless the declarer for having tithed his produce as commanded, yet by Yohanan's day the Levite

---

[7] See Lieberman, *Hellenism in Jewish Palestine*, 139–143. Compare, however, R. Wilk, "John Hyrcanus I and the Temple Scroll," *Shnaton, An Annual for Biblical and Ancient Near Eastern Studies* 9 (1985), 221–230 [in Hebrew].

[8] The instance of the ending of loud work on intermediate days of the festival is most explicit. The Mishnah notes that loud work was permitted "until his day," presumably from time immemorial up until his institution of the reform. In the case of the abolition of the declaration concerning tithes the practice being ended is commanded in the Torah.

may have been deprived of his share by the priests. Better that the
declaration be abolished than that the individual end up cursing himself
by asking God to bless him for having fulfilled obligations, which in
fact had been disregarded. The "Awakeners" were Temple officials
who opened the doors of the sanctuary at dawn, reciting the verse
from Ps. 44:24: "Arise, why do you sleep, O Lord!" The "Knockers"
used to stun animals prior to sacrifice, to make it easier to dispatch
them. These latter two groups of officials were engaging in practices
for which there were uncomfortable equivalents in pagan temples,
hence they too were abolished. As the practical problem of runaway
sacrificial animals remained (a runaway animal, one must remember,
was not only a potential source of embarrassment, but it could also
end up being sacrificed improperly, in which case the entire offering
might become invalid), Yohanan instituted a series of restraining rings
to hold them during sacrifice. The higher degree of sanctity, even on
intermediate days of the festival in Jerusalem, was underlined by
forbidding all loud work there at that time. The reasons one needed
no longer inquire concerning *demai* produce are obscure, several
explanations being offered by our sources, which are not entirely
convincing.

One question arises as a result of this data. Why did Jews need to
wait for Yohanan for these reforms to be enacted? Was there no
Jewish ruler in Jerusalem prior to his day who felt the need to put
through the changes which Yohanan legislated? The answer to this
question should not be made overly simple. Perhaps account should
be taken of the fact that Jews became cognizant of the uncomfortable similarities between the practice in their Temple and that of
pagans only as a result of the greater awareness of the outside world,
in the aftermath of independence. On the other hand, I would suggest that this greater concern for strict observance being expressed
in Yohanan's day was an expression of that same tendency which
encouraged the formation of sectarian groups. In fact, according to
one of the possibilities considered by Yadin, it may have been pres-
sure from such sectarian groups which induced Yohanan to abolish
the "Knockers" and institute the rings.[9]

Had objections to the institutions Yohanan abrogated been voiced
in the years prior to his reign? There is no way of knowing how

---

[9] Y. Yadin, *The Temple Scroll* (Jerusalem, 1983), 1.388.

ancient the opposition to these acts was when Yohanan terminated
them. Perhaps some of the opposition, as suggested above, was recent,
other parts of it of older vintage. If at least some of the objections
were old, then Yohanan's actions fit well into the framework I am
suggesting. Practices which were offensive prior to Yohanan's day
had continued on in spite of local displeasure. Jews who were unhappy
with these customs, according to the scenario outlined above, had
little choice but to grit their teeth in impotence. Once independence
was achieved, however, Yohanan the High Priest could rectify in
one fell swoop matters which had been beyond the control of the
Jews in prior generations. This ability to effect change as a result of
new circumstances, I would argue, made its impact on national life
in the Temple as a whole. In sectarian circles, as asserted above, it
served as one more impulse to the formation and maintenance of
the groups of the Maccabean era.

THE OTHER SIDE OF THE COIN

The discussion of this aspect of my thesis will close with a consideration
of the negative case. As noted in the Introduction, Jewish life will
take a dramatic turn in a different direction with the loss of independence beginning in the mid first century BCE. New groups, of a
different social composition, almost all a response of one sort or other
to the changed circumstances, entered the picture. At least one, the
early Christians, resulted in a transformed variety of sectarianism, in
which sanctity was no longer sought by means of voluntary restriction
or boundary marking of the sort promoted by all the other groups.[10]

Nevertheless, the old groups such as Sadducees, Pharisees, Essenes
and Qumran continued on. Pharisees, Saducees and Essenes had
prominent roles in the leadership of the Great Revolt, according to
Josephus. The sun did not set on this phase of Jewish sectarian activity until the era after the destruction of the Temple, at Yavneh and
thereafter. What may be the connection between these events and

---

[10] Even John the Baptist, the supposed forerunner of Jesus by Christian conception was still well within the framework of ancient Jewish sectarianism, and his practices
concerning food and dress have been cited above, as part of the argument. The
early Christians, however, were so different that full discussion of the ways in which
they differed is far beyond the scope of this book. See further above, Chapter One,
n. 19.

the waning of sectarianism? The best answer, in my view, was offered a decade ago by Shaye Cohen.[11] With no Temple whatsoever, there was much less room for agendas to be formed. There was also simply less to argue over. With Jewish life so firmly in the hands of the Romans, dependent for so much on Roman permission,[12] there was even less reason to argue. A certain degree of mutual tolerance was imposed, willy-nilly, on fractious elements in Jewish life, as in the years of autonomy prior to independence, encouraging members of the Rabbinic academies (whose records form our main body of evidence for the period) to live together in circumstances where they had little choice but to agree to disagree, that is to continue to disagree with each other, but to keep these disputes within the framework of the world of those academies. Authorities held different views, but those who held one position did not reach the point of boundary marking against those who reached other conclusions. Conflicting social tensions also endured, and they could have provided a basis for sect formation.

In sum, not only the Rabbis were left after 70, and even if they had been the only group to survive the destruction, Rabbis disagreed with each other continuously. Nevertheless, in the new situation, sects did not flourish as they had before.[13] Thus, with the basic circumstances transformed, sectarian activity among Palestinian Jews receded, not to appear again as a dominant factor until many centuries later, when conditions would once more be appropriate.

---

[11] Cohen, "Significance of Yavneh," 27–54.

[12] Note the tradition about two law students sent to Yavneh to investigate Jewish law, SifreD 344 (Finkelstein, 401), connected with Roman approval of the use of Jewish law. On this and parallel passages see M.D. Herr, "The Historical Significance of the Dialogues between Jewish Sages and Roman Dignitaries," Scripta Hierosolymitana 22 (1971), 133. In addition, note the account of the trip taken by R. Gamaliel to ask permission of the Legate of Syria (mEduyot 7:7). One would dearly like to know what sort of permission R. Gamaliel travelled to obtain.

[13] For detailed discussion of the social, political and religious circumstances in post-70 Jewish life see S. Schwartz, Josephus and Judean Politics (Leiden, 1990).

CHAPTER SEVEN

CONCLUDING REFLECTIONS

The thesis being presented in this book has been stated sufficiently in the course of its development in previous chapters so as not to need conclusion by means of reiteration. Instead, I would like to utilize this chapter for several brief concluding reflections on the path taken in the process of formulation of that thesis.

THE NATURE OF THE EXPLANATIONS OFFERED

That path has been logical, seeking to build up logical layer after layer in the process by which groups were formed, from agendas to coalescing around leaders, to factors which encouraged action. This route was taken in spite of the explicit recognition that logic (ours of two thousand years later, in particular) may not be the best guide to understanding events, and motives for action may combine in other than logical sequences. Yet, even if imperfect, logic is the only path available, hence I have followed it.

What role has been left for personal clashes, for regional loyalties or for socio-economic interest groups (to mention only three factors which often do not affect events in accordance with the rules of logic or intellect, but which are regularly invoked in explanations of the rise of sectarian groups) in the argument proposed above? The evidence in hand, unfortunately, does not permit us to see the significance of these factors very clearly, hence they have rarely been emphasized in the discussion above. Nevertheless, the framework proposed in the preceding chapters is sufficiently flexible to allow room for the operation of these causes, if more explicit evidence for their roles should ever become available. Thus I have argued for a process of interpretation of the Bible in which sectarians saw themselves and their times reflected in the Biblical text, perceiving this understanding of the Bible to be its "true" meaning, then took steps to see that their perception of the meaning of the text became a reality. Clearly, personal or regional loyalties, as well as socio-economic interests, could all thus find expression in the interpretations of the Bible proposed.

Indeed, when appropriate, these non-strictly hermeneutical considerations could play a decisive part in shaping the interpretation offered.

Another opportunity for a variety of factors to fashion the result is offered by the process of formation of groups around leaders and agendas discussed above. Existing interpersonal networks, as modern research has taught, play a decisive role in this process, perhaps an even greater one than ideological or theological commitment. Groups tend to form along the lines of existing social networks and that explanation of membership goes farther and deeper in illuminating the known results than any other. The thesis I have been presenting allows these aspects to play their part as may be needed. The ways in which groups form around agendas and/or leaders, for which I argued above, allow ample space for a variety of groups to emerge, each of which is giving expression to the perspective of some social network, whether based on personal loyalty, regional origin or economic interest.

The approach taken in the preceding chapters, virtually by default due to lack of evidence, nonetheless has an advantage. One frequent criticism of social scientific studies of religious phenomena is that they tend to reductionism, to making everything an expression of socio-economic status or other such factors. Little room, if at all, is left for theological or ideological conviction. The explanations for the rise of ancient Jewish sectarianism which I have suggested avoid that pitfall, by being sufficiently flexible to allow other social factors to play a part, if and when there is useful evidence of their role. Yet, the explanations proposed are not reductionist in the sense so often criticized.

SOCIAL COMPOSITION AND ITS IMPLICATIONS, FOR THE LAST TIME

A second focus of reflection by way of conclusion concerns the significance of the nature of the groups whose flourishing has provided the underlying question of this book. These were elitist sectarian movements, which ultimately set the tone for a whole society over an extended period of time, as indicated by their place in the mind of Josephus, the point of departure of this inquiry. All this is very unlike movements usually studied by modern social scientists, who regularly investigate lower class sectarian groups. The latter have been described as often untheological and unintellectual, as groups which accept notions from a wide variety of sources, welding them together with no real concern for consistency. The emphasis in these groups is largely on emotion, and on wide-scale campaigns to spread the word of God. How different from the ancient Jewish groups which have been the concern here, for whom detailed study of the text of the Bible, at the highest possible level, played such an important role. The response of at least some of these ancient groups to the surrounding society was one of utter disdain, so much so that one is entitled to wonder whether they seriously tried to develop a circle of supporters outside the boundaries of their committed members. Perhaps the Qumran theory of the place reserved for the "naive" to recognize the truth of the Qumran position in the end of days and thus enjoy the blessings of that era would have moved some of those considered "naive" by Qumran standards to be more sympathetically inclined towards that community, but I wonder.

In any case, the changes under consideration in this study affected the nation as a whole, but their impact would have been even more profound on the elite which ultimately joined sectarian movements. They would have been most seriously distressed by the apostasy of the old leadership and the decrees of Antiochus IV, by the breakdown of the old barriers between Jews and gentiles, as well as by the changes associated with the rise of the Maccabees. Expanded literacy as well as the move from the farms to Jerusalem would have been a much more meaningful factor in their lives. These were extraordinary times for all, but even more so for the elite. New solutions for the new times were proposed and flourished among that same pool of people, leading to the rise of sectarianism, until circumstances so changed so as to favor an era of consolidation. Thus even if some of the factors I have proposed as explanations were not as widespread in their consequences as one might want (literacy, for example, remained very restricted by modern standards), these repercussions were felt with particular force among the members of the circles which would provide the participants in sectarian movements.

It is for these reasons that I have found analogies based on Puritan Britain to be particularly insightful. Here too, as noted at the outset of this book, one encounters elitist groups, on whom the changes of the era made their most acute impact. Here too the Bible played a decisive role, and here too messianic expectations among members of the elite were prominent as forces encouraging action. Differences between the Puritan situation and that in Maccabean Palestine there were, and these have been noted as appropriate throughout this book, yet the fundamental similarity is such that I have learned much from Puritan Britain, which has helped illuminate aspects of the answers offered here.

These considerations are also important to separate between ancient Jewish sectarianism and modern fundamentalism. The circumstances which call forth fundamentalist movements in the contemporary world are very much like those which I have invoked to explain the flourishing of ancient Jewish sectarianism. For example, as was argued above, both sorts of groups are responses to a changed world, and give expression to a desire to go back to simpler days, prior to the wrenching changes. Members of both types of organizations are searching for masters to help chart the course in confusing times. Nevertheless, ancient Jewish sectarianism and modern fundamentalism should not be carelessly merged. For all the similarities, ancient Jewish sects were much more elitist, appealing to a population drawn from the natural leadership of their time and place. This difference made ancient Jewish sects more intellectual in outlook, as well as more reflective of the perspective of those at the top of society.

THE NATURE OF THE SURVIVING EVIDENCE

The explanations offered in the preceding chapters were the result of an ongoing struggle with the limitations of the surviving evidence. These limits are of many sorts, as has been noted regularly when appropriate. One further limitation remains to be discussed here: the surviving evidence is all pious in outlook, supportive of sects and their members, at most polemical on behalf of one group against others. There is no rousing defense of the Temple authorities against their critics. No apologetics for the Maccabean dynasty survived, dated later than 1 Macc. and the letters at the head of 2 Macc. There is no description of Qumran or the Essenes written by someone whose brother or son chose to live there, taking with him a substantial part of the family's assets, hence viewing these groups with a jaundiced eye. Documents of this sort, had they reached us, might have yielded further insights into the connections between context and consequence in the flourishing of sectarianism under investigation here.

To Explain is Not to Condone

Finally, explanation of the sort I have been offering is not intended to condone, certainly not to excuse. It favors neither the establishment nor the sectarian. Its sole objective is understanding. The way in which ancient Jewish sectarianism as a massive social phenomenon fitted into its social, political and intellectual context is now clearer, I hope, than at the outset − no more and no less. Yes, sectarians − both reformist and introversionist − were more extreme in their devotion to what they believed to be the proper way to be Jewish than other members of their contemporary society; the introversionist kind were very much more extreme than the average. This fact, in and of itself, is of no consequence for assessing the truth claims of the different sectarian groups. Perhaps the only conclusion to be drawn on the basis of the evidence and hypotheses presented here is that one should not be quick to dismiss Second Temple era sectarians as cranks and crackpots, unconnected with the reality of their times. While ancient Jewish sectarianism may be extraordinary in its extent, I have tried to show the very unusual epoch in which it flourished, and the ways in which it was a serious response to the dilemmas of that singular period.

Thus Far and No Further

A wall now looms on the horizon, blocking (for the moment, at least) my seeing clearly beyond it. As slight consolation I remind myself that human events regularly have a mysterious side, which historians cannot really fully penetrate. Is there any discipline in which the view is unrestricted, in which no mysteries remain unexplained? I leave that question to others. Whatever the answer to that question may be, the historian, at the very least, must know when all that he or she can reasonably say has been said, when to defer further consideration for some time and place in the indefinite future, when to hope for new sources, or that others will take up and extend the discussion on the basis of new insights − that is, when to decide that the treatment of the chosen topic has reached its end.

APPENDIX

SECTARIANISM IN SEVENTEENTH CENTURY BRITAIN FROM THE PERSPECTIVE OF BOUNDARY MARKING

Applying the perspective of boundary marking mechanisms which I am proposing to British sectarianism of the seventeenth century seems a plausible step. Scholars have already remarked on the "partly self-inflicted isolation of the godly,"[1] or commented on the "endemic separatism prevalent well before the Civil War."[2] Nevertheless, I have not seen a focused analysis of the British material from this viewpoint. I therefore present below points gleaned in passing, a number of indications of the ways British sectarianism fits this model, and of the realms of life around which the boundary marking of the groups of that time concentrated. The comparison between the British and ancient Jewish examples is instructive.

As in the case of the Jewish material it was important to divide between antecedents, forerunners and the mature phenomenon itself (Introduction, at nn. 68–79), so too in the British instances one must be sensitive to tendencies present in the late sixteenth and early seventeenth centuries, but which developed fully only later. Perhaps full fledged sectarianism in the British case did not emerge until the aftermath of the failure of the revolution, but this is a conclusion beyond my competence to reach. Again, as in the case of the Jewish groups it was important to distinguish between reformist and introversionist sects, so too must one recognize variation in the degree of separation in sixteenth and seventeenth century Britain. In accordance with these perspectives, I will record below examples of boundary marking of varying intensity, drawn from cases spread over a long period, from a hundred years or more, beginning at the end of the sixteenth century.

---

[1] Collinson, *Religion of Protestants*, 230.
[2] *Ibid.*, 273, based on the research of P. Clarke, *English Provincial Society from Reformation to the Revolution: Religion, Politics and Society in Kent* (Hassocks, 1977).

Thus, excommunication discussed in the quote from C. Hill, Introduction, at n. 119, had religious as well as social consequences.[3] Obviously, one did not worship with those who had been excommunicated, as they were no longer considered "really" Christian. As the formula of excommunication stated, those so punished were to be to a Christian as a "heathen and a publican,"[4] precisely the new sort of outsider created by boundary marking of the type I am considering. As a result of excommunication, commensality, commerce and intercourse with the excommunicate were forbidden (see below), so that families and society at large were torn asunder.[5] Replacing the old family structure was a new set of "brothers" and "sisters," the new insiders, members of one's religious family, with whom one identified, as over and against other Christians.[6]

In the realm of worship, there were objections to numerous practices which seemed to smack of Popery (such as churching of women, kneeling at the sacrament, and the wearing of the surplice at mass), and which emphasized institutional charisma, rather than personal salvation. The Godly renounced these forms of worship with stiff vows, never to participate in such again, and ministers were expelled from their parishes over issues such as these.[7]

On the other side of the coin, some Godly folks, who valued sermons and the preaching of the word above all, denied the efficacy of the sacraments as administered by a non-preaching minister.[8] Typical of this zeal for preaching was the opinion that one should move from a city where the word was inadequately proclaimed, or not pray at a church that did not provide at least two sermons a Sunday.[9]

---

[3] The discussion of excommunication below ignores the issue, much discussed at the time, of who should have the power to invoke this penalty and for what offenses. I focus on the consequences of excommunication, no matter by whom employed. For a summary of the debate over those empowered to invoke the penalty, and the reasons it should be imposed, as well as a discussion of the views of those Puritans who wanted excommunication to be a purely spiritual sanction, with no material or social consequences, see Hill, *Society and Puritanism*, 365–370, 377–381.

[4] *Ibid.*, 352.

[5] See the description of the effects of excommunication by a Scottish royalist, in C. Hill and E. Dell (Eds.), *The Good Old Cause* (London, 1969, 2nd edition), 311.

[6] Collinson, *Religion of Protestants*, 253–256. On the strong sense of community among puritans see *ibid.*, 268–269. On the use of kinship models among ancient Jewish sects see above, Chapter One, at nn. 75–76.

[7] See Hunt, *Puritan Moment*, 101–102, 111, 115.

[8] See Hill, *Society and Puritanism*, 63.

[9] *Ibid.*, 66.

Church bells pealed differently to inform congregants when there was no sermon.[10] Preaching, in the view of Puritans, was important because it was the appropriate antidote against the merry life of fellowship shunned by the zealous (see below).[11]

A sub-category of worship in ancient Jewish sectarianism was the calendar. Calendar disputes in seventeenth century Britain revolved around the question of whether one observed innumerable saint's days, scattered throughout the year, or worked regularly on the six days of every week, resting habitually on the Sabbath. No less than in ancient Judaism, this disagreement separated between people on either side of the divide.[12] Numerous ministers were suspended from their parishes for not reading the Declaration permitting sports on the Sabbath in 1633.[13] On the other side of the coin, Puritans denied access to the sacraments to those who violated the Sabbath.[14] As Hill remarks, anticipating the conclusion for which I am arguing, attitudes towards Sunday sports had become a shibboleth for distinguishing between friends and foes.[15]

Endogamy was encouraged among the pious, not as an absolute requirement, but as a practical way of ensuring marriage to the proper sort of spouse.[16] The boundary marking between sectarians and those outside their order(s) was even stronger than the marriage bonds: a sectarian wife might forsake an anti-Christian (i.e. non-sectarian) husband, and *vice versa*.[17]

Quakers refused to wear "normal" clothing and insisted on plain dress, as hallowed by the practice of their founder.[18] Drunkenness and ale-houses were much denounced, as among the worst of social ills, from which the Godly were expected to abstain.[19] In general, pious Christians were to shun the company of non-believers, as the former were to be a people apart.[20]

---

[10] *Ibid.*, 73.

[11] *Ibid.*, 69.

[12] *Ibid.*, 145–218.

[13] *Ibid.*, 200. According to a famous story, one London minister read the Declaration, as required, then read the Ten Commandments, and then announced: "You have heard now the commandments of God and man. Obey which you please," *ibid.*, 199.

[14] *Ibid.*, 205.

[15] *Ibid.*, 200.

[16] Hunt, *Puritan Moment*, 232.

[17] Hill, *World*, 311.

[18] *Ibid.*, 256.

[19] Hunt, *Puritan Moment*, 80–83, 128–129, 142–144.

[20] *Ibid.*, 231–232.

Others of the Godly were severe in their eating habits, refusing the fancy food consumed by those outside their movement, as we learn from the popular anti-Puritan ditty quoted by Hunt:

> Those who are so precise
> That they will have no Christmas pies
> It were good the crows
> Should pick out their eyes.[21]

Piping, potting and feasting, along with the mis-spending of time in pleasure, were viewed as "leprosy,"[22] a term of more than mere rhetorical significance for an audience learned in the Bible. At some level, those who indulged in these activities were as impure, and to be as excluded from the camp, as the Biblical leper. Among the restrictions imposed on an excommunicate were that no one was to eat with him, or receive him into his house.[23] This was a punishment of some significance, as Puritan private worship often ended in a meal shared by all participants.[24]

Within the movements of the elect a strong atmosphere of mutual admonition and rebuke prevailed, sometimes leading the sensitive to despair.[25] Only thus could the barrier between the pure redeemed world and that outside be maintained. Only thus might the tendency to split into further groups and sub-groups be averted.[26]

In general, as against a culture of fellowship, Puritans insisted on a culture of discipline, lived a strict life guided by precise opinions, and maintained by "painful" preachers; they abstained from the culture of fellowship and from contact with those who participated in it. Puritans, of course, had not invented moral concerns, nor had they a monopoly on attempts to eliminate bastardy or suppress drunkenness. They were not the only citizens with religious convictions, but zeal for these matters was seen as a conspicuous and essential aspect of Puritanism. It was their form of boundary marking and establishing their identity.[27]

---

[21] *Ibid.*, 151.
[22] Hill, *Society and Puritanism*, 125.
[23] *Ibid.*, 358.
[24] See Collinson, *Religion of Protestants*, 264–266.
[25] Hunt, *Puritan Moment*, 230.
[26] Hill, *Society and Puritanism*, 469.
[27] See W. Hunt, "Spectral Origins of the English Revolution: Legitimation Crisis in Early Stuart England," in Eley and Hunt, *Reviving the English Revolution*, 315–317. Cf. M. Spufford, "Puritanism and Social Control?" in A. Fletcher and J. Stevenson

One hostile witness before the Star Chamber in 1591 testified that Puritans would not eat, drink, buy or sell with persons who were not of their faction.[28] If this evidence is taken literally, the commercial implications of boundary drawing in seventeenth century Britain were no less extreme than at Qumran. As this was the evidence of a hostile witness, we are not on as firm ground as might be desired. More certain, however, was the insistence that charity be limited to members of one's own movement.[29] Commercial dealings with excommunicates were restricted: such a person could not buy or sell, be employed, sue, give evidence in the courts, give bail, make a will or receive a legacy, or serve as administrator or guardian.[30]

The examples noted thus far are ones in which British sectarianism focused on the same realms of life as the cases from Second Temple Judaism (worship, food, dress, marriage, commercial dealings and admonition). British sectarianism was also had aspects for which there are no known equivalents among ancient Jews, such as the special speech (thou forms) adopted by Quakers, or Quaker refusal to perform hat-honor.[31] Perhaps the fad for special names such as Bethankful or Sindeny should be added to this list.[32] To the extent known, ancient Jewish groups did not promote special speech forms and the names of ancient Jewish sectarians were unexceptional for their time.

The commercial aspects of British sectarianism also differed from that in Second Temple Judaism. Privateering at the expense of the Catholic Spaniards was considered a legitimate part of the war against anti-Christ).[33] British sectarians concentrated on their campaign against

---

(Eds.), *Order and Disorder in Early Modern England* (Cambridge, 1985), 41–57. The perspective of boundary maintenance for which I am arguing helps overcome Spufford's objections that social discipline and concerns were not Puritan inventions, hence were not what made Puritan groups special. What was distinctive about Puritanism, I would propose, was not discipline or social control *per se*, which had existed from time immemorial, but the perimeters erected by the pious around their way of life, which made them into elite schismatics of a new sort, criticizing the lifestyle of others (in the hope of reforming it) from that fortified position.

[28] Collinson, *Religion of Protestants*, 269.

[29] Hill, *Society and Puritanism*, 296.

[30] *Ibid.*, 357.

[31] Hill, *World*, 246–248.

[32] Collinson, *Religion of Protestants*, 240. Note also a family such as the Starrs of Cranbrook, whose children were given names such as "More-gift," "Mercy," "Suretrust," "Stand-well," and "Comfort." See further Reay, "Popular Religion," 106.

[33] Hunt, *Puritan Moment*, 161–162.

idleness, which they saw as a consequence of Popery: in the view of some radicals an idle person could not be a member of the Church of God, and such a person merited excommunication.[34] Even worse, a Godly person could be prodigal in helping those in need, if it were blindly done.[35] I know of no equivalent to these practices among Second Temple Jews.

Josephus's Essenes avoided oaths, as superfluous (*War* 2.135), especially when imposed for purposes of establishing political loyalty (*Ant.* 15.371), but took tremendous oaths on entry to the group, which bound them for life (*War* 2.139–142). The Godly of seventeenth century Britain, by contrast, seemed to have opposed oaths on principle in all contexts. This rejection of oaths was an act of anarchistic social protest, more extreme than the practice of the Essenes, and was taken as proof presumptive of sectarianism.[36]

Detailed analysis of a work such as Richard Rodgers's *Seven Treatises*, first published in 1603 and which went through seven editions before 1630, described by Hunt, as "the first systematic presentation of the Puritan conception of Godliness in its quotidian manifestations,"[37] might yield even further illustrations of the ways in which British sectarianism fits the pattern of boundary marking. As one such potential example I would note the drawing up of formal covenants between groups of the godly, specifying their obligations to each other, marking them off from those who had succumbed to wordliness and whose godliness had decayed, a practice recommended by Rogers and for which he supplied examples.[38] The authors of these documents were aware of the dangers of sectarian introversionism, which they hoped to avoid,[39] as they and their followers fell into what I have called the reformist category, but the potential for further collapsing of walls inwards was always present. The covenants themselves should be interesting to compare to sources such as 1QS or CD.

Confirmation of the conclusion for which I am arguing is provided by the response of those whom the boundaries erected were intended to distinguish as outsiders. They called the Godly folks,

---

[34] Hill, *Society and Puritanism*, 130–133, 281.
[35] *Ibid.*, 289.
[36] *Ibid.*, 383.
[37] Hunt, *Puritan Moment*, 110.
[38] Collinson, *Religion of Protestants*, 270.
[39] *Ibid.*, 271–283.

"Puritans," as a term of ironic disdain and reproach.[40] In spite of the opprobrium attached to the name, they recognized in it the professed intention of the "hotter sort of Protestants" to lead a life of purity, from which these outsiders were excluded. Portraying the consequences of boundary marking in this unfavorable light, they understood that a "Puritan" was a person who loved God with all his soul, and hated his neighbor with all his heart.[41] Recognizing the boundary marking nature of the activities of Puritans helps explain the response of the surrounding society in a way hitherto unrecognized.[42]

In noting the senses in which the model based on the Jewish cases sheds light on the British ones, my use of British examples as a source of insight into ancient Judaism approaches becoming a two way intellectual street.

---

[40] On the various meanings of "Puritan" see Hill, *Society and Puritanism*, 13–29.
[41] *Ibid.*, 24.
[42] Cf. Hunt, *Puritan Moment*, 145–146.

BIBLIOGRAPHY

Aberle, D., "A Note on Relative Deprivation Theory as Applied to Millenarian and other Cult Movements," in S. Thrupp (Ed.), *Millennial Dreams in Action* (The Hague, 1962), 209–214.

Almond, G., *Crisis, Choice and Change: Historical Studies of Political Development* (Boston, 1973).

Alon, G., "The Attitude of the Pharisees to Roman Rule and the House of Herod," *Jews, Judaism and the Classical World: Studies in Jewish History in the Times of the Second Temple and Talmud* (Jerusalem, 1977), 18–47.

Anderson, B., *Imagined Communities* (London/New York, 1991, 2nd edition).

Ankori, Z., *The Karaites in Byzantium* (New York, 1959).

Applebaum, S., "Jewish Urban Communities and Greek Influences," *Scripta Classica Israelica* 5 (1979/80), 158–177.

Arenhoevel, D., *Die Theokratie nach dem 1. und 2. Makkabäerbuch* (Mainz, 1967).

Arjomand, S., "Social Change and Movements of Revitalization in Contemporary Islam," in J. Beckford (Ed.), *New Religious Movements and Rapid Social Change* (Paris, 1986), 87–111.

———, *The Turban for the Crown – The Islamic Revolution in Iran* (New York, 1988).

Avi-Yonah, M., "Historical Geography," in S. Safrai and M. Stern (Eds.), *The Jewish People in the First Century, Volume One* (Assen, 1974), 78–116.

Aviad, J., "The Contemporary Israeli Pursuit of the Millennium," *Religion* 14 (1984), 199–222.

Avigad, N., *Discovering Jerusalem* (Jerusalem, 1980).

Balch, R., "When the Light Goes Out Darkness Comes: A Study of Defection from a Totalist Cult," in R. Stark (Ed.), *Religious Movements: Genesis, Exodus and Numbers* (New York, 1985), 11–63.

Bar Ilan, M., "Illiteracy in the Land of Israel in the First Centuries CE," in S. Fishbane (Ed.), *Essays in the Social Scientific Study of Judaism and Jewish Society, Volume II* (New York, 1992), 46–61.

Bar Kochva, B., *"Pseudo-Hecataeus" on the Jews: Legitimizing the Jewish Diaspora* (Berkeley, 1996).

Barkai, G., "Jerusalem of the Hasmonean Era," in H. Eshel and D. Amit (Eds.), *The History of the Hasmonean House*, (Jerusalem, 1995), 231–238 [in Hebrew].

Barker, E., "People Who do not Become Moonies," in R. Stark (Ed.), *Religious Movements: Genesis, Exodus and Numbers* (New York, 1985), 65–93.

Baron, S., *A Social and Religious History of the Jews* (New York, 1952–).

Barrera, J.T., "The Essenes of Qumran: Between Submission to the Law and Apocalyptic Flight," in F. García Martínez and J. Trebolle Barrera, *The People of the Dead Sea – Their Writings, Beliefs and Practices* (Leiden, 1995), 50–76.

Baumbach, G., "Schriftstellerische Tendenzen und historische Verwertbarkeit der Essenerdarstellung des Josephus," in C. Thoma, G. Stemberger, and J. Maier (Eds.), *Judentum, Ausblicke und Einsichten, Festgabe für Karl Schubert zum siebzigsten Geburtstag* (Frankfurt, 1993), 23–51.

Baumgarten, A.I., "City Lights – Urbanization and Sectarianism in Hasmonean Jerusalem", in M. Poorthuis and C. Safrai (Eds.), *The Centrality of Jerusalem: Historical Perspectives* (Kampen, 1996), 50–64.

———, "Crisis in the Scrollery: A Dying Consensus," *Judaism* 44 (1995), 399–413.

——, "Euhemerus's Eternal Gods: Or, How Not To Be Embarrassed By Greek Mythology," in R. Katzoff, Y. Petroff and D. Schaps (Eds.), *Classical Studies in Honor of David Sohlberg* (Ramat Gan, 1996), 91–103.

——, "Greco-Roman Voluntary Associations and Jewish Sects," in M. Goodman (Ed.), *The Jews of the Greco-Roman World*, forthcoming.

——, "*Hatta't* Sacrifices," *Revue Biblique*, 103 (1996), 337–342.

——, "He Knew that He Knew that He Knew that He was an Essene," *Journal of Jewish Studies*, 48 (1997), 53–61.

——, "Josephus on Essene Sacrifice," *Journal of Jewish Studies* 45 (1994), 169–183.

——, "Miracles and Halacha in Rabbinic Judaism," *Jewish Quarterly Review* 73 (1983), 238–253.

——, "Qumran and Jewish Sectarianism during the Second Temple Period," in M. Broshi, S. Japhet, D. Schwartz and S. Talmon (Eds.), *The Scrolls of the Judean Desert: Forty Years of Research* (Jerusalem, 1992), 139–151 [in Hebrew].

——, "Rabbinic Literature as a Source for the History of Jewish Sectarianism in the Second Temple Period," *Dead Sea Discoveries* 2 (1995), 14–57.

——, "Review of L. Schiffman, *Law, Custom and Messianism*," *Zion* 58 (5753), 509–513 [in Hebrew].

——, "Rivkin and Neusner on the Pharisees," in P. Richardson (Ed.), *Law in Religious Communities in the Roman Period* (Waterloo, 1991), 109–126.

——, "The Food of a Sectarian and its Implications: Finding Oneself in a Sectarian Context," in A. Baumgarten, with J. Assmann and G. Stroumsa (Eds.), *Self Soul and Body in Religious Experience*, forthcoming.

——, "The Hellenization of the Hasmonean State," in H. Eshel and D. Amit (Eds.), *The History of the Hasmonean House*, (Jerusalem, 1995), 77–84 [in Hebrew].

——, "The Legitimacy of Herod and his Sons as Kings of Israel", in I. Gafni, A. Oppenheimer & M. Stern (Eds.), *Jews and Judaism in the Second Temple, Mishna and Talmud Period Studies in Honor of Shmuel Safrai* (Jerusalem, 1993), 31–37 [in Hebrew].

——, "The Name of the Pharisees," *Journal of Biblical Literature* 102 (1983), 411–428.

——, "The Paradox of the Red Heifer", *Vetus Testamentum* 43 (1993), 442–451.

——, "The Pharisaic *Paradosis*," *Harvard Theological Review* 80 (1987), 63–77.

——, "The Rule of the Martian as Applied to Qumran," *Israel Oriental Studies* 14 (1994), 179–200.

——, "The Temple Scroll, Toilet Practices, and the Essenes", *Jewish History* 10 (1996), 9–20.

——, "The Torah as a Public Document in Judaism," *Studies in Religion* 14 (1985), 17–24.

——, "The Zadokite Priests at Qumran: A Reconsideration," *Dead Sea Discoveries*, forthcoming.

——, "Who were the Sadducees? The Sadducees of Jerusalem and Qumran", in I. Gafni, A. Oppenheimer and D. Schwartz (Eds.), *The Jews in the Hellenistic-Roman World – Studies in Memory of Menahem Stern* (Jerusalem, 1996), 393–412 [in Hebrew].

Baumgarten, J., "The Cave 4 Versions of the Qumran Penal Code," *Journal of Jewish Studies* 43 (1992), 268–276.

——, "The Disqualification of Priests in 4Q Fragments of the 'Damascus Document,' A Specimen of the Recovery of pre-Rabbinic Halakha," in J. Barrera and L. Montaner (Eds.), *The Madrid Qumran Congress: Proceedings of the International Congress on the Dead Sea Scrolls, Madrid, 18–21 March 1991* (Leiden, 1992), 2.503–514.

——, "The Pharisaic-Sadducean Controversies about Purity and the Qumran Texts," *Journal of Jewish Studies* 31 (1980), 157–170.

——, "The Purification Rituals in DJD 7," in D. Dimant and U. Rappaport (Eds.), *The Dead Sea Scrolls – Forty Years of Research* (Leiden/Jerusalem, 1992), 199–209.

——, "The 'Sons of Dawn' in Damascus Document = CD 13:14–15 and the Ban on Commerce among the Essenes," *Israel Exploration Journal* 33 (1983), 81–85.

——, "The Unwritten Law in the Pre-Rabbinic Period," *Journal for the Study of Judaism in the Persian, Hellenistic and Roman Period* 3 (1972), 7–29.

Beckford, J.A., "Accounting for Conversion," *British Journal of Sociology*, 29 (1978), 249–262.

——, "Introduction," in J. Beckford (Ed.), *New Religious Movements and Rapid Social Change* (Paris, 1986), ix–xv.

Beckwith, R., "The Pre-History and Relationships of the Pharisees, Sadducees and Essenes: A Tentative Reconstruction," *Revue de Qumran* 11 (1982), 3–46.

Ben Arieh, S., "The 'Third Wall' of Jerusalem," in Y. Yadin (Ed.), *Jerusalem Revealed – Archaeology in the Holy City 1968–1974* (New Haven/London, 1976), 60–62.

Ben Shalom, I., *The School of Shammai and the Zealots' Struggle Against Rome* (Jerusalem, 1993) [in Hebrew].

Ben Shammai, H., "Between Ananites and Karaites: Observations on Early Medieval Jewish Sectarianism," *Studies in Muslim-Jewish Relations* 1 (1992), 19–29.

——, "Methodological Remarks Concerning the Relationship Between the Karaites and Ancient Jewish Sects," *Cathedra* 42 (5747), 69–81 [in Hebrew].

Berger, K., *Das Buch der Jubiläen* (Gütersloh, 1981).

Bergmeier, R., *Die Essener-Berichte des Flavius Josephus* (Kampen, 1993).

Bernstein, M., "The Employment and Interpretation of Scripture in 4QMMT: Preliminary Observations," in J. Kampen and M. Bernstein (Eds.), *Reading 4QMMT – New Perspectives on Qumran Law and History* (Atlanta, 1996), 29–52.

——, "'Walking in the Festivals of the Gentiles' 4QpHosea^a 2.15–17 and *Jubilees* 6.34–38," *Journal for the Study of the Pseudepigrapha* 9 (1991), 21–34.

Bickerman, E.J., *Chronology of the Ancient World* (London, 1968).

——, "En Marge de l'Ecriture," *Studies in Jewish and Christian History, Part Three* (Leiden, 1986), 327–349.

——, "Faux littéraires dans l'antiquité classique," *Studies in Jewish and Christian History, Part Three* (Leiden, 1986), 196–211.

——, "Genesis and Character of Maccabean Hellenism," *From Ezra to the Last of the Maccabees* (New York, 1962), 153–165.

——, "La chaine de la tradition pharisienne," *Studies in Jewish and Christian History, Part Two* (Leiden, 1980), 256–279.

——, "La Charte Seleucide de Jerusalem," *Studies in Jewish and Christian History, Part Two* (Leiden, 1980), 44–85.

——, *The God of the Maccabees* (Leiden, 1979).

——, *The Jews in the Greek Age* (Cambridge, 1988).

——, "Une proclamation seleucide relative au temple de Jerusalem," *Studies in Jewish and Christian History, Part Two* (Leiden, 1980), 86–104.

Blenkinsopp, J., "A Jewish Sect of the Persian Period," *Catholic Biblical Quarterly* 52 (1990), 5–20.

——, "Interpretation and the Tendency to Sectarianism: An Aspect of Second Temple History," in E.P. Sanders (Ed.), *Jewish and Christian Self Definition Volume Two: Aspects of Judaism in the Graeco-Roman Period* (London, 1981), 1–26.

Bloch, J., *On the Apocalyptic in Judaism* (Philadelphia, 1952).

Bloch, M., "A Contribution Towards a Comparative History of European Societies," *Land and Work in Medieval Europe, Selected Papers by Marc Bloch* (Berkeley, 1967), 44–81.

Bowman, J., "Did the Qumran Sect Burn the Red Heifer?" *Revue de Qumran* 1 (1958), 73–81.

Broshi, M., "A Day in the Life of Hananiah Notos," *Alpayim* 13 (5757), 117–134 [in Hebrew].

——, "Anti-Qumranic Polemics in the Talmud," in J. Barrera and L. Montaner (Eds.), *The Madrid Qumran Congress: Proceedings of the International Congress on the Dead Sea Scrolls, Madrid, 18–21 March 1991* (Leiden, 1992), 2.589–600.

——, "The Archeology of Qumran – A Reconsideration," in D. Dimant and

U. Rappaport (Eds.), *The Dead Sea Scrolls – Forty Years of Research* (Leiden/Jerusalem, 1992), 103–115.

——, "The Diet of Palestine in the Roman Period, Introductory Notes," *Israel Museum Journal* 5 (1986), 41–56.

——, "The Expansion of Jerusalem in the Reigns of Hezekiah and Manasseh," *Israel Exploration Journal* 24 (1974), 21–26.

——, "Western Palestine in the Roman-Byzantine Period," *Bulletin of the American Schools of Oriental Research* 236 (1979), 1–10.

Broshi, M. and Yardeni, A., "On Nethinim and False Prophets," *Tarbiz* 62 (5753), 45–54 [in Hebrew].

Brownlee, W., *The Midrash Pesher of Habakkuk* (Missoula, 1979).

Burgmann, H., "Das umstrittene Intersacerdotium in Jerusalem 159–152 v. Chr.," *Journal for the Study of Judaism in the Persian, Hellenistic and Roman Period* 11 (1980), 135–176.

Burkert, W., "Oriental Symposia: Contrasts and Parallels," in W. Slater (Ed.), *Dining in a Classical Context* (Ann Arbor, 1991), 7–24.

Burridge, K., *New Heaven, New Earth: A Study of Millenarian Activities* (New York, 1969).

Cahill, J., "Chalk Vessel Assemblages of the Persian/Hellenistic and Early Roman Periods," *Qedem* 33 (1992), 190–274.

Callaway, P.R., *The History of the Qumran Community: An Investigation* (Sheffield, 1988).

Capp, B.S., "Extreme Millenarianism," in P. Toon (Ed.), *Puritans, the Millennium and the Future of Israel: Puritan Eschatology 1600 to 1660* (Cambridge/London, 1970), 66–90.

——, "*Godly Rule* and English Millenarism," *Past and Present* 52 (1971), 106–117.

——, "The Fifth Monarchists and Popular Millenarianism," in J.F. McGregor and B. Reay (Eds.), *Radical Religion in the English Revolution* (Oxford, 1984), 165–190.

——, *The Fifth Monarchy Men* (London, 1972).

——, "The Political Dimension," in C.A. Patrides and J. Wittreich (Eds.), *The Apocalypse in English Renaissance Thought and Literature* (Manchester, 1984), 93–124.

Caquot, A., "Ben Sira et le Messianisme," *Semitica* 16 (1966), 41–68.

Carr, E.H., *What is History* (Baringstoke, 1987, 2nd edition).

Charlesworth, J., (Ed.), *The Messiah – Developments in Earliest Judaism and Christianity* (Minneapolis, 1992).

——, "From Messianology to Christology: Problems and Prospects," in J. Charlesworth (Ed.), *The Messiah – Developments in Earliest Judaism and Christianity* (Minneapolis, 1992), 3–35.

Chiesa, B., and Lockwood, W., *Yaqub al-Qirqasani on Jewish Sects and Christianity* (Frankfurt, 1984).

Chinnery, E., and Haddon, A., "Five New Religious Cults in British New Guinea," *The Hibbert Journal* 15 (1917), 448–463.

Clarke, P., *English Provincial Society from Reformation to the Revolution: Religion, Politics and Society in Kent* (Hassocks, 1977).

Cohen. G.D., "Messianic Postures of Ashkenazim and Sephardim," *Studies of the Leo Baeck Institute* (Ungar, 1967), 117–156.

Cohen, M., "Maimonides' Egypt", in E. Ormsby (Ed.), *Maimonides and his Time* (Washington, 1989), 21–34.

Cohen, S.J.D., "A Virgin Defiled: Some Rabbinic and Christian Views of the Origins of Heresy," *Union Seminary Quarterly Review* 36 (1980), 1–11.

——, "Are There Tannaitic Parallels to the Gospels?" *Journal of the American Oriental Society* 116 (1996), 85–89.

——, *From the Maccabees to the Mishnah* (Philadelphia, 1987).

——, *Josephus in Galilee and Rome: His Vita and Development as a Historian* (Leiden, 1979).

——, "The Significance of Yavneh: Pharisees, Rabbis and the End of Jewish Sectarianism," *Hebrew Union College Annual* 55 (1984), 27–54.

Cohn, N., *The Pursuit of the Millennium* (London, 1957).

Collins, J.J., "Early Jewish Apocalypticism," *Anchor Bible Dictionary* (New York, 1992), 1.282–288.

——, "Messianism in the Maccabean Period," in J. Neusner, W. Green & E. Frerichs (Eds.), *Judaisms and their Messiahs* (Cambridge, 1987), 97–110.

——, *The Apocalyptic Imagination* (New York, 1984).

——, *The Scepter and the Star: The Messiahs of the Dead Sea Scrolls and Other Ancient Literature* (New York, 1994).

Collins, J.J., and Charlesworth, J., (Eds.), *Mysteries and Revelations – Apocalyptic Studies since the Uppsala Colloquium* (Sheffield, 1991).

Collinson, P., *The Religion of Protestants* (Oxford, 1982).

Coser, L., *Greedy Institutions: Patterns of Undivided Commitment* (New York, 1974).

Cross, F.M. Jr., "The Early History of the Qumran Community," in D. Freedman and J. Greenfield (Eds.), *New Directions in Biblical Archaeology* (Garden City, 1971), 70–89.

Cross, F.M. and Eshel, E., "Ostraca from Khirbet Qumrân," *Israel Exploration Journal* 14 (1997), 17–28.

Crown, A., "Redating the Schism between the Judaeans and the Samaritans," *Jewish Quarterly Review* 82 (1991), 17–50.

Cumpsty, J., "Glutton, Gourmet or Bon Vivant: A Response to Charles S. Liebman," *Journal for the Scientific Study of Religion* 24 (1985), 217–221.

Danby, H., *The Mishnah* (Oxford, 1933).

Davies, P.R., *Behind the Essenes* (Atlanta, 1987).

——, "Hasidim in the Maccabean Period," *Journal of Jewish Studies* 28 (1977), 127–140.

——, *The Damascus Covenant* (Sheffield, 1982).

——, "The Ideology of the Temple in the Damascus Document," *Journal of Jewish Studies* 33 (1982), 287–301.

——, "Was There Really a Qumran Community?" *Currents in Research* 4 (1995), 9–35.

Dawson, L., "Church/Sect Theory: Getting it Straight," *North American Religion* 1 (1992), 5–28.

——, "Reflection on Sociological Theories of Sects and New Religious Movements," Paper presented to the May 1990 meeting of the Canadian Society of Biblical Studies.

De Vaux, R., *Archaeology and the Dead Sea Scrolls* (Oxford, 1973, 2nd edition).

De Witt, N., "Organization and Procedure in Epicurean Groups," *Classical Philology* 31 (1936), 205–211.

Demsky, A., "Writing in Ancient Israel and Early Judaism," in J. Mulder (Ed.), *Miqra, Compendia Rerum Iudaicarum ad Novum Testamentum, Part II* (Philadelphia, 1988), 1–20.

Dexinger, F., "Die Sektenproblematik im Judentum," *Kairos* 21 (1979), 273–277; 283–286.

——, "Limits of Tolerance in Judaism: The Samaritan Example," in E.P. Sanders (Ed.), *Jewish and Christian Self Definition Volume Two: Aspects of Judaism in the Graeco-Roman Period* (London, 1981), 88–114, 327–338.

Di Lella, A., and Skehan, P., *The Wisdom of Ben Sira* (New York, 1987).

Dimant, D., "New Light from Qumran on the Jewish Pseudepigrapha – 4Q390," in J. Barrera and L. Montaner (Eds.), *The Madrid Qumran Congress: Proceedings of the International Congress on the Dead Sea Scrolls, Madrid, 18–21 March 1991* (Leiden, 1992), 2.405–448.

——, "The Qumran Manuscripts: Contents and Significance," in D. Dimant and L. Schiffman (Eds.), *Time to Prepare the Way in the Wilderness* (Leiden, 1995), 23–58.

——, "Qumran Sectarian Literature," in M. Stone (Ed.), *Jewish Writings of the Second Temple Period – Apocrypha, Pseudepigrapha, Qumran Sectarian Writings, Philo, Josephus* (Philadelphia, 1984), 483–550.

Douglas, M., "Afterword," in J. Neusner, *The Idea of Purity in Ancient Judaism* (Leiden, 1973), 137–142.

——, "Atonement in Leviticus," *Jewish Studies Quarterly Review* 1 (1993/94), 109–130.

——, *How Institutions Think* (London, 1987).

——, *Natural Symbols* (New York, 1982, 2nd edition).

——, *Purity and Danger* (London/New York, 1984).

——, "Radical Dissent, Religious Minorities and Incipient Sectarianism in the Social Sciences," paper read at Pinkhos Churgin Memorial Program, *Application of the Social Sciences to the Study of Judaism in Antiquity*, Bar Ilan University, November 1996.

Duhaime, J., "Relative Deprivation in New Religious Movements and the Qumran Community," *Revue de Qumran* 16 (1993), 265–276.

Dumont, L., *Homo Hierarchicus – The Caste System and its Implications* (Chicago/London, 1980, 3rd edition).

Efron, J., "Simon b. Shatah and Alexander Jannaeus," *Studies in the Hasmonean Period* (Leiden, 1987), 161–190.

Eley, G., and Hunt, W. (Eds.), *Reviving the English Revolution – Reflections and Elaborations on the Work of Christopher Hill* (London/New York, 1988).

Eshel, E., "4Q477: The Rebukes of the Overseer," *Journal of Jewish Studies* 45 (1994), 111–122.

Eshel, E., and Kister, M., "A Polemical Qumran Fragment," *Journal of Jewish Studies*, 43 (1992), 277–281.

Eshel, H., "The Prayer of Joseph, A Papyrus from Masada and The Samaritan Temple on *ARGARIZIN*," *Zion* 56 (5751), 125–136 [in Hebrew].

——, *The Samaritans in the Persian and Hellenistic Periods: The Origins of Samaritanism* (Dissertation, The Hebrew University, 1994) [in Hebrew].

——, "Wadi ed-Daliyeh Papyrus 14 and the Samaritan Temple," *Zion* 61 (5756), 359–365 [in Hebrew].

Eshel, H. and Amit, D. (Eds.), *The History of the Hasmonean House*, (Jerusalem, 1995) [in Hebrew].

Feldman, L., "How Much Hellenism in Jewish Palestine?" *Hebrew Union College Annual* 57 (1986), 83–111.

——, *Jew and Gentile in the Ancient World* (Princeton, 1993).

Festinger L., Riecken, H., and Schachter, S., *When Prophecy Fails* (New York, 1964, 2nd edition).

Finkelstein, L., *Sifre on Deuteronomy* (New York, 1969).

Finlayson, F., *Historians, Puritanism and the English Revolution: The Religious Factor in English Politics before and after the Interregnum* (Toronto, 1983).

Fitzmyer, J., *The Gospel According to Luke (X–XXIV)* (New York, 1985).

Fleck, L., *Genesis and Development of a Scientific Fact* (Chicago/London, 1979).

Flusser, D., "Pharisäer, Sadduzäer und Essener im Pescher Nahum," in K. Grözinger (Ed.), *Qumran* (Darmstadt, 1981), 121–166.

——, "Pharisees, Sadducees and Essenes in Pesher Nahum," in M. Dorman *et al.* (Eds.), *Essays in Jewish History and Philology in Memory of Gedaliahu Alon* (Jerusalem, 1970), 133–168 [in Hebrew].

——, "Qumran and the Famine during the Reign of Herod," *Israel Museum Journal* 6 (1987), 7–16.

——, "Some of the Precepts of the Torah from Qumran (4QMMT) and the Benediction Against the Heretics," *Tarbiz* 61 (5752), 333–374 [in Hebrew].

——, "The Half-Sheqel in the Gospels and the Dead Sea Sect," *Tarbiz* 31 (5722), 150–156 [in Hebrew].

Fraade, S., "Ascetical Aspects of Ancient Judaism," in A. Green (Ed.), *Jewish Spirituality – From the Bible through the Middle Ages* (New York, 1986), 253–288.

Friedman, M.A., *Jewish Marriage in Palestine: A Cairo Geniza Study, II, The Ketuba Texts* (Tel Aviv/New York, 1981).

Fulbrook, M., "Christopher Hill and Historical Sociology," in G. Eley and W. Hunt (Eds.), *Reviving the English Revolution – Reflections and Elaborations on the Work of Christopher Hill* (London/New York, 1988), 31–52.

Gager, J., *Kingdom and Community* (Englewood Cliffs, 1975).

García Martínez, F., "4QMMT in a Qumran Context," in J. Kampen and M. Bernstein (Eds.), *Reading 4QMMT – New Perspectives on Qumran Law and History* (Atlanta, 1996), 15–28.

——, "The Men of the Dead Sea," in F. García Martínez and J. Trebolle Barrera, *The People of the Dead Sea Scrolls – Their Writings, Beliefs and Practices* (Leiden, 1995), 31–48.

——, "The Origins of the Essene Movement and of the Qumran Sect," in F. García Martínez and J. Trebolle Barrera, *The People of the Dead Sea Scrolls – Their Writings, Beliefs and Practices* (Leiden, 1995), 77–98.

García Martínez, F., and Van der Woude, A.S., "A 'Groningen' Hypothesis of Qumran Origins," *Revue de Qumran* 14 (1990), 521–541.

Garrett, C.H., *The Marian Exiles* (Cambridge, 1966, 2nd edition).

Geiger A., *Judaism and its History* (New York, 1952).

——, *Urschrift und Ubersetzungen der Bibel in ihrer Abhänglichkeit von der innern Entwicklung des Judentums* (Frankfurt, 1928, 2nd edition).

Geller, M., "Alexander Jannaeus and the Pharisee Rift," *Journal of Jewish Studies* 30 (1979), 202–211.

Gellner, E., *Nations and Nationalism* (Oxford, 1983).

——, *Saints of the Atlas* (Chicago, 1969).

Gerlach, L., and Hine, V., "Five Factors Crucial to the Growth and Spread of a Modern Religious Movement," *Journal for the Scientific Study of Religion* 7 (1968), 23–40.

Glock, C., and Stark, R., *Religion and Society in Tension* (Chicago, 1965).

Goldstein, J., *I Maccabees* (Garden City, 1976).

——, *II Maccabees* (Garden City, 1983).

——, "How the Authors of 1 and 2 Maccabees Treated the 'Messianic' Promises," in J. Neusner, W. Green & E. Frerichs (Eds.), *Judaisms and their Messiahs* (Cambridge, 1987), 69–96.

——, "Jewish Acceptance and Rejection of Hellenism," in E.P. Sanders (Ed.), *Jewish and Christian Self Definition Volume Two: Aspects of Judaism in the Graeco-Roman Period* (London, 1981), 64–87, 318–326.

Goodblatt, D., "The Talmudic Sources on the Origins of Organized Jewish Education," *Studies in the History of the Jewish People and the Land of Israel* 5 (1980), 83–108 [in Hebrew].

Goodman, M., "A Note on the Qumran Sectarians, the Essenes and Josephus," *Journal of Jewish Studies* 46 (1995), 161–166.

Goody, J., *Cooking, Cuisine and Class – A Study in Comparative Sociology* (Cambridge, 1982).

——, *The Domestication of the Savage Mind* (Cambridge, 1977).

——, *The Interface between the Written and the Oral* (Cambridge, 1987).

——, *The Logic of Writing and the Organization of Society* (Cambridge, 1986).

Goody, J., and Watt, I., "The Consequences of Literacy," *Comparative Studies in Society and History* 5 (1962/3), 304–345.

Greenberg, M., "The Stabilization of the Text of the Hebrew Bible, Reviewed in the Light of the Biblical Materials from the Judean Desert," *Journal of the American Oriental Society* 76 (1956), 157–167.

Guelich, R., *Word Bible Commentary Mark 1:8–26* (Dallas, 1989).

Haller, W., *The Rise of Puritanism* (New York, 1947, 2nd edition).

Hanson, P.D., *The Dawn of Apocalyptic – The Historical and Sociological Roots of Jewish Eschatology* (Philadelphia, 1983, 2nd edition).

——, "Jewish Apocalyptic Against its Near Eastern Environment," *Revue Biblique* 78 (1971), 31–58.

Harrington, H., "Did the Pharisees Eat Ordinary Food in a State of Ritual Purity?" *Journal for the Study of Judaism in the Persian, Hellenistic and Roman Period* 26 (1995), 42–54.

Harris, J., "The Circumcised Heart," *Commentary* 99 (June 1995), 57–60.

Harris, W.V., *Ancient Literacy* (Cambridge, 1989).

Harrison, J.F.C., *The Second Coming: Popular Millenarianism 1780–1850* (New Brunswick, 1979).

Havelock, E., *Preface to Plato* (Cambridge, 1963).

Hazan, H., "Holding Time Still with Cups of Tea," in M. Douglas (Ed.), *Constructive Drinking* (Cambridge, 1987), 205–219.

Heinemann, M., "How the Words got on to the Page: Christopher Hill and Seventeenth Century Literary Studies," in G. Eley and W. Hunt (Eds.), *Reviving the English Revolution – Reflections and Elaborations on the Work of Christopher Hill* (London/ New York, 1988), 73–98.

Hengel, M., *Judaism and Hellenism – Studies in their Encounter in Palestine in the Early Hellenistic Period* (Philadelphia, 1981).

Hengel, M., and Deines, R., "E.P. Sanders' 'Common Judaism', Jesus and the Pharisees. A Review Article," *Journal of Theological Studies* 46 (1995), 41–51.

Herr, M.D., "Continuum in the Chain of Torah Transmission," *Zion* 44 (5739), 43–56 [in Hebrew].

——, "Political-Realistic Messianism and Cosmic-Eschatological Messianism in the Works of the Sages," *Tarbiz* 54 (5745), 331–346 [in Hebrew].

——, "The Historical Significance of the Dialogues between Jewish Sages and Roman Dignitaries," *Scripta Hierosolymitana* 22 (1971), 123–150.

Hexter, J.H., *Doing History* (London, 1971).

——, "The Burden of Proof," *Times Literary Supplement*, October 24, 1975, 1250–1252.

Hill, C., *Antichrist in 17th Century England* (London, 1971).

——, *Change and Continuity in 17th Century England* (New Haven, 1991, 2nd edition).

——, "Partial Historians and Total History," *Times Literary Supplement*, November 24, 1972, 1431–1432.

——, *Puritanism and Revolution* (New York, 1964).

——, *Society and Puritanism in Pre-Revolutionary England* (London, 1964).

——, "The Burden of Proof," *Times Literary Supplement*, November 7, 1975, 1333.

——, *The Century of Revolution* (New York, 1961).

——, *The Experience of Defeat* (New York, 1984).

——, *The Intellectual Origins of the English Revolution* (Oxford, 1965).

——, *The World Turned Upside Down: Radical Ideas during the English Revolution* (London, 1972).

Hill, C., and Dell, E., (Eds.), *The Good Old Cause* (London, 1969, 2nd edition).

Hobsbawm, E.J., *Primitive Rebels* (New York, 1959).

Horgan, M., *Pesharim: Qumran Interpretations of Biblical Books* (Washington, 1979).

Horsley, R., *Sociology and the Jesus Movement* (New York, 1989).

Humbert, J.B., "L'Espace Sacré à Qumran," *Revue Biblique* 101 (1994), 161–214.

Hunt, W., "Spectral Origins of the English Revolution: Legitimation Crisis in Early Stuart England," in G. Eley and W. Hunt (Eds.), *Reviving the English Revolution – Reflections and Elaborations on the Work of Christopher Hill* (London/New York, 1988), 305–332.

——, *The Puritan Moment* (Cambridge, 1983).

Isenberg, S.R., "Millenarism in Greco-Roman Palestine," *Religion* 4 (1974), 26–46.

Kantorowicz, E., *The King's Two Bodies: A Study in Mediaeval Political Theology* (Princeton, 1957).

Kapera, J.Z., "An Anonymously Received Pre-Publication of the 4QMMT," *The Qumran Chronicle* 2 (1990), 1–12.

Katz, J., *Halacha in Straits – Obstacles to Orthodoxy at its Inception* (Jerusalem, 1992) [in Hebrew].

——, "In Clarification of the Term 'Forerunners of Zionism'", *Jewish Emancipation and Self-Emancipation* (Philadelphia, 1986), 104–115.

Kee, H.C., "Testament of the Twelve Patriarchs," in J. Charlesworth (Ed.), *The Old Testament Pseudepigrapha* (New York, 1983–85), 1.775–781.

Kennedy, J.G., *Struggle for Change in a Nubian Community: An Individual in Society and History* (Palo Alto, 1977).

Kidd, I.G., *Posidonius, II. The Commentary: (i) Testimonia and Fragments 1–149* (Cambridge, 1988).

Kister, M., "Marginalia Qumranica," *Tarbiz* 57 (5748), 315–328 [in Hebrew].

Klawans, J., "Notions of Gentile Impurity in Ancient Judaism," *AJS Review* 20 (1995), 285–312.

Koch, K., "What is Apocalyptic? An Attempt at a Preliminary Definition," in P. Hanson (Ed.), *Visionaries and their Apocalypses* (Philadelphia, 1983), 16–36.

Kuhn, T.S., *The Structure of Scientific Revolutions* (Chicago, 1970, 2nd edition).

Kupferschmidt, U., "Reformist and Militant Islam in Egypt," *Middle Eastern Studies* 23 (1987), 404–418.

Kutscher, E.Y., *A History of the Hebrew Language* (Jerusalem/Leiden, 1982).

Laato, A., "The Chronology of the Damascus Document of Qumran," *Revue de Qumran* 15 (1992), 605–607.

Lamont, W., *Godly Rule: Politics and Religion 1603–60* (London, 1969).

——, "Richard Baxter, The Apocalypse and the Mad Major," *Past and Present* 55 (1972), 68–90.

Landes, R., "Lest the Millennium be Fulfilled: Apocalyptic Expectations and the Pattern of Western Chronography," in W. Verbeke, D. Verhelst and A. Welkenhuysen (Eds.), *The Use and Abuse of Eschatology in the Middle Ages* (Leuven, 1988), 137–211.

Lazarus-Yafeh, H., "Contemporary Fundamentalism – Judaism, Christianity, Islam," *The Jerusalem Quarterly* 47 (1988), 27–39.

Leiman, S., *The Canonization of Hebrew Scripture: The Talmudic and Midrashic Evidence* (Hamden, 1976).

Levi, I., "Les sources talmudiques de l'histoire juive. I. Alexandre Jannée et Simon b. Shetah. II. La rupture de Jannée avec les pharisiens," *Revue des Études Juives* 35 (1897), 213–223.

Levine, L., "The Political Struggle between the Pharisees and Sadducees in the Hasmonean Period," in A. Oppenheimer, U. Rappaport and M. Stern (Eds.), *Jerusalem in the Second Temple Period – Abraham Schalit Memorial Volume* (Jerusalem, 1980), 61–83 [in Hebrew].

Lewis, B., "An Apocalyptic Vision of Islamic History," *Bulletin of the British School of Oriental and African Studies* 13 (1950), 308–338.

Licht, J., "The Attitude Towards Events of the Past in the Bible and Apocalyptic Literature," *Tarbiz* 60 (5751), 1–18 [in Hebrew].

——, *The Thanksgiving Scroll* (Jerusalem, 1957) [in Hebrew].

Lieberman, S., *Hellenism in Jewish Palestine* (New York, 1962, 2nd edition).

——, "New Light on Cave Scrolls from Rabbinic Sources," *Texts and Studies* (New York, 1974), 190–199.

——, "The Discipline in the So-Called Dead Sea Manual of Discipline," *Journal of Biblical Literature* 71 (1951), 199–206.

——, *The Tosefta* (New York, 1955–88).

——, *Tosefta Kifshuta, Zeraim* (New York, 1955).

Liebes, Y., "The Ultra-Orthodox Community and the Dead Sea Scrolls," *Jerusalem Studies in Jewish Thought* 3 (1982), 137–152 [in Hebrew].

Liebman, C., "Extremism as a Religious Norm," *Journal for the Scientific Study of Religion* 22 (1983), 75–86.

Lilienblum, M., *Autobiographical Writings* (Jerusalem, 5730).

Liu, T., *Discord in Zion* (The Hague, 1973).

Liver, J., "The Half-Sheqel Offering in Biblical and Postbiblical Literature," *Harvard Theological Review* 56 (1963), 173–198.

——, "The 'Sons of Zadok the Priests,'" *Revue de Qumran* 6 (1967/70), 1–30.

Mack, B., *Wisdom and the Hebrew Epic* (Chicago/London, 1985).

Magen, I., *The Stone Vessel Industry in Jerusalem during the Second Temple Period* (Jerusalem, 1988) [in Hebrew].

Main, E., "Les Sadducéens vus par Flavius Josephe *Revue Biblique* 97 (1990), 161–206.

Mannheim, K., "The Problem of Generation," *Essays on the Sociology of Knowledge* (London, 1952), 276–320.

Mantel, H., "The Sadducees and Pharisees," in M. Avi-Yonah & Z. Baras (Eds.), *Society and Religion in the Second Temple Period. World History of the Jewish People Volume VIII* (New Brunswick, 1977), 99–123.

Manuel, F., "Towards a Psychological History of Utopias," in F. Manuel (Ed.), *Utopias and Utopian Thought* (Boston, 1966), 69–100.

Marböck, J., "Das Gebet um die Rettung Zions Sir 36, 1–22," in J. Bauer and J. Marböck (Eds.), *Memoria Jerusalem – Freundesgabe Franz Sauer* (Graz, 1977), 93–115.

Marcus, J., "Modern and Ancient Jewish Apocalypticism," *Journal of Religion* 76 (1996), 1–27.

Margaliot (Margulies), M., *Midrash Wayyikra Rabbah* (Jerusalem, 1972).

Marrou, H., *A History of Education in Antiquity* (New York, 1956).

Mason, S., *Flavius Josephus on the Pharisees* (Leiden, 1991).

——, "Greco-Roman, Jewish and Christian Philosophies," in J. Neusner (Ed.), *Approaches to Ancient Judaism, New Series, Volume Four* (Atlanta, 1992), 1–28.

——, "Josephus, Daniel and the Flavian House," in F. Parente and J. Sievers (Eds.), *Josephus and the History of the Greco-Roman Period – Essays in Memory of Morton Smith* (Leiden, 1994), 161–195.

——, "Was Josephus a Pharisee? A Reexamination of *Life* 10–12," *Journal of Jewish Studies* 40 (1989), 31–45.

McGinn, B., *Visions of the End: Apocalyptic Traditions in the Middle Ages* (New York, 1979).

McGregor, J.F., "Seekers and Ranters," in J.F. McGregor and B. Reay (Eds.), *Radical Religion in the English Revolution* (Oxford, 1984), 121–139.

Meeks, W., *The First Urban Christians – The Social World of the Apostle Paul* (New Haven, 1983).

Meens, R., "Pollution in the Early Middle Ages: The Case of the Food Regulations in Penitentials," *Early Medieval Europe* 4 (1995), 3–19.

Meier, J., "Jesus in Josephus: A Modest Proposal," *Catholic Biblical Quarterly* 52 (1990), 76–103.

Mendels, D., "Hellenistic Utopias and the Essenes," *Harvard Theological Review* 72 (1979), 205–222.

——, *The Rise and Fall of Jewish Nationalism* (New York, 1992).

Metso, M., "In Search of the *Sitz im Leben* of the Community Rule," forthcoming in the Proceedings of the 1996 International Dead Sea Scrolls Conference, Provo, Utah, July, 1996, to be edited by E. Ulrich and D. Parry.

Momigliano, A., *Alien Wisdom: The Limits of Hellenization* (Cambridge, 1975).

Murphy-O'Connor, J., "The Critique of the Princes of Judah (CD VIII, 3–19)," *Revue Biblique* 79 (1972), 200–216.

Na'aman, N., "Historiography, the Fashioning of the Collective Memory, and the Establishment of Historical Consciousness in Israel in the Late Monarchical Period," *Zion* 60 (5755), 449–472 [in Hebrew].

Neusner, J., *From Politics to Piety – The Emergence of Pharisaic Judaism* (Englewood Cliffs, 1973).

——, *Judaism: The Evidence of the Mishnah* (Chicago, 1981).

——, *Rabbinic Traditions about the Pharisees Before 70* (Leiden, 1971).

——, "Rabbinic Traditions About the Pharisees Before 70: The Problem of Oral Transmission," *Journal of Jewish Studies* 22 (1971), 1–18.

——, *The Idea of Purity in Ancient Judaism* (Leiden, 1973).

——, "The Use of the Later Rabbinic Evidence for the Study of Paul," in W.S. Green (Ed.), *Approaches to Ancient Judaism, Volume II* (Chico, 1980), 43–64.

Neusner, J., Green, W., and Frerichs, E., (Eds.), *Judaisms and their Messiahs* (Cambridge, 1987).

Nicklesburg, G., "Enoch, First Book of," *Anchor Bible Dictionary* (New York, 1992), 2.508–516.

——, "Social Aspects of Palestinian Jewish Apocalyptic," in D. Hellholm (Ed.), *Apocalypticism in the Mediterranean World and the Near East* (Tübingen, 1983), 641–654.

——, "The Apocalyptic Construction of Reality in *1 Enoch*," in J.J. Collins and J. Charlesworth (Eds.), *Mysteries and Revelations – Apocalyptic Studies since the Uppsala Colloquium* (Sheffield, 1991), 51–64.

Nitzan, B., *Pesher Habakkuk* (Jerusalem, 1986) [in Hebrew].

Nock, A.D., "On the Historical Importance of Cult Associations," *Classical Review* 38 (1924), 105–109.

Ong, W., *Orality and Literacy: The Technologizing of the Word* (London/New York, 1982).

Oppenheimer, A., *The Am Ha-aretz – A Study in the Social History of the Jewish People in the Hellenistic-Roman Period* (Leiden, 1977).

Parente, P., "Onias III's Death and the Founding of the Temple of Leontopolis," in F. Parente and J. Sievers (Eds.), *Josephus and the History of the Greco-Roman Period – Essays in Memory of Morton Smith* (Leiden, 1994), 69–98.

Penton, M.J., *Apocalypse Delayed* (Toronto, 1985).

Puech, E., "Une Apocalypse Messianique (4Q521)," *Revue de Qumran* 15 (1992), 475–519.

Qimron, E., "Halakhic Terms in the Dead Sea Scrolls and their Contribution to the History of the early *Halakha*," in M. Broshi, S. Japhet, D. Schwartz and S. Talmon (Eds.), *The Scrolls of the Judean Desert: Forty Years of Research* (Jerusalem, 1992), 128–139 [in Hebrew].

——, "The Chicken, The Dog and the Temple Scroll – 11QTᶜ (Col. XLVIII)," *Tarbiz* 64 (5755), 473–475 [in Hebrew].

Qimron, E., and Strugnell, J., "An Unpublished Halakhic Letter from Qumran," *Israel Museum Journal* 2 (1984–85), 9–12.

——, "An Unpublished Halakhic Letter from Qumran," *Biblical Archeology Today: Proceedings of the International Conference on Biblical Archeology Jerusalem, April 1984* (Jerusalem, 1985), 400–408.

——, *Discoveries in the Judean Desert X, Qumran Cave 4. V – Miqsat maase ha-Torah* (Oxford, 1994).

Rabin, C., *Qumran Studies* (New York, 1957).

Rabinowitz, L.I., "Names, In the Talmud," *Encyclopedia Judaica* 12.807.

Rajak, T., "Cio che Flavio Giuseppe vide: Josephus and the Essenes," in F. Parente and J. Sievers (Eds.), *Josephus and the History of the Greco-Roman Period – Essays in Memory of Morton Smith* (Leiden, 1994), 141–160.

——, "The Hasmoneans and the Uses of Hellenism," in P.R. Davies and R.T. White (Eds.), *A Tribute to Geza Vermes – Essays on Jewish and Christian Literature and History* (Sheffield, 1990), 261–280.

Rappaport, U., "On the Hellenization of the Hasmoneans," *Tarbiz* 60 (5751), 447–503 [in Hebrew].

Ravitsky, A., *Messianism, Zionism and Jewish Religious Radicalism* (Tel Aviv, 1993) [in Hebrew].

Rayner, S., "The Perception of Time and Space in Egalitarian Sects: A Millenarian Cosmology," in M. Douglas (Ed.), *Essays in the Sociology of Perception* (London, 1982), 247–274.

Reay, B., "Introduction: Popular Culture in Early Modern England," in B. Reay (Ed.), *Popular Culture in Seventeenth Century England* (London, 1985), 1–30.

——, "Popular Religion," in B. Reay (Ed.), *Popular Culture in Seventeenth Century England* (London, 1985), 91–128.

——, "Quakerism and Society," in J.F. McGregor and B. Reay (Eds.), *Radical Religion in the English Revolution* (Oxford, 1984), 141–164.

——, "Radicalism and Religion in the English Revolution: An Introduction," in J.F. McGregor and B. Reay (Eds.), *Radical Religion in the English Revolution* (Oxford, 1984), 1–22.

——, *The Quakers and the English Revolution* (London, 1985).

Redkop, C., "A New Look at Sect Development," *Journal for the Scientific Study of Religion* 13 (1974), 345–352.

Reed, S.A., "Genre, Setting and Title of 4Q477," *Journal of Jewish Studies* 47 (1996), 146–147.

Regev, E., "Ritual Baths of Jewish Groups and Sects in the Second Temple Period," *Cathedra* 79 (5756), 3–21.

——, "The Use of Stone Vessels at the End of the Second Temple Period," in Y. Eshel (Ed.), *Judea and Samaria Research Studies, the 6th Annual Meeting (24 March 1996)*, forthcoming [in Hebrew].

Reich, R., "A Note on the Function of Room 30 (the 'Scriptorium') at Khirbet Qumran," *Journal of Jewish Studies* 46 (1995), 157–160.

Risberg, B., "Textkritische und exegetische Anmerkungen zu den Makkabäerbüchern," *Beiträge zur Religionswissenschaft* 2 (1915), 26–31.

Rist, J., *Epicurus: An Introduction* (Cambridge, 1972).

Rochford, E.B., "Factionalism, Group Defection and Schism in the Hare Krishna Movement," *Journal for the Scientific Study of Religion* 28 (1989), 162–179.

Rofé, A. "The Beginnings of Sects in Post-Exilic Judaism," *Cathedra* 49 (1988), 13–22 [in Hebrew].

Rowland, C., *The Open Heaven – A Study of Apocalyptic in Judaism and Early Christianity* (New York, 1982).

Rowley, H.H., *The Relevance of Apocalyptic* (London, 1947).

Runciman, W., *Relative Deprivation and Social Justice* (London, 1966).

Saldarini, A.J., *Pharisees, Scribes and Sadducees in Palestinian Society: A Sociological Approach* (Edinburgh, 1988).

Sanders, E.P., *Jewish Law From Jesus to the Mishnah* (London, 1990).

——, *Judaism: Practice and Belief 63 BCE–66 CE* (London/Philadelphia, 1992).

——, *Paul and Palestinian Judaism* (London, 1977).

——, "Puzzling out Rabbinic Judaism," in W.S. Green (Ed.), *Approaches to Ancient Judaism Volume II* (Chico, 1980), 65–80.

Schäfer, P., "Der vorrabinische Pharisaismus," in M. Hengel & U. Heckel (Eds.), *Paulus und das antike Judentum* (Tübingen, 1992), 125–175.

——, "Die messianischen Hoffnungen des rabbinischen Judentums zwischen Naherwartung und religiösem Pragmatismus," *Studien zur Geschichte und Theologie des rabbinischen Judentums* (Leiden, 1978), 214–243.

Schechter, S., *Aboth de Rabbi Nathan* (New York, 1967).

Scheerson B.S. (Ed.), Eleazar of Worms, *Sefer ha-Rokeah* (Jerusalem, 5727).

Schiffman, L., "Jewish Sectarianism in Second Temple Times," in R. Jospe and S. Wagner (Eds.), *Great Schisms in Jewish History* (New York, 1981), 1–46.

——, *Law, Custom and Messianism in the Dead Sea Sect* (Jerusalem, 1993) [in Hebrew].

——, "Legislation Concerning Relations with non-Jews in the Zadokite Fragments and in Tannaitic Literature," *Revue de Qumran* 11 (1983), 379–389.

——, *Reclaiming the Dead Sea Scrolls* (New York, 1994).

——, *The Halakhah at Qumran* (Leiden, 1975).

——, "The New Halakhic Letter (4QMMT) and the Origins of the Dead Sea Sect," *Biblical Archaeologist* 53 (1990), 64–73.

——, "The Place of 4QMMT in the Corpus of Qumran MSS," in J. Kampen and M. Bernstein (Eds.), *Reading 4QMMT – New Perspectives on Qumran Law and History* (Atlanta, 1996), 81–98.

Scholem, G., *The Messianic Idea in Judaism* (London, 1971).

Schürer, E., *The History of the Jewish People in the Age of Jesus Christ*, Revised and Edited by G. Vermes, F. Millar & M. Black (Edinburgh, 1979–).

Schwartz, B., *Queuing and Waiting: Studies in the Social Organization of Access and Delay* (Chicago, 1975).

Schwartz, G., *Sect Ideologies and Social Status* (Chicago, 1970).

Schwartz, H., *The French Prophets: The History of a Millenarian Group in Eighteenth-Century England* (Berkeley, 1980).

Schwartz, S., *Josephus and Judean Politics* (Leiden, 1990).

——, "On the Autonomy of Judaea in the Fourth and Third Centuries BCE," *Journal of Jewish Studies* 45 (1994), 157–168.

Segal, A., "Conversion and Messianism: Outline for a New Approach," in J. Charlesworth (Ed.), *The Messiah – Developments in Earliest Judaism and Christianity* (Minneapolis, 1992), 296–340.

Sewell, W., Jr., "Marc Bloch and the Logic of Comparative History," *History and Theory. Studies in the Philosophy of History* 6 (1967), 208–218.

Shepperson, G., "The Comparative Study of Millenarian Movements," in S. Thrupp (Ed.), *Millennial Dreams in Action* (Hague, 1962), 44–54.

Sievers, J., *The Hasmoneans and their Supporters* (Atlanta, 1990).

Simmel, G., *Conflict: The Web of Group Affiliations* (Glencoe, 1955).

Simpson, J., "The Stark-Bainbridge Theory of Religion," *Journal for the Scientific Study of Religion* 29 (1990), 367–371.

Sivan, E., "Enclave Culture," in M. Marty (Ed.), *Fundamentalism Comprehended* (Chicago, 1995), 11–68 = *Alpayim* 4 (5752), 45–98 [in Hebrew].

Smith, M., *Jesus the Magician* (New York, 1978).

——, "Pseudepigraphy in the Israelite Literary Tradition," in K. von Fritz (Ed.), *Pseudepigrapha I, Entretiens sur l'antiquité classique, Tome XVII* (Geneva, 1972), 192–227.

——, "Review of *The Cambridge History of the Bible, Volume I: From the Beginnings to Jerome*," *American Historical Review* 77 (1972), 94–100.

——, "The Dead Sea Sect in Relation to Ancient Judaism," *New Testament Studies* 7 (1960), 347–360.

——, "What is Implied by the Variety of Messianic Figures?" *Journal of Biblical Literature* 78 (1959), 66–72.

——, "Zealots and Sicarii: Their Origins and Relations," *Harvard Theological Review* 64 (1971), 1–19.

Spufford, M., "Puritanism and Social Control?" in A. Fletcher and J. Stevenson (Eds.), *Order and Disorder in Early Modern England* (Cambridge, 1985), 41–57.

Stark, R., *The Rise of Christianity – A Sociologist Reconsiders History* (Princeton, 1996).

Stark, R., and Bainbridge, W., "Networks of Faith: Interpersonal Bonds and Recruitment to Cults and Sects," *American Journal of Sociology* 85 (1980), 1376–1395.

——, *The Future of Religion: Secularization, Revival and Cult Formation* (Berkeley, 1985).

Stegemann, H., "The Qumran Essenes – Local Members of the Main Jewish Union in Late Second Temple Times," in J. Barrera and L. Montaner (Eds.), *The Madrid Qumran Congress: Proceedings of the International Congress on the Dead Sea Scrolls, Madrid, 18–21 March 1991* (Leiden, 1992), 1.83–166.

Stein, S.J., *The Shaker Experience in America* (New Haven, 1992).

Stendahl, K., *Paul Among Jews and Gentiles and other Essays* (Philadelphia, 1976).

Stern, M., *Greek and Latin Authors on Jews and Judaism* (Jerusalem, 1976–84).

——, *Studies in Jewish History – The Second Temple Period* (Jerusalem, 1991) [in Hebrew].

——, "Zealots," *Encyclopedia Judaica Yearbook, 1973* (Jerusalem, 1974), 135–152.

Steudel, A., "'The End of Days' in the Qumran Texts," *Revue de Qumran* 16 (1993), 225–246.

Stock, B., *The Implications of Literacy: Written Language and Models of Interpretation in the Eleventh and Twelfth Centuries* (Princeton, 1983).

Stone, L., "Literacy and Education in England 1640–1900," *Past and Present* 42 (1969), 69–139.

Stone, M., "Apocalyptic Literature," in M. Stone (Ed.), *Jewish Writings of the Second Temple Period – Apocrypha, Pseudepigrapha, Qumran Sectarian Writings, Philo, Josephus* (Philadelphia, 1984), 383–441.

Strack, H., and Billerbeck, P., *Kommentar zum neuen Testament aus Talmud und Midrasch* (Munich, 1922–61).

Strugnell, J., "MMT Second Thoughts on a Forthcoming Edition," in E. Ulrich and J. VanderKam (Eds.), *The Community of the Renewed Covenant – The Notre Dame Symposium on the Dead Sea Scrolls* (Notre Dame, 1994), 57–76.

Strugnell, J., and Dimant, D., "4Q Second Ezechiel," *Revue de Qumran* 13 (1988), 45–58.

Sussmann, Y., "Research on the History of the Halacha and the Scrolls of the Judean Desert," *Tarbiz* 59 (5750), 11–76 [in Hebrew].

Syme, R., *Colonial Elites* (Oxford, 1958).

Szittya, P., "Domesday Bokes: The Apocalypse in Medieval English Culture," in R.K. Emmerson and B. McGinn (Eds.), *The Apocalypse in the Middle Ages* (Ithaca, 1992), 374–397.

Szmeruk, C., "The Social Significance of Hassidic Shekhita," *Zion* 20 (5715), 47–72 [in Hebrew].

Talmon, S., "The Emergence of Jewish Sectarianism," in *King, Cult and Calendar* (Jerusalem, 1986), 165–201.

——, "Qumran Studies: Past, Present and Future," *Jewish Quarterly Review* 85 (1994), 1–31.

Talmon, Y., "Millenarian Movements," *Archives Européennes de Sociologie* 7 (1966), 159–200.

——, "The Pursuit of the Millennium: The Relation Between Religious and Social Change," *Archives Européennes de Sociologie* 3 (1962), 125–148.

Tapper, R., and N., "'Thank God We're Secular,' Aspects of Fundamentalism in a Turkish Town," in L. Caplan (Ed.), *Studies in Religious Fundamentalism* (London, 1987), 51–78.

Tarn, W.W., *Hellenistic Civilization* (New York, 1952, 3rd edition).

Taylor, D., "The Lord's Battle: Paiselyism in Northern Ireland," in R. Stark (Ed.), *Religious Movements: Genesis, Exodus and Numbers* (New York, 1985), 241–278.

Taylor, J., "John the Baptist and the Essenes," *Journal of Jewish Studies* 47 (1996), 256–285.

Tcherikover, V., *Hellenistic Civilization and the Jews* (Philadelphia, 1959).

Theissen, G., *Sociology of Early Palestinian Christianity* (Philadelphia, 1978).

Theodor, J. and Albeck, C., *Midrash Bereshit Rabba – Critical Edition with Notes and Commentary* (Jerusalem, 1965, 2nd edition).

Thomas, K., *Religion and the Decline of Magic* (New York, 1971).

Thompson, E., "On the Rant," in G. Eley and W. Hunt (Eds.), *Reviving the English Revolution – Reflections and Elaborations on the Work of Christopher Hill* (London/New York, 1988), 153–160.

Thrupp, S., "A Report on the Conference Discussion," in S. Thrupp (Ed.), *Millennial Dreams in Action* (The Hague, 1962), 11–30.

Tov, E., *Textual Criticism of the Hebrew Bible* (Minneapolis, 1992).

Tuveson, E.L., *Millennium and the Utopia* (New York, 1964).

van der Woude, A.S., "Wicked Priest or Wicked Priests? Reflections on the Identification of the Wicked Priest in the Habakkuk Commentary," *Journal of Jewish Studies* 33 (1982), 349–359.

VanderKam, J., *The Dead Sea Scrolls Today* (Grand Rapids, 1994).

Vermes, G., "Preliminary Remarks on Unpublished Fragments of the Community Rule from Qumran Cave 4," *Journal of Jewish Studies* 42 (1991), 250–255.

Wacholder, B., "The Letter from Judah Maccabee to Aristobulus: Is 2 Maccabees 1:10b–2:18 Authentic?" *Hebrew Union College Annual* 49 (1978), 89–133.

Wacholder, B., and Abegg, M., *A Preliminary Edition of the Unpublished Dead Sea Scrolls, The Hebrew and Aramaic Texts from Cave Four, Fascicle One* (Washington, 1991).

Walzer, M., *The Revolution of the Saints* (Cambridge, 1965).

Watson, F., *Paul, Judaism and the Gentiles – A Sociological Approach* (Cambridge, 1986).

Weinfeld M., "The Crystallization of the Community of the Exiles (קהל הגולה)," paper read at Pinkhos Churgin Memorial Program, *Application of the Social Sciences to the Study of Judaism in Antiquity*, Bar Ilan University, November 1996.

——, *The Organizational Pattern and the Penal Code of the Qumran Sect* (Fribourg, 1986).

——, "The Origin of the Apodictic Law," *Vetus Testamentum* 23 (1973), 63–75.

Weinstein, D., *Savonarola and Florence* (Princeton, 1970).

——, "The Savonarola Movement in Florence," in S. Thrupp (Ed.), *Millennial Dreams in Action* (The Hague, 1962), 187–206.

Wertheimer, A., *Batei Midrashot* (Jerusalem, 5728).

White, S.A., "A Comparison of the 'A' and 'B' Manuscripts of the Damascus Document," *Revue de Qumran* 48 (1987), 537–553.

Wilk, R., "John Hyrcanus I and the Temple Scroll," *Shnaton, An Annual for Biblical and Ancient Near Eastern Studies* 9 (1985), 221–230 [in Hebrew].

Wilson, B., *Magic and the Millennium* (London, 1973).

——, *Religious Sects: A Sociological Study* (London, 1970).

——, *Sects and Society* (Berkeley, 1961).

——, *The Social Dimensions of Sectarianism* (Oxford, 1990).

Wilson, S., *Pulpit in Parliament* (Princeton, 1969).

Wintermute, O., "Jubilees," in J. Charlesworth (Ed.), *The Old Testament Pseudepigrapha* (New York, 1983–85), 2.35–51.

Worsley, P., *The Trumpet Shall Sound: A Study of "Cargo" Cults in Melanesia* (New York, 1968, 2nd edition).

Wuthnow, R., "World Order and Religious Movements," in E. Barker (Ed.), *New Religious Movements: A Perspective for Understanding Society* (Toronto, 1982).

Yadin, Y., *The Temple Scroll* (Jerusalem, 1983).

Zeitlin, I., *Jesus and the Judaism of his Time* (New York, 1988).

Zeitlin, S., "The Am Haarez," *Jewish Quarterly Review* 23 (1932/3), 45–61.

Zubaida, S., "The Quest for the Islamic State: Islamic Fundamentalism in Egypt and Iran," in L. Caplan (Ed.), *Studies in Religious Fundamentalism* (London, 1987), 25–50.

SUBJECT INDEX[1]

Admonition 7, 91, 110–112, 204
Africa 132–133, 147
Afterlife 114
Agriculture 64, 74, 104–105,
  132–133, 136, 137, 143–145, 147
Akiba 182, 186–187
Akribeia 56, 133
Alcimus 72, 83, 190
Alexander Balas 88, 90
Alexander Jannaeus 2, 12 n. 30, 13,
  21, 63, 119, 173, 174 n. 83
Alexander the Great 19, 26 n. 78,
  31, 38 n. 121, 46
Alexandria 119, 142, 145
Anan son of Anan 50
Antigonus 174 n. 83
Antigonus of Socho 21, 46, 148
Antiochus III 81, 168 n. 65
Antiochus IV 7, 26, 58, 69, 72, 83,
  86 n. 19, 89, 90 n. 26, 91, 113,
  144, 169, 176, 190, 191, 198
Apocalyptic 154
  Definition 153, 155–156
Araq el Amir 69 n. 98
Aristeas, Letter of 120
Aristobulus I 22, 88, 174 n. 83
Ashkenazim 160–161
Augustine 63 n. 80

Bannus 2–3, 11, 44 n. 8, 45, 49, 51,
  63, 93, 97, 101
Bar Kochba 181–182, 186–187
Ben Sira 20, 26–27, 69, 105,
  118–119, 144–145, 168–169, 189
  n. 1
  Social Outlook 169
Bible 37, 48, 114–136, 196–198
  Fixing Text 130
  New Readers 124–129
Boethusians 21
Boundary Marking 7–11, 35, 38, 60,
  80, 81, 90–113, 150, 195, 201–207
Brain Washing 61
Bridge Building 55 n. 58, 74 n. 114
"Builders of the Wall" 89 n. 25, 90

Calendar 36 n. 116, 57 n. 64, 78,
  85–86, 109, 115, 190, 203
Celibacy 44, 102, 104
Charity 61, 96 n. 40, 104
Choice 66–67, 73–74
Chosen People 67
Christians 2, 3, 19, 26 n. 78, 35
  n. 109, 37 n. 120, 42–43, 45, 50
  n. 42, 56, 63 n. 80, 112, 148 n. 35,
  157, 164, 181, 190 n. 5, 194
Chronology 21–22, 33
Circumcision 100
Cleopatra III 12 n. 30
Coexistence, Old & New 71–72
Commerce 7, 91, 104–107, 205–206
Common Judaism 34 n. 107, 56, 68
  n. 96
Communism 47, 61–62
Comparative History 35–39, 207
Contingency 66–67, 70–73
Copper Scroll 173 n. 81
Ctistae 58–59
Cynics 59 n. 70

Damascus 90
Damascus Document = CD 2 n. 1,
  21–22, 25–26, 31, 43 n. 6, 44–45,
  76 n. 123, 89–91, 132, 206
Daniel 84, 169–171, 180 n. 99
Dead Sea Scrolls/Sect 1, 2 n. 1, 4,
  11, 12, 13, 19, 21–23, 25, 28, 30,
  31–32, 34–35, 39, 42–43, 44–45,
  46–47, 48, 50–51, 53, 54–55, 56,
  58–62, 63–66, 73–74, 75, 95–96, 97,
  99–100, 102–104, 105–107, 109,
  110–112, 114–116, 132–133, 151,
  174–180, 181, 190, 205
  Accounts of Past 21–22, 33
  Date for Redemption 177–180
  Origins 2 n. 1, 32–33, 73
Demetrius III 32 n. 102
Demography 44
Determinism 38 n. 121, 53, 110 n. 83
Discipline, Breakdown 57 n. 64
Doctors 48 n. 36

---

[1] For all authors, see also Passage Index.

PASSAGE INDEX

Greek Authors

Philo

Josephus

Latin Authors

Rabbinic Literature

Qumran Literature

MODERN AUTHORS INDEX

SUPPLEMENTS

TO THE

JOURNAL FOR THE STUDY OF JUDAISM

Formerly Studia Post-Biblica

49. LIETAERT PEERBOLTE, L.J. *The Antecedents of Antichrist.* A Traditio-Historical Study of the Earliest Christian Views on Eschatological Opponents. 1996. ISBN 90 04 10455 0

50. YARBRO COLLINS, A. *Cosmology and Eschatology in Jewish and Christian Apocalypticism.* 1996. ISBN 90 04 10587 5

51. MENN, E. *Judah and Tamar (Genesis 38) in Ancient Jewish Exegesis.* Studies in Literary Form and Hermeneutics. 1997. ISBN 90 04 10630 8

52. NEUSNER, J. *Jerusalem and Athens.* The Congruity of Talmudic and Classical Philosophy. 1996. ISBN 90 04 10698 7

53. LARSON, E.W. *The Translation of Enoch from Aramaic into Greek.* ISBN 90 04 10690 1 (In preparation)

54. COLLINS, J.J. *Seers, Sibyls & Sages in Hellenistic-Roman Judaism.* 1997. ISBN 90 04 10752 5

55. BAUMGARTEN, A.I. *The Flourishing of Jewish Sects in the Maccabean Era: An Interpretation.* 1997. ISBN 90 04 10751 7

56. SCOTT, J.M. *Exile: Old Testament, Jewish, and Christian Conceptions.* 1997. ISBN 90 04 10676 6 (In preparation)

ISSN 1384-1261